D0139770

HEALING WAYS

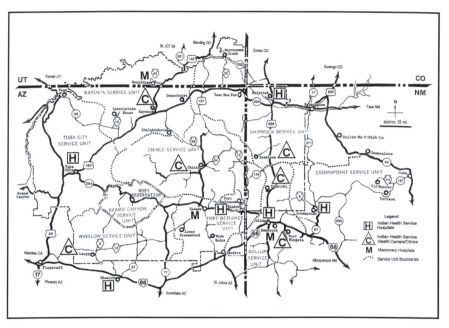

Navajo Health Facilities, 1961

HEALING WAYS

Navajo Health Care in the Twentieth Century

WADE DAVIES

University of New Mexico Press
Albuquerque

Marianne Jewell Memorial Library
Baker College of Muskegon
Muskegon, Michigan 49442

For my parents

© 2001 by Wade Davies
All rights reserved.
First paperbound printing, 2009
Paperbound ISBN: 978-0-8263-2441-2

15 14 13 12 11 10 09   1 2 3 4 5 6 7

Library of Congress Cataloging-in-Publication Data

Davies, Wade, 1969–
   Healing ways : Navajo health care in the twentieth century /
Wade Davies.—1st ed.
       p.   cm.
Includes bibliographical references and index.
   ISBN 0-8263-2276-x (cloth : alk. paper)
      1. Navajo Indians—Rites and ceremonies.   2. Navajo Indians—Religion.
3. Navajo Indians—Medical care.
4. Native American Church of North America—History.
I. Title: Navajo health care in the twentieth century. II. Title.
   E99.N3 D32 2001
   610'.89'972—dc21   2001001844

CONTENTS

LIST OF ILLUSTRATIONS

LIST OF MAPS

LIST OF TABLES

PREFACE

Over the past century, people of the Navajo Nation have found ways to combine the benefits of many forms of healing to care for their minds and bodies. This history of health care among the Navajos, or the Diné as they call themselves, focuses on this central point; it considers the process by which Navajos have adopted Western medicine without compromising their reliance upon Navajo healing ceremonies and other forms of medical care. This incorporative process has occurred on individual and group levels. Patients have sought the services of physicians, Navajo healers, and other health care providers in combination. In recognition of this trend, the tribal leadership has been increasingly active in trying to preserve and promote these medical options on the Navajo reservation.

Western medicine is just one of many practices Navajos have adopted from non-Navajos to improve their quality of life. Preserving the old ways, while adopting new ones, however, has never been easy. The pace of societal change has been rapid over the past one hundred years, especially since World War II. Mass culture, fast food, gradual urbanization, youth gangs—all of these things have changed the texture of life in Navajo country, making it more difficult for young people to learn the traditional ways. Yet despite change and adaptation, the old beliefs and practices, including traditional healing ceremonies, endure among the Navajos. Navajo-Modoc author, Sonlatsa Jim-James, has summed up well this process of change and continuity:

Even in the modern world we live in today, these ceremonies, stories, and customs are still kept among the Navajo. Undoubtedly, they are not as strong as they were a long time ago, but they are not forgotten. The land is now distributed among the Navajo, and modern technology has taken its toll on the reservation. Food is produced faster, people can get to ceremonies faster, and the Diné get healing faster. This does not mean that the cultural identity of the Navajo is lost. It just means that the Diné are learning to function in two different worlds. They are getting the best of both worlds: the spiritual ways and the modern ways.[1]

Non-Indian medical providers have sometimes hindered and sometimes assisted the Diné in their effort to use Western medicine on their own terms. Especially prior to the 1940s, medical professionals, U.S. government officials, and Christian missionaries tried to dissuade Diné patients from utilizing their indigenous forms of healing. By doing so, they often did more to repel Navajos from their Western services than to eclipse Navajo medical practices. In part because they eventually recognized this dilemma, many health care workers and federal policymakers, as the twentieth century progressed, saw the utility in breaking down cultural barriers.

One of the most poignant examples of cross-cultural accommodation in Navajo medical care occurred in 1997, when the U.S. Indian Health Service placed a Navajo healer on its payroll. Outside of a government health center in Winslow, Arizona, Jones Benally took referral cases from physicians in a healing hogan he erected. Such an arrangement would have been unthinkable half a century before, but it reflected decades of Navajo efforts to convince the federal government that Western medicine should complement rather than replace Navajo healing.[2]

Navajo reactions to Western medicine have largely been based on the perceived medical benefits those services have offered. There is evidence that Western medicine has performed well among the Navajos, who have suffered greatly from infectious disease and high infant death rates since non-Indians arrived in the American Southwest. Delivering medical care on the Navajo reservation has always been a challenging prospect, given its dispersed population, its geographical expanse of over 25,000 square miles, and contrasting cultural perspectives between patients and providers. A comprehensive medical system, combining preventive and clinical care, has proven to be an effective approach for dealing with such a health environment, but serious medical problems remain. Infectious diseases, diabetes, and accidental injuries continue to plague the Navajos.

Since the late nineteenth century, Western medical services have been offered to the Navajos by a variety of providers, including traders, Christian missionaries, state health departments, and private practitioners. The federal government, however, has been the main source of health care through its Bureau of Indian Affairs (BIA) and, later, its Indian Health Service. Administrative and budgetary decisions made by Congress and the federal bureaucracy, therefore, have largely determined the extent and form of Western medical care on the Navajo reservation.

Western medical services were not always accessible or effective for Navajo patients. In the early 1900s, the government had relatively little to offer to Navajo patients in regard to health care, either in terms of the quantity or quality of its services. During the 1930s and early 1940s this situation changed, as BIA Commissioner John Collier drew upon New Deal funds to increase the federal commitment to Indian health care and as medical technology made medical services more effective. World War II brought new challenges to Navajo country by placing demands on BIA finances and personnel, devastating medical gains made on the reservation. A concomitant rise of conservative politics after the war led to a call for the gradual termination of federal services to American Indians. Foremost among the terminationists' targets was the BIA, which symbolized the special relationship between the federal government and American Indians. The politicians were unable to eliminate the Bureau, but they did reduce its duties, eliminating its medical role and ushering in the Public Health Service, and its subagency, the Indian Health Service (IHS), as a replacement. Terminationists pushed for this transfer in hopes that the Indian Health Service could quickly bring Indian health patterns up to the national average and allow the federal government to withdraw from its medical obligation to the Navajos and other Indian groups. There were, however, no hasty solutions to Indian medical problems, and more liberal federal policies in the 1960s expanded the IHS's role in reservation medical care.

The 1970s witnessed an increased federal commitment to Indian health care, and U.S. officials willingly allowed tribal groups to play larger roles in the administration of those services. But new threats to Navajo health care surfaced during the 1980s and 1990s, as federal budget cuts forced IHS representatives and tribal leaders to fight to retain gains already achieved. In spite of such financial obstacles, Navajo medical care continued to improve, thanks in part to better medical technology and more cooperative relationships between Navajo and non-Indian leaders and healers.

As Western medical services increased in availability and quality during the twentieth century, so did the Navajo desire to take advantage of them. The Navajos' growing reliance on Western medicine posed dilemmas for them. They had to depend on the U.S. government's willingness and ability to maintain medical services and on the providers to respect their views on health and healing. Because Navajos often perceived federal health care as inadequate and unresponsive to their concerns, the tribe asserted its role as an advisor to the BIA and IHS, and provided additional Western medical services. A growing number of qualified and experienced Navajo physicians, nurses, and medical administrators after mid-century made it easier for the Navajos to influence Western medical care. As they developed their skills as government negotiators, medical administrators, nurses, and physicians, the Diné drew closer to true self-determination in medical care. Funding woes and cultural conflicts remained, but to a much greater extent at the end of the twentieth century than at the beginning, the Navajos had the ability to shape Western medicine to fit their perceived needs and their way of life.

Navajo efforts to preserve traditional healing, and their continued adherence to it in large numbers, prevented them from becoming entirely dependent on Western medicine and the outsiders that often accompanied it. Traditional healing provided medical, emotional, and cultural benefits to the Diné that Western medicine could not. Similarly, the Native American Church, which began to attract Navajo participants in the 1930s, in part because it offered holistic healing benefits, broadened Diné health care options. By drawing on these healing forms as alternatives to each other or, more often, in combination with each other, Navajo patients controlled the fashion in which they sought healing.

Many scholars, including anthropologists, sociologists, demographers, and historians, have written about Navajo health care, providing us with a strong sense of how health patterns and medical services developed on the reservation in the nineteenth and twentieth centuries. This book hopes to complement that body of scholarship by providing a general overview of the history of health care, in its many forms, on the Navajo reservation. Particular attention is given to the years from the 1940s to the end of the century, when the combined use of Western medicine and traditional healing became most common. Because many Navajos view health and healing in a broad context, this work attempts to do the same. It explores changing and complex relationships between health providers and patients; among federal, state, and tribal governments; and between medical doctors and medicine men. It attempts to illuminate the complex process the Navajo Nation and various individuals undertook, and continue to undertake, to expand and shape medical care as a crucial part of their quest for self-determination and the preservation of the their way of life.[3]

A note here on my use of terms may aid the reader. Navajos have used different terms to refer to themselves, as have outsiders in reference to the Navajos. For stylistic reasons and a desire not to alienate people who prefer one term to another, I sometimes use different terms interchangeably. Because most scholars, and perhaps most indigenous people in the United States, prefer the terms "American Indian" or "Indian" over "Native American," I most commonly use the former two, but all appear in the text. Similarly "Diné," which is the word Navajos use for themselves in their own language, is used interchangeably with "Navajo," originally a non-Navajo term, but one which many Navajos adopted in place of or in conjunction with "Diné." "Diné Bikéyah" and "Navajo country" are used both in reference to the Diné traditional land base and to the official reservation. In later chapters "Navajo Nation" is sometimes used to refer to the reservation itself, but most often to designate the Navajo people and their government collectively.

In choosing what terms to use, what sources to consult, and how to interpret the information available to me, a number of people offered invaluable assistance. Dr. Peter Iverson devoted countless, and seemingly endless, hours to this project, both during my time as a graduate student at Arizona State University and in the years since. He deserves credit for helping me to conceive this project and to see it through. I also want to thank him for connecting me to a wide variety of scholars, tribal leaders, and health care workers who were able to guide me further. But most importantly, I wish to thank him for his friendship.

I am pleased to have shared an interest in American Indian history, and especially Navajo health care, with Dr. Robert Trennert, whose direction and example proved invaluable to this study. Dr. Philip VanderMeer also assisted me in this project, and perhaps even more importantly, contributed greatly to my development as a historian.

A number of individuals took the time and effort to sit down and speak with me about their experiences with Navajo health care. The strongest aspects of this work, I believe, are attributable to what they gave me. Not only did they offer essential factual information, they helped me to understand the human reality behind the facts. I thank Beulah Allen, M.D.; Lori Arviso Alvord, M.D.; Geri Bahe-Hernandez; Patrick Bohan; Steven Borowsky, M.D.; Ellouise DeGroat; Henry Dobyns; Raymond Estrada; Lena Fowler; Lou Fox; Edward Hardiman, M.D.; Jennie Joe; John King; Fran Kosik; Jim Lang; Alexander Leighton; Don Lewis-Kratsik, M.D.; Taylor McKenzie, M.D.; Barbara Munn; Peggy Nakai; Elton Naswood; Doug Peter, M.D.; Mary Roessel, M.D.; Robert Roessel; Tom Sasaki; Thomas Todacheeny; and Robert Young for inviting me into their homes and places of work. I apologize if I have misrepresented them in any way and take full blame for any errors that may appear in the text. The views expressed herein are the interpretations of this author, the individuals listed above, or both, and do not necessarily represent the views of any organization with which these people may be involved, including Diné College, the Navajo Area Indian Health Service, Navajo Division of Health, the Navajo Nation Health Foundation, Rehoboth-McKinley Hospital, or the U.S. Public Health Service.

I would also like to acknowledge the archival staffs at the University of Arizona Special Collections, Arizona Historical Society in Tucson, the Arizona Historical Foundation, the Arizona State Museum, the Arizona State University Labriola Center, the Arizona State University Southwest Collections, the Museum of Northern Arizona, the various branches of the National Archives, the Navajo Nation Museum, the Northern Arizona University Special Collections and Archives Department, and the University of New Mexico Center for Southwest Research. I especially appreciate the help given to me by James Allen, Clarenda Begay, Evelyn Cooper, Marjorie Ciarlante, Laurie Devine, William Dobak, Pat Etter, Alan Ferg, Richard Fusick, Marlene Jaspers, Mark Leutbecker, Laura McCarthy, Chris Marin, Joyce Martin, Fred Nicklasen, Dennis Preisler, Stephen Phalen, Robert Spindler, and Karen Underhill.

I am also grateful for the University of New Mexico Press's interest in this work, and especially thank Durwood Ball and David Holtby for offering their guidance, encouragement, and insightful advice. I also thank Barbara Kohl for her skilled editorial work.

Many friends and colleagues critiqued my writing, offered their emotional support, and helped me to locate relevant materials. I have not the room to acknowledge them all, but Mike Baker, Rhonda Barbone, Charlotte Frisbie, Jerri Glover, Valerie Griffiths, Larry King, Steven Laurent, Ron Smith, Martin Weissert, and Scott Zeman deserve my special thanks.

Finally, I thank my parents, Dr. William Davies and Norma Davies. My father inspired my love for history and he and my mother offered the emotional support and encouragement, not to mention the research assistance, that made this book possible. I dedicate it to them.

NAVAJO HEALING
AND WESTERN MEDICINE

The Navajos call themselves the Diné, the Earth Surface People, and in-habit a homeland they call Diné Bikéyah, Home of the People. These terms unambiguously demonstrate that the Navajos and their land are in-separable. Diné Bikéyah is a vast area circumscribed by sacred moun-tains—Blanca Peak, Colorado, to the east; Mount Taylor, New Mexico, to the south; San Francisco Peaks, Arizona, to the west; and Mt. Hesperes, Colorado, to the north. Spanning hundreds of miles between these moun-tains, it is a ruggedly beautiful land.

In Diné Bikéyah, less than ten inches of rain may fall in a year. By erod-ing the landscape into washes and canyons, water makes its presence known, but springs are scattered and often difficult to find. It is a place of sage-covered deserts and pine-forested mountains, a place where heat and violent thunderstorms in the summer give way to the heavy snows of win-ter. Movement has been a necessary part of life for the Navajos. Without physical and mental strength, the Diné could not meet the demands of a hunting existence, and later, a pastoral life spent migrating as the seasons and the sheep and goats required. They also needed strength to protect themselves from their enemies, first Indian and later non-Indian as well, who could rob them of their livelihood, their freedom, and their lives.

Long before the United States took control of the Southwest in 1846, the Diné had learned how to adapt to this environment. In the process, they drew on knowledge from their ancestors and the Holy People who cre-ated them, and learned from their own trial and error. Like all cultures do, the Navajos also acquired healing beliefs and practices from outsiders, but they adopted only those beliefs and practices that fit their needs and world-view, while rejecting others. In doing so, they looked to other Native peoples for what they had to offer in a similar way as they would to non-Indians in later years. Through this complex process, the Diné established elaborate health care practices that included exercise, sanitation, physical protection from injury, herbalism, and holistic healing ceremonies.

When Anglo-American observers first paid notice to Navajo healing ways late in the nineteenth century, they saw them as "superstitious" and harmful. As they began trying to change Navajo healing, they failed to see that the people had put centuries of thought into their ways. These non-Indians had confidence in their own medical customs, but they did not see the benefits of alien customs and looked for weaknesses rather than strength and complexity in Navajo healing.

The points of dissimilarity between these medical traditions contributed to conflicts between Navajos and American physicians, Christian missionaries, and government administrators. But even in these early years, the potential for compromise existed. As dissimilar as the health care traditions were, they could conceivably coexist in the Diné world. Navajos viewed Western medicine as serving a different role than their healing ways, so they could accept the former, without rejecting the latter.

Navajo Traditional Healing

Although literature on Diné healing is voluminous and often well researched and respectful, many Navajo healers believe that the traditional concepts and practices cannot and should not be related in their entirety through writing. Because the healing ceremonies are considered sacred and imbued with power, Navajos have hesitated to relate information about them to non-Indians. When they have done so, they have purposefully omitted certain details out of respect for the ceremonies. Nor is writing the ideal means to represent the body of Navajo ceremonial knowledge, which is traditionally passed down orally from one generation to another. Unlike Western medicine in modern times, Navajo healing is not an easily compartmentalized subsection of life, separate from education, politics, family, or religion, making it even more difficult for scholars to define academically. Nevertheless, it is important to include at least a few general details about Navajo healing to provide a reference for understanding the evolution of Navajo health care in the twentieth century.[1]

A typical Navajo home (hogan) during the winter, date unknown. Hogans were well suited to protect the Navajos in a sometimes harsh and desolate environment, and they were also important parts of the Navajo ceremonial ways. Courtesy of the Arizona Historical Foundation, University Libraries, Arizona State University, RW-94.

Navajo traditional healing evolved and continues to survive because it reflects Diné history and culture, and the struggle by the people to make Diné Bikéyah their home. As such, Navajo ceremonialism has proved durable and invaluable, and perceived threats to it have never been taken lightly. The Navajo healing rituals have changed over the past two hundred years, with new ceremonies emerging and others fading, but change does not reflect weakness. That Diné healing has endured over centuries attests to the commitment Navajo healers and patients have made to maintaining the integrity of their ways. Of course, Navajos do not share perfectly uniform views of health and healing, and presumably, they never have, but even today the majority retain at least some connection to these ways.

Navajo ceremonial healing is complex, but there are helpful ways to think about it. The most basic principle of Navajo healing is that of *hózhǫ.* Hózhǫ cannot be translated exactly in other jjlanguages, but is best defined as "harmony," "order," and "beauty." The Diné origin story teaches them of a universal harmony. After much trial and error in the chaotic underworlds, the Navajo Holy People, including First Man and First Woman, ascended to this world through a reed. Using songs, prayers, and rituals, they affected the power in all things to create this world and set everything into a state of hózhǫ. After Changing Woman created the Earth Surface People (Diné) from her own body, using First Man's medicine bundle, the Holy People withdrew. If the Diné maintain hózhǫ by following their creators' examples, they find fortune and good health, but harm comes to them if they forsake those examples. "We are told by the singers who teach us that these Holy People, although they are no longer visible on earth, are still aware of how we are conducting ourselves here," explained Frank Mitchell, a well-known Navajo healer of the twentieth century. "If we are in trouble, they are there to protect us from misfortune."[2]

Healing is central to Navajo ceremonialism, but not because the Diné fear death. Their stories, and the words *sǫ'ah naagháii bik'eh hózhǫ,* teach them to seek long life, not to deny mortality, but to live in a state of beauty and harmony, and to obtain knowledge. Dying of old age is accepted because elders then share their knowledge and make way for a new generation, a new cycle of life.[3]

Navajo healing is holistic; the focus is on restoring harmony to the patient rather than on curing specific symptoms. Healing is brought about through ceremonies involving songs, rituals, and prayers that invoke the Holy People who can help restore harmony. Navajos, however, do not simply communicate with the Holy People through the ceremonies; they *use the same powers* the Holy People used. Spoken words, songs, and other ceremonial acts have powers to help establish harmony and good health if used properly, but also have powers to bring harm if used improperly. Healing acts can take the form of herbal remedies, or they can be more elaborate chantways, lasting up to nine days and nights and incorporating the use of dry paintings that represent images of the Navajo deities. Like words, these symbols are a means to access power and must be respected because they can bring benefit or harm. Ceremonies are often performed in the traditional Navajo dwelling, the hogan, a domed structure that represents a microcosm of the universe, carefully oriented to the four sacred directions and with a doorway that always faces east.[4]

Those who conduct the chantway ceremonies and other rites are known as *hataałii*, "singers," also referred to as traditional healers or as "medicine men," although they are sometimes women. There are dozens of different chantways and other ceremonial rites, and their length and complexity require a great deal of time and effort on the part of each singer to learn. Most singers are able to learn only a few in their lifetime, and no one knows all of them. To become a singer, a young man or woman may spend years studying with someone who already possesses the required knowledge. The apprentice also assembles the medicine bundles, or *jish*, that the singer and apprentice need to perform the ceremonies. The apprentice assists the teacher until deemed ready to perform on his or her own. The Navajo healer is unlike many American Indian medicine people in that he or she does not gain personal powers through visions, but rather facilitates a transfer of power from the Holy People to the patient. If the ceremonies are done incorrectly or out of season, or if they are compromised in any way, this spiritual power may fail to work or might cause further harm to the people involved.[5]

Illness is manifested mentally or physically, or in both ways simultaneously, but the true cause is a disruption of harmony. It can be the result of taboo transgression, excessive behavior, improper contact with animals or other forces of nature, inappropriate or improper use of the ceremonies, or contact with malignant entities (spirits and witches).[6]

Breaking taboos can cause illness because humans are committing transgressions against those principles that create harmony between them and their environment. These rules are handed down by the Holy People who learned from their own experiences how improper conduct can yield misfortune. Sexual taboos are among the most serious. The Holy People were plagued by the birth of monsters following their own sexual misconduct. And the Navajos are inflicted with "moth sickness" seizures if they commit incestuous acts with fellow clan members.[7]

Illness can be a punishment, but it is not always brought about by misguided or malevolent deeds. The sick person may simply have made an error in judgment or come into contact unintentionally with something disruptive, including wind, snakes, bears, coyotes, lightning, and other forces that are common in his or her environment. In an often-unforgiving landscape such as Diné Bikéyah, to respect, know, and sometimes fear the environment is a necessity. "The whole thing is interwoven, the way of life of the Navajos is interwoven with nature," said Howard Gorman, a respected Navajo leader of the twentieth century. Because all creatures are linked as a whole, they must be dealt with properly, lest imbalance occur.[8]

Malignant spirits of the dead and malevolent humans can also cause illness. In such cases, the patient may not have broken any taboos or done anything to bring disease upon him or herself. Some non-Navajos have scorned the Diné for these beliefs, but they are essential parts of the Navajo universe and way of life, as well as manifestations of other aspects of the ceremonial world and universal power. Hózhǫ́ exists because there is also hóchxǫ'—sometimes translated as "chaos" and "sickness." The belief in hóchxǫ' reinforces the need for traditional healing and helps explain why people, who are intended to be in harmony with their surroundings, sometimes do things that run counter to this ideal.[9]

A deceased person can affect the living as a ch'į́įndi (ghost). After death, the spirit is guided to the underworld in the north, but the body must be buried properly to ensure that this journey will be undertaken

Navajos gather for a traditional ceremony, probably around the turn of the century. In addition to healing an individual patient, ceremonies served to unite the extended family and community. Courtesy of the Arizona Historical Foundation, University Libraries, Arizona State University, McH-415.

without disturbance. People are taught to avoid contact with the dead whenever possible, because of the *ch'įįndi*. Deceased elders are not as dangerous, because they have led successful lives and respected the power of their knowledge. And a newborn's death is less threatening because he or she has yet to acquire knowledge. Those who die in the prime of their lives are the most dangerous, because their *ch'įįndi* can cause "ghost sickness" in others, leading to death if not treated by the proper ceremonies. Because the spirit may return to its previous place of dwelling, Navajo tradition insists that the survivors abandon any hogan or other structure where a person has died. A small group of relatives conducts the burial and must follow a very strict ritual to prevent the ch'įįndi from bringing harm. As part of that ritual, the burial party is prohibited from having contact with others for many days. Such an inconvenient and hazardous undertaking prompted many Navajos, especially in the late nineteenth and early twentieth centuries, to have non-Navajos inter the dead for them.[10]

The living can also bring harm to others if they draw upon spiritual power to acquire wealth, seduce lovers, or harm their enemies and rivals. Anthropologist Clyde Kluckhohn called these actions "witchcraft," the inverse of ceremonial healing. Witches are thought to commit incest and murder, and to use "ghost powder" from the dead to inflict ghost sickness on others. They may also misuse ceremonies intentionally, causing illness rather than curing it.[11]

Many laypeople and healers know enough to diagnose illness themselves, but quite often a special Navajo diagnostician will be called in. Unlike the singers, who must learn to invoke outside sources of power through ceremonies, diagnosticians receive their divining abilities through a gift of power that they connect to Gila Monster. They may also use songs, prayers, and herbs, and they listen to what the patient and others have to say, but they draw upon the power within themselves to find a solution for the problem. There are different varieties of Navajo diagnosticians, but the most common are the "hand tremblers." Hand tremblers may trace symbols in the dirt floor of a hogan and hold a trembling arm over the patient. The movement changes when the trembler thinks of the real cause or when a certain symbol is drawn. Diagnosticians sometimes treat the illness themselves or suggest appropriate herbal remedies or chantways. It is then up to the individual and his or her family to seek out a qualified herbalist or singer. Because ceremonies require a great deal of time, effort, and expense, a patient may first choose to take part in some short prayer ceremonies related to the larger ceremony to "test" the validity of the diagnosis.[12]

There are no fewer than twenty-six chantway ceremonies known to have existed among the Navajos, and at least ten are still practiced. In addition, there are many minor rites that are not as elaborate as the chantways but are still crucial to Navajo healing. Each chantway or rite is linked to the spiritual force that caused the illness. For example, Evilways and the Enemyway rite can be used to counteract ghost sickness and the negative effects of contact with non-Navajos.[13]

While the ceremonies focus on healing, they are valuable to the Navajos in other ways. For instance, they help reinforce the familial bonds that are so vital in Navajo society. Although chantways are often done on behalf of an individual, community and family members play active roles in preparing for the complex and expensive sings. Certain ceremonies can be conducted only at certain times of the year, and there is no guarantee that a patient or his or her family will be able to locate a healer who knows the particular chantway or rite. Without help from the family, the patient can rarely afford to pay the healer and diagnostician, or to supply food for the many people who might attend. Yet, as burdensome as the healers' fees can be, they are necessary. Even a singer who is related to the patient must be paid or the ceremony will be ineffective. In the early days, singers were paid in goods, sometimes animals or blankets. In more recent years, cash has become an acceptable form of payment.[14]

The ceremonies also serve broader social functions. The Yeibichai portion of the Nightway ceremony is used to initiate Navajos into adulthood. After reaching a certain age, young Navajos are invited to enter the ceremony at a certain point during its nine-night course. There, the Yei dancers reveal secrets to them that signify their passage from children to adults. In such ways, healing ceremonies focused on individuals are used for larger community purposes. In fact, each chantway and rite helps restore harmony simultaneously to the individual, the tribe, and the entire universe.[15]

In addition, by telling the Diné where they came from and how they fit into their surroundings, the ceremonies contribute to the Navajo sense of identity. Healing and history are interwoven in the sings, and many healers take their roles as teachers and historians as seriously as their role as curers. It is crucial that they instruct apprentices. In this way, they pass information from generation to generation, and they live on through those who learn from them. Singers "are not entirely gone when they pass away," said Frank Mitchell. "Their stories are still here for the future use of the People. It is like the plants, like corn and beans. When they mature you pick the seed and you plant it again. It comes up again and produces some more seeds."[16]

Ceremonial knowledge teaches about the creation of the earth; each chantway is linked in some form to the origin story. This is especially true of the Blessingway rite, the most central of all Navajo ceremonies, and one that is more focused on prevention than curing. By conducting this ceremony, the singers perform the same acts that the Holy People used to create the world and establish harmony. In some instances, it may be sung over a pregnant woman or a new hogan to ensure good health and happiness. Every other ceremonial rite and chantway is connected to the Blessingway through shared songs and prayers, and each has a link to a specific story about the Holy People. Singers are not required to know these stories in order to conduct the ceremonies, but those who do know them are usually the most highly esteemed. Mitchell knew the Blessingway and the importance of understanding the creation stories. These stories gave meaning to what he did, and in memorizing them, he found it easier to remember the songs and prayers that related to them. "The story is like a trail," he said.[17]

Other Traditional Navajo Medical Practices

The chantways are not the only methods the Navajos have used to guarantee good health. Long before Navajos came into contact with non-Indians, they had established public health methods that were well suited to their environment and lifestyle. From the point of birth to the moment of death, Navajos relied, and still rely, on nurturing, education, exercise, good diet, sweat baths, and herbal remedies to protect them from injury, to treat medical problems, and to ensure mental health.[18]

According to Navajo tradition a baby receives a wind soul, the source of its thoughts and deeds, its "goodness" and "badness." The Holy Wind helps distinguish the individual and connects him or her to the Holy People. "It is said that the wind enters each newborn, / a whoosh of breath inside, and the baby gasps," wrote Navajo poet Luci Tapahonso. "It is wet with wind. It is holy. It is sacred. / Such energy we are, with wind inside." Made alive by the sacred wind, the new baby finds itself surrounded by

A Navajo mother and a baby in a cradle board. Cradle boards helped protect
infants from injury and allowed them to observe adults close up as they worked
and took part in ceremonial life. Courtesy of the Arizona Historical Foundation,
University Libraries, Arizona State University, IN-8.

members of the extended maternal family—parents, brothers and sisters, mother's brothers and sisters, and grandparents. For the rest of its life, the strong bonds of family sustain this individual mentally and physically.[19]

Centuries before contact with Anglos, Navajo mothers learned how to care best for their children in a rural environment. A mother placed the newborn in a cradle board to protect it from snakes and insects, the harsh sun, and injuries that could be caused by a fall from a horse or inflicted by the feet of others while they worked. The baby's arms and legs may have been restricted, but the infant could begin learning from the surrounding world while sitting, or propped up against a hogan wall or a loom as the mother worked close by. When the baby cried, the mother would nurse and hold him or her, and when relatives passed in and out of the hogan, they would greet the baby with a smile and jostle the cradle.[20]

When the infant laughed for the first time, a sister or brother placed salt, bread, and meat on his or her hands to bring health and hasten the first steps and words. As the child aged, he or she began to understand Navajo beliefs and ceremonial ways. Boys and girls learned about objects and actions that could cause illness, and they probably observed the importance of disposing of their bodily waste properly to prevent witches from using it to bring harm to them. Learning these ways not only protected them from harmful forces, it ensured a more sanitary environment.[21]

After weaning, children learned to eat like adults, usually from their own trial and error. The Navajo diet has changed throughout the centuries. During the first years in the Southwest, they depended on piñon nuts and other desert plants as well as small game. They later grew corn, squash, and beans, which contributed to their high-fiber, low-fat diet. When the Spanish arrived in New Mexico, the Navajos added to their diet sheep and other European livestock taken in raids or trade. The meat nourished them well and helped ease periods of famine. It has been suggested that the animal proteins served them in later years by helping them withstand imported diseases.[22]

Navajo youths might get enough exercise doing their daily chores and tending the flocks, but boys and girls were encouraged to toughen up through other strenuous activities. Running before dawn, sometimes with ice in their mouths, rolling in the snow, and jumping into icy ponds helped them to build up endurance. Pushed by their elders and their inner drive, young Navajos devoted hours a day to running through snow, rain, and heat. "I used to race by myself early in the morning while it was still dark, and in the middle of the day and in the evening," recalled a man named Left Handed in the 1930s. "In the middle of the day when it got real hot, when the sun was right in the middle of the sky, I used to run a race under the sun, while the sun was looking down on me."[23]

Navajo adults learned how to care for themselves physically even without the aid of healers. As was the case with many American Indian groups, the Navajos used medicinal herbs. Although healers used them in their ceremonies, they never monopolized such knowledge. Navajo "herbalists" specialized in administering herbal remedies and offered temporary relief to those awaiting ceremonial cures. Navajos also practiced home medicine and learned to use herbs, set bones, purify their bodies with sweat baths, and care for the immediate needs of the sick. As practical as these methods seem, they were all linked to the more general ceremonial beliefs. Sweat baths, for instance, were accompanied by their own spiritual songs.[24]

In all of these ways, the Navajos had learned how to become one with Diné Bikéyah, to fulfill their quest to live healthy harmonious lives. Indeed, their ways seem to have been well suited to their environment. The Navajos were not disease free before they came into contact with Europeans, but they had little reason to be dissatisfied with their medical practices. Navajos and other Indians did suffer from digestive problems, pneumonia, dysentery, eye problems, and other ailments. Nonetheless, they were free from influenza, typhoid, cholera, smallpox, and other diseases imported by the Europeans, and they apparently experienced little cancer, heart disease, or tuberculosis.[25]

Comparisons and Contrasts

By the 1860s, American missionaries and agents began to focus considerable attention on the Navajos. As will be seen, this contact set in motion a process of interchange between the different healing ways. To understand how Navajos reacted to this contact between their healing practices and those of non-Indians, it is necessary to compare the two medical traditions.

Scholars of Native American medicine and Western medicine have tended to focus on the dissimilarities between the forms of healing. This emphasis is not surprising because the differences *are* striking. In general, American Indian medical beliefs, and Navajo healing in particular, are holistic, with a focus on the entire individual. Conversely, Western medicine, as it existed by the late nineteenth century, focused on specific or-gans in the body and on microorganisms as the chief cause of sickness, rather than holistic harmony.

This basic difference in the way the cultures viewed health and healing helps explain why so many conflicts occurred between Navajo healers and non-Indian medical practitioners and adds meaning to the Navajo insis-tence that their traditions be preserved. On the other hand, because the two forms of medical care appeared to be so different, the adoption of one did not necessarily imply the rejection of the other. Western medicine, as Navajos began to understand it, could never replace traditional healing, because it was not spiritual. It could be adopted, therefore, without threat-ening to co-opt traditional healing's central position in Diné life.

The temptation to oversimplify the philosophies underlying Navajo traditional healing and Western medicine makes those healing forms ap-pear more rigid than they really were, or are. In fact, neither has been static over time, and both encompass a variety of styles, beliefs, and prac-tices. Terms like "Navajo traditional healing" and "Western medicine" are academic generalizations that help us to discuss these complex and evolv-ing views of health and illness. They are not meant to represent uniform and unchanging systems. The healing forms have always been more adapt-able than they have sometimes appeared.

Non-Indian Americans generally think of Native Americans in a his-torical context that does not allow them to change without losing their identity as "real" Indians. Yet all cultures change over time, and the Navajos are well known for their willingness to try new things. Accepting Western medicine has not represented a deviation from Navajo ways be-cause Navajo ways have always incorporated change. Furthermore, Diné beliefs and practices have not been uniform geographically. Leland Wyman, a respected student of Navajo healing, contends that there is not a single Navajo ceremonial system. Different healers have their own vari-ations on ceremonies depending on their personalities, where they learned them, and where they were raised. And as scholar Charlotte Frisbie has explained, the otherwise exacting ceremonies allow for varia-tions in overall length and degree of elaborateness.[26]

A certain degree of flexibility allowed Navajo healing to change over the years, to evolve and to grow, but adding new elements did not change the fundamental beliefs underlying traditional healing nor the fact that it belonged to them. Once they began practicing something new, it became

Navajo. Navajo healing has traditionally accepted the need to treat symptoms while waiting for a ceremony to be performed. Here, it is permissive because the patient can take advantage of anything that works to find relief. This attitude compelled Navajos to adopt herbal remedies and other physical treatments from non-Navajo Native Americans, and would later encourage them to pay notice to Western medicine.[27]

Western medicine has also been in flux from the beginning. It, too, represents a long process of sharing among many cultures. It, too, is characterized by regional variations and allows for disagreements among its practitioners. Western medicine reflects centuries of intercultural sharing among Europe, Asia, and the Americas. Egyptians, Greeks, Arabs, Western Europeans, and even indigenous peoples of the Americas have contributed to its beliefs and practices. And like Navajo healing, Western medicine has continued to change and evolve.[28]

Even though Western medicine has been distinguished by its "scientific" emphasis, it has never been as far removed from spirituality as it appeared. Despite the fact that physicians such as Galen had emphasized empirical principles in health and healing as far back as the second century A.D., monks carried responsibilities for health care in early medieval Europe, and they related illness to sin. Until the post–Civil War era, American clergymen often doubled as physicians, and even in modern times, religious denominations have played a large role in American hospitals. The rising popularity of "new age" medicine in the United States in recent decades also underscores the fact that Euro-Americans have remained concerned with the spiritual side of healing. In this case, a similarity between the two healing traditions may have hindered Navajo acceptance of Western medicine. But because the overt influence of religion on Western medicine had declined enough by the late nineteenth century, Navajos were less likely to perceive it as conflictive with their own beliefs. Although Christian missionaries, as is discussed later, tied their medical services to the Navajos to their evangelical aims, many Navajos proved able to separate the medical benefits from the ultimate missionary goals.[29]

Although they stem from evolutionary processes rooted in different hemispheres, cultures, and histories, Western medicine and Navajo healing have never had irreconcilable differences on a philosophical level. Based on healing beliefs alone, there was no reason why Navajos could not and would not find value in Western medicine from the beginning.

▾ 2 ▴

TOWARD ACCEPTANCE,
1864–1940

Although the potential always existed for the Navajos to accept Western medicine, the Diné had little incentive and few opportunities to make use of it in the first decades after its introduction to the reservation. Western medicine had little impact on the Diné Bikéyah before 1920. Between the forced removal of the Navajos to Fort Sumner in 1864 and the end of the nineteenth century, the U.S. federal government dispatched a few poorly qualified and inadequately equipped physicians. Minimal government health care in these early years left room for other non-Indians to play large roles in introducing Western medicine to the Navajos, including traders and Christian missionaries. Even working in conjunction, however, these non-Indians offered few medical benefits to the Navajos. Instead, they did more to antagonize the population they were there to serve by criticizing their healing beliefs and attempting to overcome the singers' influence.

After roughly half a century of exposure, Western medicine began to take root among the Diné; the potential for Navajo acceptance of the alien medicine began to play out by the 1920s as the quality and quantity of physicians' services improved. The New Deal years that followed brought even greater change to medical care in Navajo country. An expanding federal commitment to Indian health care led to substantial growth in the federal government's Bureau of Indian Affairs (BIA) Medical Division on the reservation, making Western medical care more accessible. At the same time, improving medical technology made government health care more effective, and a more culturally tolerant atmosphere made Western medicine appear less threatening to the Navajo way of life. In recognition of these changes, Navajos proved more willing to utilize Western medicine. Realizing that the people were incorporating government health care more readily, the tribal leaders subsequently initiated efforts to promote and shape its delivery.

Western Medicine Comes to the Navajos

Although the U.S. government initiated contact with the Navajos and offered vaccinations to them during the 1850s, few Navajos had contact with physicians until the American Civil War. In an effort to establish total authority over American Indians in the Southwest, the U.S. Army subjugated the Navajos and moved them 300 miles southeast to an area in New Mexico known as the Bosque Redondo. Union troops, led by Colonel Christopher "Kit" Carson, set upon Navajo land, destroying livestock, burning crops, and killing hundreds of people. By the end of 1864, more than 8,000 Navajos had made the miserable journey, the "Long Walk" as they called it, to the Bosque Redondo. There, at the newly erected Fort Sumner, living in cramped and unhealthy conditions, the Navajos faced a plague of infectious diseases and many met Anglo physicians for the first time.[1]

The U.S. Army provided physicians and built a small hospital at Fort Sumner in 1865, but these measures were not enough to overcome health problems caused by overcrowding and tainted water. Diseases, including dysentery, cholera, smallpox, measles, and syphilis were rampant. Inconsistent rations and the Navajos' unfamiliarity with techniques for preparing new food items led to problems of malnutrition that compounded the situation. Yet Navajos were understandably reluctant to utilize government medical services. Vaccination was about the only method that proved successful in fending off disease and was one of the few Western medical practices for which Navajos saw a use. Otherwise, medical treatments were painful and offered few benefits, and some Navajos feared contact with ch'įįndi from those who had died in the hospital, which one Navajo referred to as a place where "all who go in never come out."[2]

For three decades after 1868, when the Navajos were allowed to return to their homeland, Western medicine made even fewer inroads, in part because the federal government did not give medical services a high priority

A typical road through Navajo country during the 1950s. Rain and snow frequently made reservation roads impassable, and patients even found it difficult to reach medical facilities during good weather. Courtesy of Virginia Brown, Ida Bahl, and Lillian Watson Collection, Cline Library, Northern Arizona University, NAU.PH.92.14.122.

on the Navajo reservation. Minimal health care efforts proved impotent against the range of infectious diseases that inflicted the Navajos. As historian Robert Trennert has argued, the early government health activities for the Navajos were "half-hearted at best, underfunded, unfocused, and largely ineffective." Although the Treaty of 1868 between the United States and the Navajos provided for a physician, the government did not supply one until 1872. And the small staffs that followed, no matter how dedicated and qualified, could do very little for people whose scattered residences were often inaccessible because of primitive roads and inclement weather.[3]

The paucity of federal health care services on the Navajo reservation reflected larger trends in U.S. Indian affairs. Until the twentieth century, federal medical care for American Indians functioned largely on an ad hoc basis. Even though federal policymakers viewed medical care as part of a larger effort to assimilate Indians into "American" society by compelling them to give up their own forms of healing, the government devoted only scarce funds to this feature of their Indian program. The first government physicians to serve American Indians usually fulfilled specific treaty obligations that varied from tribe to tribe. The War Department, which originally carried out federal Indian affairs, showed little interest in social services. The Department of the Interior, which succeeded it, established the Education and Medical Division in its Office of Indian Affairs in 1873, but otherwise devoted scant attention to Indian health care. As late as 1900, the Medical Division had only eighty-three physicians—enough for only half of the Indian agencies. No nurses were employed before 1890, and only twenty-five served on reservations by the turn of the century.[4]

Those government physicians who were assigned to the Navajos usually resided at Fort Defiance, Arizona, near the center of the 1868 reservation, where they could service boarding school students and dispense medicinal remedies. The majority of Navajos, however, lived miles away and were not likely to actively seek out the agency physician. Facilities were crude and few in number. Supplies were so scarce that truly dedicated physicians had to find ways to procure remedies and instruments using their own wits and, sometimes, finances. Except for pain relievers (such as cocaine) and vaccines, they had little to offer of medicinal value. Most physicians displayed the requisite contempt for Navajo traditional healing, but their cultural arrogance was only a minor contributor to their general ineffectiveness. Physicians who served the Navajos in the late nineteenth and early twentieth centuries varied in their levels of dedication and qualification, but conditions dictated that even the most dedicated usually ended up frustrated and embittered.[5]

Not willing or able to sponsor a sizable effort on its own, the Indian Office (later known as the BIA) accepted assistance from nongovernment traders and missionaries. Traders, whose posts were increasingly common on the reservation between 1886 and 1910, often served as middlemen between the Navajos and non-Indians and provided some basic medical services. They were ultimately businessmen, and had vested interests in winning community respect and in keeping their Navajo customers healthy and productive. As a result, traders were willing to spare Navajo families the expense and emotional strain of burying the dead, and they also sold patent medicines.[6]

Perhaps no group in the late 1800s and early 1900s had more to do with introducing Western medicine to the Navajos than did Protestant missionaries. A number of the various denominations supplied their own personnel and hospitals to the reservation, often at the invitation of the U.S. government. The first government physician, John Menaul, actually came to Navajo country a year earlier as a Presbyterian missionary and medical doctor. In 1897, missionaries also claimed credit for the first hospital built specifically to serve the Navajos when, at the request of Agent Lt. Edward H. Plummer, the Episcopalians established the Good Shepherd Hospital at Fort Defiance. In the early twentieth century, Seventh Day Adventists, the Christian Reformed Church, and Presbyterians also included medical work in their larger mission programs. The Presbyterians escalated their medical commitment to the Navajos in 1906 with the construction of a small hospital on eighty acres granted to them by the federal government. In 1910, the Christian Reformed Church followed suit, constructing a ten-bed hospital at Rehoboth, New Mexico, serving Navajos living off the reservation around Gallup, New Mexico.[7]

Missionary medical care was primarily an evangelical tool. Christian missionaries believed that it would be easier to introduce the Navajos to new spiritual and social ideas after gaining their confidence through physical treatment. Whereas they viewed education as the best disseminator of the evangelical message to children over a sustained period of time, physicians and hospitals could be employed to introduce Christianity to adults and children alike. They also believed that health care would help implant Christianity by drawing the Navajos away from their adherence to traditional ways. Early missionaries, regardless of their denomination, fully intended to wipe out ceremonial healing and had little sympathy for Navajo traditional fears and concerns. As was the case with other medical missionaries, the Christian Reformed Church missionaries rarely lost sight of their greater purpose. As Reverend John Dolfin explained, the medical missionary "must first be a missionary and then a doctor," and medical service "is and must always continue to be a preparer of the way for the message of salvation."[8]

Rather than medical care opening the way for conversion, however, the missionaries' religious and cultural attitudes tended to hinder Navajo acceptance of their medical services. Navajo healers and patients surely noticed that the missionaries had declared war against traditional healing. Protestants, such as Rehoboth physician Dr. J. D. Mulder, clearly viewed the Navajo healers as their adversaries, believing that the ceremonies were endangering lives by keeping patients away from hospital care. Much to his dismay, Mulder admitted that the mission had not wiped out Navajo healing by the end of its first decade. "The sick among the Navahoes are still to a very great extent taken care of by their own medicine men," he claimed. "Very few patients come to me that have not first been under their care." He saw patients entering his hospital in larger numbers as the years passed, but the frustration remained. "The fact, however, that we are gaining ground may not put us off our guard," he wrote. "Superstition still hangs as a shroud over these people. And no sooner are the bonds loosened, but Satan stands ready to cast the heathen, awakening from superstition, into agnosticism and doubt."[9]

The missionaries' cultural and religious arrogance, no doubt, did little to foster Navajo trust, and probably restricted the flow of potential patients, but for many Navajos, the medical missionaries and traders were the first providers of Western medicine they would come to know. In a time when the U.S. government offered little in the way of health care and epidemic diseases were prevalent, the missionaries played an invaluable role as health care providers. Their services were utilized by a few Navajos who accepted Christianity and many more who rejected the missionaries' religious and social messages but, as the quality of Western medicine improved, saw tangible benefits in what they were offering.

A Growing Government Commitment, Early 1900s

Missionary medicine continued to expand across the reservation in the early 1900s, but the federal government gradually became the reservation's dominant Western medical provider. Even before the turn of the century, the BIA had noted the need for a stronger medical program on the Navajo reservation as well as for American Indians nationwide. Medical efforts for the Navajos increased with the addition of the first government hospitals and tuberculosis sanitoriums. Staff levels increased, and physicians improved qualitatively as they were brought under Civil Service regulations in late 1891, replacing political patronage with standardized hiring procedures.

As the federal government placed greater emphasis on its assimilation program at the turn of the century, Indian health care became a larger issue. Concern for Indian health increased as policymakers began to consider it inextricably linked to their boarding school efforts, which they felt were more important. Illness and death spread rapidly among the confined students, giving American Indians good cause to resist sending their children to government schools. If these educational efforts were to succeed, something had to be done about the high incidence of disease.[10]

At the end of the nineteenth century and beginning of the twentieth, Congress and the BIA attempted to improve medical care for American Indians in a variety of ways. The BIA gave greater emphasis to preventive measures by issuing a directive in 1889 informing its physicians that they would have to venture into the field to treat, examine, and educate their service population. The Bureau also gave health care a higher profile in 1908 by adding a chief medical officer to coordinate and regulate agency medical programs, and in 1911, Congress appropriated funds specifically for Indian health care for the first time, setting aside $40,000 for building new facilities and increasing staff levels on reservations nationwide.[11]

These policy changes, though seemingly meager, had noticeable effects on Navajo health care. Increasing appropriations allowed the BIA to begin adding hospitals to the Navajo reservation. By 1920, small hospitals had been established at Shiprock in New Mexico, and Fort Defiance, Tuba City, and Leupp in Arizona. Fort Defiance also received a tuberculosis sanatorium in 1915. Altogether the number of hospital beds available to the Navajos increased from about a dozen in 1900 to 184 in 1920. The 1920s saw further construction, with the total number of government hospital beds rising to 268 in 1929. Staff increased in general, and the BIA began hiring women as field matrons after 1890 to carry the medical program to Navajo hogans. In addition to caring for the sick, the matrons, who usually lacked formal medical training, pushed forward the government's assimilation effort by teaching sanitation, hygiene, and moral habits to Navajo women.[12]

Government officials on the reservation were encouraged by signs that the Navajos were receptive to the growing medical presence. A 1915 report by one such official claimed that "Indians now come for treatment voluntarily who heretofore would not have come except by force which is not advisable. It is no uncommon feature to have patients brought in voluntarily to the hospitals from distances up to 100 miles."[13]

But optimistic reports about Navajo willingness to use the hospitals told only part of the story. Statistics showing thousands of Navajo patients per year were somewhat misleading. Many of those patients were the same people coming back numerous times. Thousands more stayed away. Some may simply have lived too far away to seek care at the hospitals. And other Navajos continued to view the hospitals as places of death. Patients were often brought to hospitals only when they were dying, either because they and their families had tried all other remedies and were desperate for help, or because they knew death was imminent and wanted the hospital to take care of the burial. Either way, dying patients perpetuated the hospitals' dubious reputations and dissuaded others from seeking care.[14]

Field matrons also faced problems finding and keeping willing patients. The matrons had more direct contact with traditional healers who often resented their efforts to transform Navajo ways. Matrons were also ill equipped and improperly trained to deal with a variety of health emergencies, including epidemics that swept across the reservation in the early twentieth century. Navajo seasonal movement and transportation problems further frustrated their attempts to maintain long-term connections with particular Navajo families.[15]

Regardless of increasing utilization rates at the hospitals, health conditions on the reservation remained poor. Shortcomings in field health had very obvious effects on conditions in the hospitals and boarding schools. As one superintendent argued in 1912, school children were in constant danger of acquiring infectious diseases from Navajo adults when they went home for visits. "Too little attention is paid to epidemics among the camp Indians," continued the report, "and epidemics sweep unchecked from one side of the reservation to the other, causing great loss of life among children." Agency superintendents (local government officials who supervised federal programs on the reservation) were less likely to point out that epidemics frequently spread from the school children to the adults. Navajos had resisted some infectious diseases in the past because of their scattered residency patterns, but grouping students together compromised this traditional advantage and a variety of diseases thrived among their compacted ranks. At least a few government employees could see this dynamic. "The Indian Office was collecting and taking Indian children off to non-reservation schools," remarked Dr. Albert Wigglesworth. "It was a terrible mistake, for they began returning them dying of TB. I was frantic. I had no place to keep them."[16]

World War I made poor health conditions on the reservation even worse. The war effort drew much-needed federal funding away from the Navajos and decimated an already overburdened medical staff as physicians and nurses left reservations to serve in the military. The Navajos also fell victim to the influenza epidemic during World War I. Killing over twenty million people globally, influenza struck the Navajos between October 1918 and the end of 1920, killing over two thousand.[17]

A variety of infectious diseases were common among the Navajos in the early 1920s. Pneumonia, influenza, and other diseases reemerged time and again, and trachoma and tuberculosis remained endemic. Indian Service employees worried that these health threats could compromise other aspects of Indian policy. "The health situation has become the basic problem amongst these people and its successful solution is a pre-requisite to all other phases of the Navajo problem," argued Navajo Commissioner H. J. Hagerman in 1924, "for it is quite evident that if the Navajos are rapidly drifting into a state of universal infection by a virulent disease, industrial and educational activities can be of little avail amongst them."[18]

Despite continued funding woes, there were signs of an increasing federal commitment to Indian health care in the 1920s. The passage of the Snyder Act in 1921 made the "relief of distress and conservation of health" an official goal of Indian policy, thereby committing the government to end its patchwork approach to Indian medical programs. Another federal action in the decade had a more direct effect on Navajo health care. The BIA sponsored a regional effort, beginning in 1924, to address trachoma, an infectious disease which had become endemic among southwestern Indians, painfully attacking the lining of their eyelids and causing loss of vision.[19]

No single document better summed up problems in Indian health care, or had a greater influence on future policies, than did the Meriam Report in 1928. In response to criticism of federal policies, Secretary of the Interior Hubert Work commissioned Lewis Meriam and a team from the Brookings Institution to conduct an extensive survey of all BIA-administered programs, including health care. The final report offered a scathing assessment of federal Indian policy in general and Indian health care in particular, arguing that "practically every activity undertaken [by the national government] for the promotion of the health of the Indians is below a reasonable standard of efficiency." Meriam criticized the medical program for its poor staff training and its overemphasis on clinical care while indicting Congress for failing to provide sufficient funds to meet even the most basic needs. The report also expressed more general concerns about the BIA's cultural arrogance: "[The survey staff] would not recommend the disastrous attempt to force individual Indians or groups of Indians to be what they do not want to be, to break their pride in themselves and their Indian race, or to deprive them of their Indian culture."[20]

The Meriam Report proposed solutions as well. It argued that more hospitals and tuberculosis sanatoriums were needed and that existing ones should be improved. Professional field nurses should replace overwhelmed and undertrained matrons, it said, and standards and wages would have to be increased to attract better physicians. By bringing deficiencies in Indian health care to the forefront, the report paved the way for a growing BIA medical care program in the 1930s, and its criticism of assimilation policy foreshadowed attempts on the part of government officials to break down cross-cultural barriers between Western and Navajo healing.

Navajo Healing, 1864–1930

While Western medicine gradually found a foothold among the Navajos, traditional healing continued to dominate Diné health care. Against the wishes of missionaries and the U.S. government, Navajo patients were not trading in their traditional beliefs when they came to the hospitals. Meanwhile, non-Indian influences did place a strain on Navajo society and thereby affected Diné healing.

The Long Walk and exile in Fort Sumner posed great threats to Navajo healing because those episodes exacted a physical toll on its practitioners and removed the Diné from their sacred land in the center of the four mountains. The elderly, who held a wealth of ceremonial knowledge, and the young, who were responsible for carrying that knowledge into the future, were often the hardest hit by the physical strains. Some ceremonies may have disappeared forever as their practitioners succumbed. The Bosque Redondo's flora also failed to provide many of the herbs and other natural remedies used by Navajo healers in Diné Bikéyah.[21]

Nonetheless, many singers survived and healing ceremonies continued at Fort Sumner. Enemyways and Evilways were used to counteract the ill effects of daily exposure to non-Navajos and their own dead. Healers and herbalists devised new remedies to combat syphilis and other recently introduced diseases with plant and animal materials found nearby. Even when cures failed, Navajo healers could deflect criticism by pointing out that Army treatments were just as ineffectual. Meanwhile, other singers who had eluded capture waited hundreds of miles to the northwest, holding on to sacred knowledge until the rest returned.[22]

Throughout the early reservation years, Navajo traditional healing remained central to Diné life. In many ways, Navajo traditional healing proved versatile. When new challenges presented themselves, Navajos found ways to conceptualize them in traditional ways, and dealt with them accordingly. During the early 1900s, ceremonialism grew in new ways as Navajos employed it to explain and treat recently introduced diseases. For example, diagnosticians associated tuberculosis with lightning sickness and found ways to treat it traditionally. "We went through many expenses having ceremonies for those with tuberculosis," Frank Mitchell remembered. "At the beginning there were no doctors, so we depended on the singers to cure these sicknesses. . . . We just had one-, two-, or five-night ceremonies, one- or two-hour sandpaintings." Similarly, healers implemented a variety of traditional methods, from the Yeibichai to herbal remedies, to deal with influenza. David Lansing recalled the post–World War I flu epidemic hitting his Navajo community near Aneth, in southern Utah:

One old man and wife were not affected by the sickness. The man was a medicine man; so this couple went around from home to home praying for the people. One day they came to our house because all of us were ill. He brought something that looked like a piece of tree bark. He advised all of us to spit in this thing, and we did. He told the same thing to all the real sick people. I do not know what he did with this collected sputum, but about two days after the medicine man paid us his visit, we were all up and around again. The other people he had visited all got well, too. This seemed mysterious, but we were glad to be well again.[23]

Navajos still had faith in their healers, and increased utilization rates in the hospitals no more reflected Navajo acceptance of the government's assimilation program than it did of the missionaries' evangelism; nor did it indicate that patients fully trusted the non-Indian practitioners. Government physicians were just as likely as missionaries to insult their patients' beliefs well into the 1920s. The BIA's Navajo Agency superintendents were some of the most outspoken opponents of the traditional healing system, having been entrusted with the responsibility of guiding the Navajos to assimilation. This antitraditional attitude may have even increased after the turn of the century as the government's presence grew. In the first decade of the twentieth century, superintendents Samuel Daire and Peter Paquette clearly stated their intentions to overcome traditional healing and Navajo witchcraft, and Paquette went so far as to sanction the arrest of practicing singers. Some physicians understood that these policies repelled potential patients and showed greater tolerance for the traditional ways, but they seem to have been in the minority.[24]

Navajo healers' opinions of Western medicine, on the other hand, varied. Diagnosticians and singers rarely faced the prospect of becoming rich from their work, but they had reasons to oppose anybody or anything that antagonized them and threatened to draw the Navajos from their beliefs. Many healers ignored Western medicine, either because it scarcely existed in their part of the reservation or because it seemed to offer little of value. Others were conscious of its presence but opposed it as a threat to Navajo ways. Even those singers who were more open to the physicians' presence were aware of the battle lines that had been drawn between them. Manuelito Begay, a Navajo healer who cooperated willingly with Western medical providers in the twentieth century, explained that he had been well aware of the white physicians and their attitudes:

> When the doctors and hospitals were first established among us, the doctors thought they were the only ones who knew how to apply medicine to patients. The Navajo people were not recognized at all and, in that connection, we thought the same way, we could not agree as to whose treatment should be recognized. The doctors thought they were the ones, and we thought we were the ones.[25]

Singer Sam Yazzie remembered those early days as a time when he was more gracious toward the physicians than they were toward him. "I have a great respect for the doctors. I would not have done to them as they have done to us and try to shame many of us from practicing our own medicine. At one time the American physicians would have all of us medicine men put out of business. I have never felt that way towards the white doctors."[26]

U.S. Government Medicine during the New Deal

The Great Depression and New Deal years brought significant changes to medical care in Navajo country. An expanding federal commitment to Indian health care, prompted by the Meriam Report, led to substantial growth in the BIA Medical Division on the reservation, making Western medical care more accessible. Simultaneously, improving medical technology made government health care more effective. Indian Commissioner John Collier also encouraged BIA employees to be more accepting of Navajo views on health and healing. Although Collier's cross-cultural vision yielded only limited results during the 1930s, it opened the way for better relations among physicians, healers, and patients. In recognition of these changes, Navajos proved even more willing to utilize Western medicine.

Perhaps what is most remarkable about increasing Navajo acceptance of government medicine during the era, is that it came at a time when tensions between the Navajos and the BIA were high. New Deal programs supplied jobs and better services during the Depression, but they were accompanied by a BIA livestock reduction program that caused great distress for countless Navajo families. Encouraged by Collier, the livestock reduction program compelled Navajos to sell percentages of their livestock holdings in

A field nurse pays her weekly visit to a Navajo family in 1936. Field nurses were often the first Western medical providers Navajos met. Courtesy of Arizona State Library, Archives and Public Records, Archives Division, Phoenix, no. 93-9917.

order to reduce the strain that overgrazing placed on the reservation soil. Conceived with seemingly good intentions, the program failed to take into account Navajo ways of relating to their animals. Nor did Collier and other officials pay sufficient attention to Navajo attitudes about and proposed solutions for the soil erosion problem. Some families were not even aware of the program's existence until government workers came to slaughter their sheep, goats, and horses. Largely because of the livestock reduction, many Navajos hated Collier, and Navajo distrust of federal intentions showed through in Tribal Council meetings. Yet tribal leaders had comparatively few conflicts with the BIA Medical Division.

At the beginning of the Great Depression, tuberculosis, trachoma, and infant mortality rates for the Navajos far surpassed national averages. Despite a growing federal commitment to Indian health care, Western medical services for the Navajos were woefully inadequate. Existing facilities were understaffed and lacked the technology to help curb high death rates. Of nine hospitals, only three had x-ray machines, and the BIA Medical Division had no laboratory facilities of its own. In addition, the Navajo population continued to grow, reaching roughly 40,000 in 1930, which limited the BIA's ability to meet their medical needs.[27]

Appointed as BIA commissioner in 1933 under Franklin Roosevelt's presidency, John Collier promised to provide better medical services for American Indians. In 1934, the commissioner chose Dr. W. W. Peter to supervise the Navajo medical program, because the physician shared Collier's vision, enthusiasm, and drive, and had a strong background in public health. Peter planned to revamp the medical delivery system, injecting New Deal funding to improve and expand reservation medical facilities, and promising higher standards for health care workers. He placed a greater emphasis on preventive health with a particular focus on health education efforts and intensified campaigns against trachoma, tuberculosis, and venereal disease. Immunization and field nursing programs were to be stepped up and a laboratory added. He planned a centralized medical system, extending out into the field and including multiple facilities.[28]

Under Peter's direction, the BIA expanded its medical facilities network on the Navajo reservation, supporting a total of eleven hospitals and two tuberculosis sanatoriums by 1940. Among these was the Navajo Medical Center at Fort Defiance containing 140 beds, constructed in 1938 with $450,000 of Works Progress Administration funds. The Medical Center took the most difficult medical and surgical cases from other reservation hospitals, served as a base for staff training, and provided housing for dental and laboratory services. In all, the number of hospital beds for the Navajos more than doubled throughout the 1930s, expanding from 268 in 1929 to 564 in 1940. The hospitals were also better equipped than before, with new x-ray machines at the facilities in Crownpoint (New Mexico) and Fort Defiance. In addition, dispensaries were established at multiple points across the reservation.[29]

As the quantity and quality of medical facilities improved, so did the medical staff during the 1930s. By 1940, the Indian Service employed 326 medical workers, including a growing number of Navajos as ancillary staff. Included in this number were over a dozen medical doctors (all still non-Navajo) who were, in general, better trained and had stronger qualifications than their predecessors. The BIA found it easier to attract skilled physicians because more stringent Civil Service requirements weeded out less qualified applicants and the Great Depression made the $3,200 annual salary more appealing.[30]

In conjunction with changes in the size and quality of its clinical facilities and staff, government-sponsored Western medicine became more comprehensive by focusing more on preventive health. To some extent, field dentists (who traveled to see their patients) played a role in this process, but that medical service remained largely inadequate throughout the 1930s. The primary players in preventive health were, without a doubt, the field nurses, who were responsible for reaching Navajo patients far from the nearest medical facilities.[31]

Field nursing in the New Deal capitalized on a program that had developed prior to Collier and Peter's appointments. The BIA originally had been coaxed into implementing field nurses by the New Mexico Association on Indian Affairs (NMAIA), a private organization founded in 1922. With the BIA's consent, the group had hired a few field nurses, including Elizabeth Forster and Mollie Reebel, to serve a number of New Mexico pueblos. In 1930, the NMAIA dispatched Forster and Reebel to care for Navajos living to the west and south of Shiprock. They took to the job with great enthusiasm and ingenuity. Whereas the BIA's field matrons had been frustrated by Navajo seasonal migrations, the NMAIA nurses began following Navajos to their summer camps in the mountains, where they conducted clinics. The field nurses also proved more adept than many of the matrons at earning Navajo acceptance. They chipped away at Navajo shyness and suspicion by caring for Navajo livestock and

playing active roles in the Navajo communities—including sponsoring
Christmas parties and coaching Navajo basketball teams.[32]

Reebel and Forster also showed a respect for Navajo beliefs and practices rarely displayed by non-Indian medical providers in that era. They
did not interfere with traditional Navajo healing practices and sometimes
worked in close cooperation with Navajo practitioners. "It was in June
that I was called to a hogan to help a Navajo midwife deliver a baby!"
reported Forster in 1932. "I wouldn't have missed the experience for anything. I had mostly to do the lady's bidding but was able to introduce a few
hygienic measures of my own. We had no less than eighteen interested
spectators (men, women, and children) and more arrived too late for the
real excitement." Forster found that the Navajo healers were more than
willing to respect and welcome her in return:

> When I came here a year ago I soon realized that the Navajos here-
> abouts expected to find me antagonistic to their religious customs
> and were slow to consult me about illness until the medicine man
> had failed to help, but gradually they are showing more confidence
> in my good will and often notify me that they are having a sing and
> invite me to attend. Sometimes I am invited to practice medicine
> with the medicine man, sometimes I am asked to await the conclu-
> sion of the sing so as to be on hand to take the patient to the hos-
> pital. I am surprised and gratified to find my medicine men friendly
> and often cooperative. One of them tells me with a serious twinkle
> that he is glad to have me attend his sings and see good medicine
> practiced.[33]

The NMAIA nurses' successes helped convince the BIA to take a more
active role in field nursing. The Bureau took over full responsibility for
field nursing in 1935. Reebel stayed on as a BIA staff member and helped
the government medical service institutionalize the use of temporary clinics and other methods she and Forster had pioneered. The new nurses
drove hundreds of miles annually, ferrying patients to and from hospitals,
conducting health and hygiene seminars, administering first aid, and dispensing medicine. Often living in tents they took with them into the
mountains, the nurses were the front line of the medical program. They
worked long hours and rarely knew what would be expected of them from
week to week.[34]

Dedication of the BIA hospital for Navajos at Fort Defiance, Arizona, 20 June 1938. Courtesy of Dodge Collection, Labriola National American Indian Data Center, Arizona State University Libraries, SPC 125:1.

Field health services were closely tied to the government school system. Boarding schools had long served as bases for extending Western medicine to Navajo children, and ten of them on and around the reservation continued to do so. As day schools became more prevalent during the New Deal, the BIA Medical Division turned its attention toward them. Commissioner Collier wanted the new school buildings to serve as community centers, medical clinics, and subagencies as well as educational institutions.[35]

The BIA relied heavily on school teachers to provide medical services to students. Even though they lacked formal medical training, teachers were encouraged to instruct children in proper hygiene habits, sanitation, and infant care, and when field nurses and physicians were not present, it fell upon them to administer daily treatments to children suffering from trachoma. No doubt, these efforts had a significant impact on many Navajo students, but most children did not attend school, in part because of transportation problems and seasonal migration patterns.[36]

During the 1930s, the Medical Division enjoyed some success combating disease, especially trachoma. Hospital and field nursing reports early in the decade estimated that one-third of all Navajos suffered from the eye disease. The Southwestern Trachoma Campaign initiated in the 1920s had failed to prevent the ailment from inflicting pain and blindness on thousands of American Indians. But the BIA Medical Division finally achieved a breakthrough with trachoma between 1938 and 1940, using new sulfanilamide drugs. Previous treatments that included painful surgeries and caustics ended as the drug therapies proved effective. The gains against trachoma were neither complete nor permanent, but served as a key step in convincing Navajos that non-Indian doctors and nurses had real healing power.[37]

Western medicine proved less effective against tuberculosis. A 1938 estimate showed about 900 active cases of tuberculosis on the reservation, in spite of a variety of BIA efforts to combat the disease. In an attempt to provide better clinical care for tuberculosis patients and to separate them from the rest of the population, the BIA added a new sanitorium at Winslow, Arizona. In addition, in 1935, Navajo school children began receiving the new Bacillus-Calmette-Gruerin vaccine on a volunteer basis. Field nurses also began a campaign to check students for the disease using x-rays.[38]

The increased efforts produced few results. Government personnel laid part of the blame for the disease's persistence on insufficient federal services, but Navajo reluctance to seek BIA treatment proved more problematic. Hundreds of patients who needed treatment simply were not seeking care, in large part because sanatorium treatment required long stays far from home. Many patients who did agree to accept medical care waited until the disease had reached an advanced painful stage, and little could be done for them. BIA superintendents and physicians worried that those who refused institutionalized care posed a continuing threat to others as well as to themselves.[39]

Although the Navajo response to sanatoriums proved discouraging to the BIA, the government employees could find encouragement in the Navajos' growing willingness to accept their other health care services during the 1930s. The average number of Navajo patients entering BIA hospitals remained relatively high during the decade in comparison to the number of beds available. Hospitals with official bed capacities of between twenty and fifty consistently showed average daily patient loads ranging from forty to fifty. A wider variety of patients seemed to be using the hospitals than in previous years, although most were still boarding school children and maternity patients. Overcrowding became a real problem for the BIA facilities. In addition to finding room for patients, hospitals had to accommodate family members who often stayed at their side. Family support helped patients overcome misgivings about entering the alien hospital environment; sometimes loved ones waited outside or in hallways and occasionally mothers occupied the same bed as their sick children.[40]

Dr. Peter delighted in the "very large numbers" of Navajos who came each year to BIA facilities, including approximately nine thousand patients between 1935 and 1936. Clearly, increased medical accessibility, links established with patients by the field health program, and Western medicine's proven ability to deal with trachoma, prompted many Navajos to accept government treatment more regularly.[41]

The Navajo Tribal Council

The New Deal also marked the beginning of the Navajo Tribal government's advisory and participatory involvement in Western medicine, in part because of Dr. Peter's willingness to work closely with them, and in part because they had come to realize the importance of Western medical services on the reservation. Council delegates came to know Peter well and they were well informed about medical activity on the reservation. Influential leaders such as Chee Dodge (the first tribal chairman and long-time liaison between traditional Navajos and U.S. officials), Pete Price (a traditional healer), Jacob C. Morgan, Dashne Cla Chiscschillige, and Howard Gorman numbered among those who were willing to accept new approaches, and were interested in what Peter had to say about health care. These tribal leaders represented a wide variety of viewpoints on different issues. They often disagreed about politics, religion, and education. And they rarely shared common attitudes about traditional healing and the role that it should play in their people's future. Yet, remarkably, they were all advocates of Western medicine.[42]

Many Tribal Council delegates recognized that their constituents were using government hospitals in increasing numbers, and they frequently asked for new facilities and better funding. Influential members, including Dodge and Morgan, sought treatment in government and missionary hospitals, thereby demonstrating their confidence in Western medicine. With Peter's encouragement, the Council also contributed financially to

Chee Dodge, the first Navajo tribal chairman. Dodge favored, and worked tirelessly to promote, a wide variety of healing options for his people, including the traditional ways, BIA services, and missionary medicine. Courtesy of the Arizona Historical Foundation, University Libraries, Arizona State University, KR-78.

the medical program and increasingly played the role of intermediary between the BIA Medical Division and the Navajo population. The Council did not command the respect of every Navajo on the reservation, but its cooperation and advocacy proved important to the Medical Division's efforts.

A working relationship between the BIA and Tribal Council on health issues had begun in the 1920s when agency officials tried to win their cooperation in the antitrachoma and tuberculosis efforts. Throughout the 1920s, BIA representatives worked to develop a relationship with the Navajo leaders, reporting on Medical Division activity and stressing the importance of health and hygiene during Council meetings. The Council delegates listened thoughtfully and voiced their own opinions, demonstrating that they cared deeply about health issues and wanted to see a larger medical presence on the reservation.[43]

Peter tried to capitalize on this relationship and to encourage an even greater unity of purpose. He delivered detailed reports and planned elaborate demonstrations for each Council meeting. When typhoid fever hit the reservation in 1938, for example, Peter stepped out in front of the Council and invited Price, Dodge, and others to look at the organism through a microscope. Price proclaimed that what he saw "looked like a vision." While Dodge looked into the microscope, Peter explained that these little dots that appeared through the microscope "as big as a spot on his hat" had probably infected forty-five reservation residents by way of their food or drink. Peter took the test tube and held it over the flame of an alcohol lamp:

> You can see what is happening in there. Do you see them? There are bunches of them together rolling up and dying by the million[s] as I boil them over this flame. There are millions now who are dead. This is the biggest funeral we have ever had on the Navajo Reservation. Much of the water on this Reservation apparently has the typhoid germs in it. What I am doing here on the stage is something that should be done in every hogan. Boil your drinking water.[44]

Taking the tube away from the flame, Peter poured it into a glass and drank it. "You would have to hold a gun to my head to make me drink living germs," he said. Such tactics may have led some delegates to question Peter's sanity, but they seemed pleased to take part in his demonstrations, and willingly spread the word to their constituents.[45]

Peter also encouraged the tribe to institutionalize the cooperative relationship with a formal body. In November 1934, Peter proposed that the tribe establish its own committee on health. "The purpose of such a designated group," Peter later explained, "would be to acquaint themselves with all existing facilities available for health service; for interpreting these facilities and modern health concepts to the people; and enlisting their understanding and participation." He then handed the responsibility for its creation to a Navajo committee composed of Morgan, Henry Taliman, Luke Bradley, and the new Tribal Council Chairman Thomas Dodge (Chee Dodge's son). In 1938, the Council voted on the proposed committee along with similar committees for education and trading and accepted it, by a tally of fifty-four to zero. Five committee members were selected with Teddy Nez as its chairman and given the responsibility for advising the tribe on health issues.[46]

The Council also committed limited tribal funds to health care. Tribal leaders knew that they depended heavily on the U.S. government and the missionaries to provide the bulk of medical services, but they saw the value in supplementing those services in special cases. Peter frequently approached the Council with the hope that it would support medical services with tribal money, and the Council delivered. Twice, in 1937 and again in 1940, by a unanimous vote, they allocated funds to help the BIA support a dentist at Fort Defiance. These first appropriations were relatively small ($5,000 in this particular case), but the tribe's role in reservation health care had begun.[47]

New Deal Attitudes About Traditional Healing

As part of his "Indian New Deal," John Collier hoped to restore the power of traditional culture to American Indian societies. This reversal in federal Indian policy promised better relations between Navajo healers and the BIA based on coexistence if not necessarily cooperation. To aid this process, Collier dispatched psychiatrists and anthropologists to study Navajo traditions in greater detail as the 1930s drew to a close. Many medical employees, however, were not ready for these changes and either accepted them half-heartedly or rejected them outright.[48]

Even those employees who felt that the BIA should establish a cordial relationship with Navajo singers tended to be acting pragmatically rather than out of interprofessional respect. Peter exemplified this generally ambivalent attitude. He seems to have genuinely respected Navajo beliefs and practices and understood from a tactical standpoint that winning the approval of Navajo healers was no less important than winning approval from the Tribal Council. The best publicized instance of official amiable relations with the healers came in 1938 when, with Chee Dodge's blessings, Peter asked Pete Price to dedicate the new Fort Defiance Medical Center with a Blessingway ceremony. But, in official reports, Peter tended to refer to the healers as competitors, and he believed that the healers still held the advantage.[49]

Some government physicians and nurses continued to oppose the healers openly. One physician admitted that he had intentionally disrupted healing ceremonies in order to persuade a patient to go to his hospital. The physician disliked a policy that directed BIA employees to keep patients with contagious tuberculosis from entering general hospitals because he worried that this would drive them into the arms of a healer, who he believed could only do harm. "Our job," he declared, "is to accept all patients as far as possible to our institutions and in that way give less work to the medicine man and keep this up until there is no work for him at all."[50]

A few Navajo leaders also opposed Collier's policy of coexistence because they favored assimilation policies. J. C. Morgan, a conservative Christian, particularly disliked the idea of granting government recognition to the healers. "Mr. Collier is very strong for the continued performance of the medicineman of the tribe," said Morgan. "He says that a white man learns and is being educated thru Indian ceremonials. Now let me see about this. Who is a medicineman? . . . [H]e is a judge, loafer, a gambler and often times a drunkard." Morgan also offered multiple examples of the dangers healers presented to Navajo health. He argued that Yeibichai dancers spread trachoma by sharing masks and that healers only exacerbated the disease with their treatments. Soon after the ceremony, Morgan contended, the dancers' eyes were all "red as beets" from the disease.[51]

Even though Collier's policy changes achieved only limited headway, the transition was significant. For the first time, the BIA had thrown its official support behind Navajo efforts to seek the benefits of traditional as well as Western medicine.

Missionary Medicine in the New Deal

Just as the BIA Medical Division grew in size and improved the quality of its services in the 1930s, so did the missionary medical efforts. Overall, missionary health care became more accessible and more effective during the 1930s, and Navajos began to utilize their facilities in greater numbers. To some degree, the secular and sectarian medical presences competed against each other as government hospitals spread out across the reservation. The Episcopalians, for instance, finally closed their Good Shepherd Hospital in 1930 after years of competing with the BIA's Fort Defiance hospital. Nevertheless, as the Navajo demand for health care services continued to rise, missionaries elsewhere on the reservation found ample opportunities for their medical programs.

No mission took greater advantage of the medical approach than the Presbyterians at Ganado, and few missionaries were as influential on the reservation as its superintendent and physician, Clarence Salsbury. Together with his wife Cora, Salsbury took over the Ganado mission in 1927, and under their direction, the mission and its medical effort grew impressively. While the Episcopalian hospital disappeared and the

Dr. Clarence Salsbury and a newly purchased ambulance for Sage Memorial Hospital, Ganado, Arizona, 1932. Courtesy of Arizona State Library, Archives and Public Records, Archives Division, Phoenix, no. 93-9911.

Ruth Henderson (left) and Adele Slivers (right), Navajos and the first two nurses to graduate from the Sage Memorial School of Nursing, 29 November 1933. Also included, back row, from left to right: BIA Superintendent of the Southern Navajo Reservation John G. Hunter, Singer Red Point, Dr. Salsbury, and Arizona Governor B. B. Moeur. Courtesy of Arizona State Library, Archives and Public Records, Archives Division, Phoenix, no. 93-9903.

Christian Reformed Church's remained relatively small, the Presbyterians constructed a new one that rivaled the largest government facilities. By the end of the New Deal, neither the BIA nor the Navajo Tribal Council could ignore Salsbury or his medical program.[52]

Salsbury understood the importance of traditional healing in Navajo country. At first, Salsbury showed little interest in learning about Navajo healing, but he soon found that the singers he hoped to replace could be useful allies. In fact, if it had not been for a healer named Red Point, Salsbury's practice would have ended in failure after a little girl died of an embolism on the operating table. It did not help his situation that, up to that point, no Navajo had agreed to go under his knife, and it had taken him three days to persuade the girl's parents to grant permission for the surgery. Upon hearing about the death, every patient in the hospital left. Soon after, an angry crowd began to form outside, and Salsbury feared for his own safety, but Red Point intervened on his behalf and reminded the gathered people that healers had also had patients die. This event made an obvious impression on Salsbury, who soon began working to improve relations with local singers.[53]

A Franciscan missionary examining a Navajo girl, date unknown, but probably in the 1930s or early 1940s. Although the Catholics did not have a hospital for the Navajos, as did many of the Protestant missionaries, they offered limited medical care. Original photograph by George Thompson. Courtesy of Center for Southwest Research, Zimmerman Library, University of New Mexico, no. 000-461-0433.

Salsbury convinced victims of a 1929 flu and diphtheria epidemic to come to Ganado, by taking a picture of five healers who had sought care in the hospital and distributing it as an endorsement. Soon the Presbyterians had difficulty keeping up with the demand for their medical services, especially during epidemics, and they were forced to put up tents adjacent to the building to handle the overload.[54]

Salsbury also proved to be a skilled administrator and fund raiser. At his urging, the church gave the mission $50,000 to construct a new seventy-five–bed facility in 1930, named Sage Memorial after its primary benefactor, the Russell Sage Foundation. Salsbury had similar success with tribal leaders. Although a Catholic, Chee Dodge frequently used the facility, and after Salsbury treated his son, he contributed $500 to the hospital. Using donations from Dodge and other Navajos who had taken an interest in Sage Memorial, Salsbury added a new x-ray machine. With its new hospital and technology, Ganado became the gem of the Presbyterian home missions.[55]

Salsbury capitalized on this success in 1934 by sponsoring four-day Chautauquas, inviting local Navajos to attend social events, hear the Christian message, and attend clinics run by dentists and physicians the Presbyterians brought in for the occasion. Clarence and Cora Salsbury also established the first nursing school for Native American women, hoping that Indian nurses would help win over Indian patients. The school graduated its first two registered nurses in 1933 with a ceremony attended by Red Point and Arizona Governor B. B. Moeur. By 1940, the school had forty-two students and had extended its program to include women from Japan, China, Cuba, and other countries.[56]

The mission's purpose did not change in this process. The missionaries could not be satisfied with healthy patients if they had not been saved spiritually. Even though Salsbury openly cooperated with traditional healers, he still believed that they would have to eventually yield to Christianity and modern medicine. Anyone in Ganado would have understood this attitude by observing a conspicuous sign in front of the mission that read, "Tradition is the Enemy of Progress." While Salsbury sought out new patients, his wife and others at the mission worked on their souls. Patients who came to the hospital could expect to hear from a full-time evangelist assigned to bring them spiritual enlightenment while they were in the ward. Daily services were held in the Navajo language in which patients were taught Bible stories, Christian hymns, and simple prayers. According to Cora Salsbury, "the opportunity, privilege, and influence, of this quiet, persistent work" was "inestimable."[57]

The missionaries' goals now clashed with the BIA's. Most missionaries were not pleased with Collier's efforts to reverse assimilation policy, fearing that the commissioner's encouragement of traditional Indian cultures would steer the Navajos away from Christianity, economic progress, and good health. Of all the denominations, the Christian Reformed Church was the most openly opposed to Collier's program. In 1936, the General Conference of Missionaries of the Christian Reformed Church published an open letter to Collier that denounced him for encouraging a return to pagan religions and cultures. Among many concerns, they expressed serious misgivings about Collier's attitudes toward traditional healers. "Are you, Mr. Collier, taking a 'positive' attitude toward the medicine-man

Navajo patients wait for medical attention at Sage Memorial Hospital's dispensary, Ganado, Arizona, ca. 1948. Courtesy of Arizona State Library, Archives and Public Records, Archives Division, Phoenix, no. 93-9902.

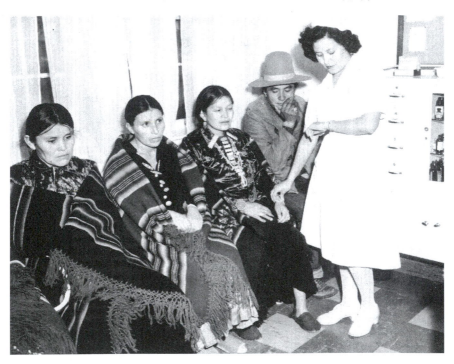

The Presbyterian mission at Ganado, Arizona, 1940. Sage Memorial Hospital is the large building in the lower right. Courtesy of Arizona State Library, Archives and Public Records, Archives Division, Phoenix, no. 93-9916.

also?" the letter asked with sarcastic disbelief. "Do you really wish to 'encourage' him and do you want to 'cooperate' with him?" Dr. Richard Pousma at Rehoboth made his opinion of traditional healers and those Anglos who supported them perfectly clear, claiming that those who encouraged their patients to attend sings were "idiotic, exceedingly stupid, and ignorant of conditions among the Indians."[58]

Not all missionaries echoed Pousma. Franciscan Father Berard Haile at St. Michael's showed a great deal of respect for Navajo beliefs and healers. He also had a more cordial relationship with Collier; he even helped draft a doomed tribal constitution in 1936. The Franciscans offered only basic medical services to Navajo parishioners, but Haile played an active role in the developing relations between Western and traditional medicine. Father Haile intently studied Navajo ceremonial ways and wrote prolifically about the culture. He believed that the missionaries could not understand the heart of the people they served without first understanding their traditions and ceremonies. Despite his understanding and patience, however, Haile saw no room for Navajo ceremonialism in the lives of those Navajos who converted to

Marianne Jewell Memorial Library
Baker College of Muskegon
Muskegon, Michigan 49442

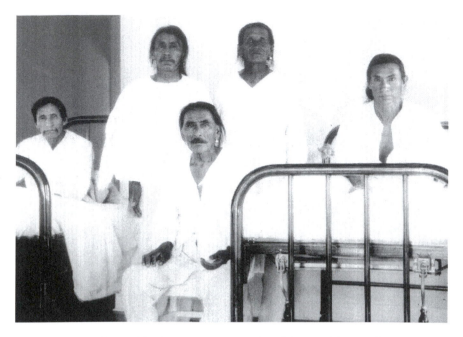

Five Navajo traditional healers as patients at Sage Memorial Hospital, 1940.
Dr. Salsbury distributed this picture widely across the reservation to win greater
Navajo acceptance of his hospital. Courtesy of Arizona State Library, Archives
and Public Records, Archives Division, Phoenix, no. 98-9889.

Catholicism. Catholics could attend "morally clean" dances, but he argued that they could not participate in the healing ceremonies. "While our Catholics do not fully perhaps understand that the practice of native religion is incompatible with the Catholic religion, they must be warned repeatedly on this point. If that is of no avail and they persist in demanding ceremonials and in practicing as singers they cannot be recognized as Catholics."[59]

The divergent missionary and government ideologies stirred tensions between them, but fortunately for Navajo patients, these were played out verbally and seemed not to interfere with their medical activity. For the most part, Salsbury and the other missionaries cooperated with the BIA Medical Division. Peter had his staff attend seminars at Sage Memorial on occasion. In turn, Salsbury gave physical exams to government Civil Conservation Corps workers, and BIA field nurses were allowed to conduct medical surveys at Ganado. Behind the scenes Salsbury and Collier had a less-than-amiable relationship. The commissioner disapproved of Salsbury's advertising that government agents would attend his Chautauquas, because he wanted to avoid any association between government programs and Christian proselytizing. According to historian Donald Parman, Salsbury also believed that Collier had encouraged the Navajos to begin holding tribal fairs in 1938 to draw attention away from his Chautauqua.[60]

Peter had little patience for missionary tirades against official policy or interference with his activities. He was particularly irritated by a Protestant minister's hesitation to appear with Pete Price at the medical center dedication. Reverend G. W. Helms informed Peter that he could not attend unless he had a clear idea of what Price would say, lest he be associated with a pagan ceremony. Peter replied that he would no more interfere with Price's ceremony than he would with the missionary's invocation:

Dr. Clarence Salsbury (right), Dr. W. D. Spining (left), and nurses operating at Sage Memorial Hospital, about 1945. Courtesy of Arizona State Library, Archives and Public Records, Archives Division, Phoenix, no. 93-9901.

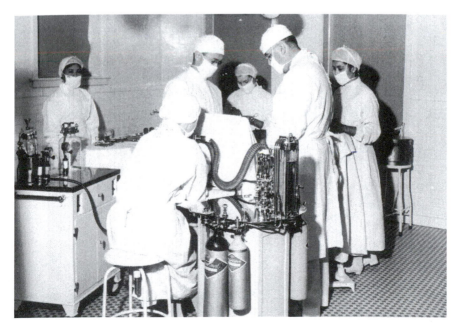

If they want to sing portions of ancient chants, I shall listen respectfully. If they want to sprinkle lintels of the hospital doors with corn meal or pollen, I shall accept that symbolism as their way of expressing their hopes that this new hospital shall serve the health of the Navajo people. If they lead us in a march around the outside of the building, I shall fall in line. If they want to dance, I shall probably keep time with my foot without thinking that their rites are either funny or Pagan. . . . Whatever these medicine man's rites may be, I am almost positively certain that they will not be Episcopalian, Presbyterian, Methodist, Baptist, Reformed Church, Independent Evangelistic, or Catholic. I have a very strong suspicion that they will be purely Navajo—which to some Whites engaged in the business of religion will probably spell nothing short of Pagan.[61]

The Rise of the Peyote Religion

The New Deal years also witnessed the coming of another form of healing to the Navajos. It has been stated previously that the Navajos were willing to incorporate new healing ways when they proved medically effective and nonthreatening to traditional practices and beliefs. The rise of the peyote religion during the 1930s as both a form of spiritualism and healing, and the negative reception it received not only from missionaries and the U.S. government, but from nonpeyotist Navajos, seems to complicate that assertion.

When one considers only those who adopted the religion, the rise of peyotism appears to be a perfect example of how focused Navajos were on health issues and how willing they were to try new methods. Indeed, many of those who practiced the peyote religion continued to use traditional ceremonies and Western medicine. Yet if Navajos were so willing to accept new forms of healing, why did the majority, who did not use peyote, react so negatively to the new religion during the New Deal era? The answer, perhaps, is that the majority of Navajos perceived the peyote religion as threatening to their way of life. It appeared relatively quickly, and it could not be accepted on a simply secular level as could Western medicine.

The peyote religion had become a part of American Indian societies long before it came to the Navajos. The small cactus plant, which contains mescaline and produces both psychological and physiological effects, first came to the attention of Native peoples in Mexico. Centuries after it became common in Mexico, it spread northward to the plains tribes, such as the Comanches and Kiowas who, in the late nineteenth century, began to incorporate the plant into a new form of spiritualism. Unlike Navajo traditional ceremonialism, this new form of spirituality grew as a pan-Indian movement. Yet the peyote religion allowed for variation from tribe to tribe, community to community, and person to person. Originally, the various peyote priests, or "roadmen" as they are known, operated independent of any overseeing body other than God and peyote. Oklahoma practitioners created a central organization known as the Native American Church (NAC) in 1918, for the sole purpose of providing legal protection from federal and state harassment.[62]

As anthropologist David Aberle contends, the peyote religion addresses traditional concerns and beliefs at the same time that it responds to changes brought about after European contact. It is truly a Native American religion in that it stresses differences between Indians and non-Indians and unity among Native peoples, yet in a sense, it bridges Indian and Western culture. The peyote religion, at least in some varieties, incorporates Christian elements, including a belief in Jesus and a heavenly afterlife. It also includes symbolic elements and beliefs that are distinctly Indian.[63]

Aberle has attributed the growth of peyotism among the Navajos in the 1930s to the economic and mental deprivation caused by livestock reduction and the Great Depression. Navajos began turning to the religion as a new source of power in a time of great confusion and distress. It had a special appeal to people caught up in a changing society and economy that focused on the individual, contends Aberle, because it provided a sense of community and belonging while also speaking to the individual's needs. For the individual it offered spiritual redemption, self-empowerment, and a heightened sense of familial duty. For many, peyotism did not replace their traditional beliefs, or Christian ones in some cases, so much as it gave them an added sense of power and well-being.[64]

Navajos in the north became familiar with the peyote religion from contacts they had with neighboring Utes, and a few began to learn how to become roadmen. The religion spread to Shiprock and other northern communities in the mid-1930s, and by 1938 it began gaining participants farther south, including those living around Window Rock and Fort Defiance. By the end of the 1930s the number of Navajos who participated in the peyote religion probably did not exceed 10 percent of the population, but those numbers were growing.[65]

In surveys he conducted in the late 1940s and early 1950s, Aberle found that the majority of new converts had been first attracted by the peyote religion's curing aspects. Like traditional ceremonialism, many of the peyote meetings focused on healing an individual, but the religion appeared to offer advantages that Western medicine and traditional healing did not. NAC meetings were sometimes used to reverse the effects of witchcraft and provide a sense of mental well-being—things that Western medicine could not do. The peyote religion also addressed concerns over modern ailments more directly than traditional ceremonialism, including problems with tuberculosis and, later, cancer. Participants also claimed that peyote helped them to remain sober, which made the religion particularly appealing during years in which alcoholism presented a growing challenge to the Navajo people, especially in and around Gallup.[66]

It did not take long for the peyote religion to attract criticism in Diné Bikéyah. Tensions began increasing between the minority of Navajos who did practice the religion and their neighbors around the reservation, but the issue did not come to a head in the Tribal Council until J. C. Morgan, now chairman, made it a point of debate. Aberle suggests that Morgan may have taken interest in the matter after he heard that Collier supported peyotist rights. In the late 1930s, Roger Davis and Howard Gorman, who were also Christians, joined Morgan in an effort to win Council support for a resolution suppressing the new religion.[67]

In June 1940, Morgan initiated a debate in the Tribal Council about the peyote religion and what should be done about its spread. He made particular use of a report Howard Gorman prepared on the issue. Gorman presented the peyote religion as a "foreign" and insidious threat, not just to Christian beliefs, but to Navajo tradition. "A marriage of Ute, Navajo, Pueblo, Catholic and Protestant rites," Gorman wrote, "peyote ceremonies among the Navajos threaten to destroy the beautiful traditional rites of our people, undermine the health of the tribe, cripple our economy and morality and sever family ties." The report also included testimonies from various Navajo men, some of whom had observed the practices or said they had taken part in them. Any evil effect, it seemed, could be associated with the practice. The peyote rites, they claimed, led to insanity, laziness, lascivious behavior, and health problems, and Roy Kinsel blamed peyote for taking control of his wife and breaking up his home.

Those who practiced, according to some statements, were "dope fiends" and even "murderers."[68]

Non-Christian Navajos also spoke out against the new religion. John Harvey, a traditional healer, considered it a threat to traditional religion and claimed that it had "impaired the wonderful Blessingway." There appears to have been a basis for Harvey's contention. As Aberle has pointed out, the peyote religion and traditional ceremonialism were distinct from one another, but the peyote rites could also be used to achieve the same goals as a Blessingway, and peyotists occasionally used a peyote rite to pray for a successful traditional ceremony. There were some healers who were also roadmen, but in those early years, most traditional practitioners apparently opposed the new religion. Whereas peyotists viewed these connections as mutually supporting, others feared that introducing such foreign ways would corrupt the traditional ways.[69]

Other Navajos openly defended the peyote religion. They claimed that the new "medicine" had real healing power and none of the negative side effects attributed to it. John Curley, for instance, told the Council that the religion had helped some to stop drinking. But the negative arguments overwhelmed the support articulated in the Tribal Council, and the members voted in 1940 to prohibit the religion as a threat to the "traditional way of life." Violators faced up to nine months incarceration and a fine of $100. The resolution passed with nearly unanimous support, fifty-two to one. Only Hola Tso, a NAC member, voted against it.[70]

The passage posed a dilemma for Collier. As a champion of tribal self-government, he could hardly overturn the decision, for to do so would be to strike a blow against tribal autonomy. But the commissioner had also been a proponent of religious freedom and cross-cultural sensitivity and had previously backed peyotist rights. Collier also doubted the accuracy of Gorman's report, especially the assertion that peyote was a "hurtful and habit-forming drug." In the end, however, Collier decided to consent to the resolution.[71]

· 3 ·

ACCEPTANCE, LOSS,
AND NEW EXPECTATIONS,
1941–54

Western medicine provided an important supplement to traditional healing for the Navajos by the early 1940s, but it came with a serious catch.
Traditional healing had been steadfast through the years, but Western
medicine at mid-century proved undependable. The more American Indian people demanded Bureau of Indian Affairs medical care, the more reliant they were on Congressional appropriations and the more affected
they were by broad changes at the national and global levels. Just as
quickly as the New Deal had enhanced BIA medical care for the Navajos,
World War II and its immediate aftermath threatened to reverse the
process, to pull the rug out from underneath them.

World War II meant short-term decreased funding and small medical
staffs, and started a long-term shift toward postwar conservatism. This
shift threatened the very existence of the BIA and its medical division.
Navajos tolerated a shrinking federal commitment to Indian health care
during the war, but in the next decade they and the BIA Medical Division
tried to rebuild and expand health care services for the Diné.

Navajo Health Care, 1940s and Early 1950s

The Navajo population continued to grow rapidly in the 1940s, ap-
proaching 60,000 by the end of the decade, and the government and missionary medical programs were struggling to meet the demand for their
limited services. The BIA's prospects for keeping pace with Indian health
needs were already bleak, as FDR's New Deal came under assault at the

end of the 1930s, and the global conflict made matters much worse. Wartime demands drew funds and personnel away from domestic agencies and crippled their ability to maintain prewar services. The BIA Medical Division found itself a branch of an agency that commanded little attention—so little that the main BIA offices actually had to relocate to Chicago to make room for war-related agencies in Washington, D.C. In such an environment, Peter and his staff had little hope of limiting threats to Navajo health. By the middle of the decade, the Navajo reservation had lost five government hospitals and dozens of physicians and nurses to wartime demands.[1]

The BIA's decreasing ability to maintain its services during the war was offset somewhat by a massive drain of the Navajo population. More than 3,000 Navajos served in the military during World War II, including the famed Marine Corps Code Talkers, and at least 10,000 others took jobs off the reservation. Were it not for this one-fifth of all Navajos who temporarily departed, the health care crisis on the reservation would have been more severe, and it did indeed intensify when thousands of Navajo veterans and workers returned home after the war. Veterans, who acquired a greater appreciation for Western medicine because of their contact with military physicians, returned home only to find a devastated reservation medical program.[2]

Federal expenditures on Indian health care remained stagnant throughout the war years, despite increasing medical costs. The budgetary strains began to show on the Navajo Agency hospitals in 1942 when Leupp Hospital had to close its doors, leaving people on the southwestern corner of the reservation with no medical facilities. The BIA converted the Winslow Sanitorium into a general hospital in an attempt to combine its duties with those of the defunct hospital, but this option did not provide adequate services. The conversion meant fewer beds for Navajo tuberculosis patients across the reservation and left Leupp Navajos with a greater distance to travel to obtain medical care. To add insult to injury, Superintendent James Stewart announced that "in view of the nationwide shortage of automobiles and tires," the Winslow facility would no longer provide transportation assistance to Navajo patients.[3]

Leupp's misfortune was soon repeated elsewhere. The Toadlena and Kayenta hospitals closed in 1944 and the facility at Fort Wingate ended services in 1946. The Medical Division did not close the Tohatchi facility

Navajo girls suffering from both trachoma and tuberculosis, inside a hogan in 1951. Despite Western medical services and traditional healing, these diseases plagued the Navajos throughout the twentieth century. Courtesy of the Arizona Historical Foundation, University Libraries, Arizona State University, RW-92.

entirely, but had to downgrade it and designate it as a health center rather than a hospital. All together the Navajos lost local access to 113 hospital beds.[4]

World War II also meant increased demands on the government medical staff. Dozens of physicians and nurses entered military service, either as volunteers or conscripts. BIA physicians under the age of forty-five were informed that they could either sign up immediately for commissions in the military or be designated Class 1-A to await the draft. This decision hit the BIA particularly hard because its physicians tended to be younger men. W. W. Peter knew that sixteen of his physicians could disappear at any moment. "This new ruling leaves only three of us over the age group," he observed, "and paragraph 5 of the circular of May 20th indicates that we old buzzards are not being left out in the cold for it says that instructions will be issued later covering physicians over 45 years of age." During the war, only the Fort Defiance hospital had more than one physician on staff. The BIA had little hope of recuperating from these staff losses after the war because its wages were not competitive with the private sector or the U.S. Public Health Service.[5]

The field health program especially felt the pinch. The field nurses contributed to the war effort by looking after Navajo women employed in ordnance camps. They helped them with child care and mended broken fingers and toes injured by dropped ammunition, yet neither they nor other field medical providers nor the Navajo depot workers gained the recognition they deserved. Instead, the BIA allowed the field medical staff to dwindle. By the end of the war, the Navajo Agency supported one field nurse and one field dentist and no itinerant physicians.[6]

Peace in 1945 did not signal an end to the staff shortages. A nationwide nursing shortage continued into the late 1940s. The paucity of nurses prevented the BIA from operating hospitals at their prewar capacity and forced many of them to either reduce their patient loads or close down. Even the Fort Defiance Medical Center had to cordon off its third floor and sacrifice thirty-five beds in order to stay open. It became a cyclical problem; the more serious the shortages were, the harder things became on BIA nurses and the more difficult it became to entice new ones to enter the service. "Our nurses are being worked to the point of exhaustion and I fear that some will quit if they do not soon obtain relief," complained Crownpoint physician Raymond Mundt.[7]

The BIA Medical Division had to face a variety of difficult decisions as its operating costs exceeded its funding during and after the war. In 1946, Dr. D. J. Hunt summed up the frustration he and his colleagues on the Navajo reservation experienced over the inadequate budget. "Almost every Agency that I visit is certain that the funds are going to be considerably short of enough to finish out the year," he commented. "What advice should I give them as to this situation, which I know is of great concern to all? Should I advise the immediate curtailment of activities, or should we continue to run until we have to close down entirely?"[8]

The quality of remaining BIA health care services also deteriorated during the decade. As clerical staffs were cut, medical record keeping essentially ceased. In 1947, the Bureau instructed its physicians to defer elective surgery until the end of the fiscal year because of an absence of funds. Administrators were forced to cut corners wherever possible. The strain took its toll on the shrunken staff. Mundt complained in 1948 that the BIA had promised to provide physicians and nurses at Crownpoint for two years, and he volunteered to pay for a help-wanted advertisement in the *Journal of the American Medical Association*. Mundt suggested that the BIA might have to find a replacement for him as well if the agency did not take action on the matter.⁹

Congress finally increased appropriations for Navajo health care in 1948, but only after severe blizzards on the Navajo and Hopi reservations in the winter of 1947–48 made national news. The Indian Rights Association, American Medical Association, and other groups began studying conditions on the Navajo reservation in great detail, and their accounts of malnutrition, high tuberculosis and infant mortality rates, inadequate housing, and ineffective preventive measures added to the public's growing awareness and concern. A wave of criticism followed, directed at federal Indian policy and the BIA in particular. Non-Indian Americans wrote angry letters to Congress chastising the government for neglecting American Indians while sending massive amounts of aid to postwar Europe.¹⁰

Perhaps prompted by the public outcry, Congress requested that

American Indian nurses caring for Navajo infants at Sage Memorial Hospital, ca. 1948. Courtesy of Arizona State Library, Archives and Public Records, Archives Division, Phoenix, no. 93-9924.

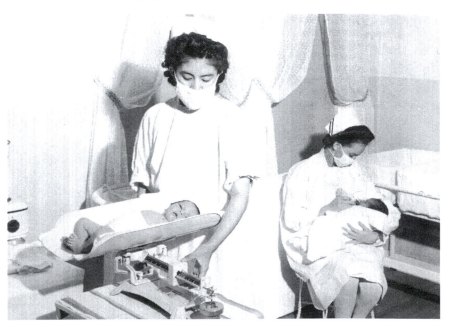

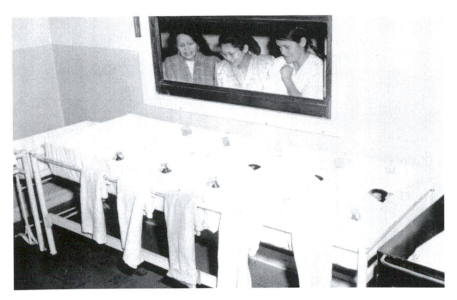

New mothers look at their babies in the Sage Memorial Hospital nursery, ca. 1948. Maternity patients often made up the bulk of missionary and government hospital patients on the Navajo reservation. Courtesy of Arizona State Library, Archives and Public Records, Archives Division, Phoenix, no. 93-9926.

Secretary of the Interior J. A. Krug assess the Navajo-Hopi situation and make recommendations. In March 1948, Krug submitted a plan that became the basis for the Navajo-Hopi Long-Range Rehabilitation Act, which President Truman signed into law in 1950. It authorized $90 million for the Navajo and Hopi reservations over a ten-year period for social programs and infrastructure improvements. The Act promised to improve Navajo and Hopi health conditions by authorizing $4,750,000 specifically for medical care programs. The health funds were designated for updating hospitals and increasing the number of beds, establishing field health clinics, hiring more itinerant physicians and dentists, and establishing a stronger public health program. Other aspects of the Act promised to affect health care delivery less directly. For instance, it authorized nearly $40 million for road construction and over a million for sanitation.[11]

The BIA Medical Division took advantage of the Long-Range Rehabilitation Act to gain back some of the ground it had lost during the war. New construction included a seventy-five–bed hospital for Tuba City, and more than three dozen new wells for the Navajo reservation. Staff levels increased as well. By 1955, the Navajo Agency supported more than four hundred health care workers, including twenty-three physicians, half a dozen dentists, eighty public health nurses, and three sanitation aides. But the Navajo population continued to grow as well, and the new funds stopped far short of solving the BIA Medical Division's funding crisis.[12]

The BIA's woes came at an inauspicious time for the Navajos. Infectious diseases, malnutrition, and infant mortality were still rampant among the Navajos, while problems with alcoholism and auto accidents were increasing. Only a few years after Navajos had accepted the utility of Western medicine, their demand and need for it were as high as ever.[13]

Missionary Medical Care

While BIA medical services plodded along, other forms of healing were still available to the Navajos. Traders were still key players, dispensing remedies and serving as uncertified paramedics. When accidents occurred, traders often administered first aid before the patients traveled to the nearest hospital. In 1946, Dr. R. B. Snavely, who replaced W. W. Peter as supervisor of medical services to the Navajos in 1942, expressed concern that traders, lacking any formal medical training, were diagnosing Navajo patients and administering penicillin to them; but he had to admit that they were helping the medical program weather difficult times.[14]

The missionaries also continued to play a vital role in Navajo health care. With help from Harry Goulding, a trader at Monument Valley, the Seventh Day Adventists added their resources to the medical missionary effort. The denomination offered first aid to the Navajos as early as 1917, but was little involved in reservation health care until a married couple arrived in 1941: Marvin Walter, an experienced missionary, and Gwen Walter, a registered nurse. They carried on with field health and, in 1945, helped to open a small clinic in Farmington, New Mexico. Goulding saw in the Seventh Day Adventists an opportunity to answer a desperate need for medical care in southern Utah. Navajos there had little access to Western medicine of any kind, living about seventy-five miles from the nearest government facility in Tuba City. In 1951, the trader offered the Seventh Day Adventists a grant of land and water rights, and in exchange the Walters agreed to offer basic health and education services for the population. It took them six years to establish a small clinic for the area, but with Goulding's help, they worked to meet a need that a war-weakened BIA could not address.[15]

The Christian Reformed Mission at Rehoboth and the Presbyterians at Ganado continued to work among the Navajos in the 1940s and 1950s, but they also felt the war's pinch. When the conflict began, Sage Memorial had four physicians, a dentist, and ten graduate nurses on staff, but gas and tire rationing forced the mission to cut back its medical fieldwork, and staffing problems threatened its clinical activity. Two of the four physicians were called to military duty. One went to the Army and the other, Dr. McPherson, was performing surgery when a Japanese kamikaze smashed into his ship, killing him. Sage Memorial's nursing staff suffered as well. Salsbury, although pleased by the opportunity for his students to distinguish themselves internationally, lamented that the Red Cross, Navy, and Army robbed the hospital of all fifteen nurses the Sage nursing school graduated in 1943.[16]

The smaller staff found ways to work through the difficulties and kept the hospital functioning. Salsbury took pride in Sage's contributions on the home front as well as overseas. In one instance, Cora and Clarence Salsbury and two of their graduate nurses helped rescue and treat a bomber crew that crashed in Canyon de Chelly during maneuvers. Following the war, Sage's two physicians and depleted nursing staff administered care to more than 2,000 inpatients and over 3,000 dispensary patients annually. In 1948, the staff performed a record-breaking 415 operations and 185 deliveries and followed that up with 552 operations and 231 births the next year.[17]

The Salsburys retired in 1950 and moved away from Navajo country, leaving Dr. W. D. Spining as medical director at Sage and Joseph Poncel as the mission administrator. Salsbury came out of retirement in 1952 to accept an appointment as chief of the Bureau of Preventive Medical Services for the Arizona State Health Department. From Phoenix, he continued to reach out to the Navajos. In the early 1950s his agency conducted a syphilis survey on the reservation, and he took advantage of a Public Health Service grant to study the reasons for low cancer rates among the Diné.[18]

Breaching Cross-Cultural Barriers

Although the 1940s were difficult times for reservation health care, the decade did see some encouraging changes regarding cross-cultural relations

between Western medical providers and the Navajos. As the 1940s progressed, the Medical Division gained access to anthropological studies that
Commissioner Collier had encouraged in the late 1930s. Two psychiatrists
from the Phipps Psychiatry Clinic at Johns Hopkins, Alexander and Dorothea Leighton, and an anthropologist from Harvard, Clyde Kluckhohn,
played important roles in sensitizing BIA medical employees to Navajo
culture.

Kluckhohn and the Leightons had prior interests in Navajo culture.
Kluckhohn had begun formal fieldwork in Navajo country in 1936. The
Leightons, with Kluckhohn's assistance, turned their attention to the
Navajos a few years later, believing that they could better understand patients from their own culture if they studied the lifeways of individuals in
other cultures. In 1940, the Leightons began working with Collier and his
administrative assistant, D'Arcy McNickle, a Salish-Kutenai man who
shared the commissioner's belief that American Indians could adapt to
change without rejecting traditional ways. With McNickle's administrative guidance, the Leightons were asked to produce a manual for Indian
Service health care workers that would help them to understand and respect their Navajo patients.[19]

The Leightons spent four months in 1940 collecting research for what
became *The Navaho Door*. Their conclusions in the book and preliminary
articles met with Collier's expectations. The Navajos were intensely concerned about health, the Leightons argued, and were pragmatic when it
came to medical care. The researchers claimed that traditional healing offered real benefits, particularly emotional and psychological ones, but
they also contended that ceremonies could be potentially dangerous if
they prevented or delayed a hospital visit. The Leightons believed that
the best results would be obtained if physicians and nurses helped Navajo
patients and healers distinguish between cases that needed immediate
medical attention and those that did not. In this process, the healers were
to be treated as colleagues rather than competitors. Perhaps the
Leightons' most central premise was that Western medicine would gain
greater acceptance only as long as it did not appear overbearing:

> If our medicine is to help and not harm the Navajo, we must avoid
> clean sweeps. We must get them to accept and use our pertinent,
> practical knowledge without undermining their faith. That faith
> must grow and adjust also, but it must not be ruthlessly attacked sim-

ply because it offers some obstacles to medicine. Instead, white medicine should be expressed to the Navajos in terms of their own culture, in ways that fit into their understanding of the world and their scale of values.[20]

The Leightons also offered practical advice to BIA employees to help them apply these principles. Care givers, they said, should be aware that Navajos considered excessive questioning to be rude and should work harder at listening to their patients. Because Navajos were accustomed to traditional healing's exactness, claimed the Leightons, doctors could expect them to follow directions if they were translated properly and devoid of overly technical terms. In fact, whenever possible, physicians and nurses should explain medical concepts by comparing them to traditional beliefs. The book provided sample dialogues to assist in this process. For example, a physician could explain that a patient had been infected with syphilis even though no symptoms had appeared, just as a taboo transgression might have no apparent ill effect on a person's health until later in life. They also suggested that physicians pay attention to the realities of Navajo life. It would be useless, for instance, to tell Navajos to take pills at certain times or to wash before meals if their patients had no clocks or did not have easy access to water.[21]

The commissioner hailed the Leightons' work as a great breakthrough for Navajo health care. "For the first time," Collier declared, "we began to see the practicability of utilizing the inherent values of the native culture to improve health and living conditions among a primitive group in which the incidence of disease and the death rate continue high in spite of every effort of modern medicine."[22]

Collier had hoped that the Leightons could stay on to help see their recommendations through to fruition. In 1941, he hired Dorothea Leighton as a consultant psychiatrist to the BIA but lost Alexander Leighton to World War II when the Naval Reserves called him to active duty in December. Clyde Kluckhohn avoided military service because of a heart lesion and stayed on the Navajo reservation long enough to coauthor two books with Dorothea Leighton. Together, Kluckhohn and Leighton published *The Navaho* in 1946 and *Children of the People* in 1947, in which they offered a detailed look at Navajo culture, health, and healing.[23]

It is difficult to know if these studies had a significant effect on BIA medical personnel and their attitudes regarding Navajo patients and

healers. After Collier departed in 1945, the BIA did not show great enthusiasm for cross-cultural studies or applied anthropology. McNickle
claimed in 1959 that BIA professionals in the postwar era came to the
agency with better college credentials than ever before, but lamented that
they still had not been prepared sufficiently to deal with other cultures.
Nonetheless, anthropologists, psychiatrists, and other scholars continued
to contribute to a growing wealth of published material about Navajo culture. BIA personnel also had access to a Navajo-English medical dictionary, thanks to Father Haile and Robert Young's work on a written Navajo
language during Collier's tenure. In short, if physicians and nurses were in-
clined to learn more about Navajo culture and were willing to reach out
across cultural gulfs, the tools were available.[24]

In the early 1950s, physicians and healers were indeed beginning to
find ways to work together with greater ease. A few physicians in particular seemed to make a difference. In 1952, Dr. Walsh McDermott from the
Cornell Medical School came to help the BIA treat boarding school students suffering from hepatitis and tuberculosis at Tuba City, beginning a
long-term relationship with the Navajos. McDermott also found a com-
patriot in Dr. Kurt Deuschle, a Public Health Service medical officer at
the Fort Defiance sanatorium who had arrived in August 1952.
McDermott and Deuschle continued to play key roles in Navajo health in
the following years and were among a new crop of physicians serving the
Navajos after World War II who were more open to the Navajo healers.[25]

Deuschle and John Adair, an anthropologist who spent time on the
reservation before and after the war, claimed that young physicians in that
era were generally more receptive to cross-cultural issues than their predecessors. They argued that young doctors and nurses were more exposed
to social science educations and more open to cultural experiences.
Deuschle, for one, had learned that arrangements could be made that better enabled patients to use traditional healing without interfering with
hospital service. If medically feasible, patients might be encouraged to
have a Blessingway before coming to the hospital. If health problems were
more serious, he found that occasionally healers were willing to conduct a
temporary ceremony over articles of the patient's clothing.[26]

Navajo healers were often willing to reciprocate when physicians
showed a willingness to cooperate with them. In February 1954,
Manuelito Begay spoke to the Tribal Council, reporting that he and other
healers had met with a group of physicians and come to an agreement.

Previously, Begay said, physicians had always tried to prevent patients from leaving hospitals in order to attend sings, and when healers asked physicians to temporarily discharge their patients, they were told that the patients would not be allowed back. Things had changed. "If you bring a child to the hospital and they cannot do it any good with their medicine, they will have the child returned for our treatment," Begay explained. "[I]f we make no progress with our medicine, then we return the child to the hospital. By understanding each other to help one another, we help the third party."[27]

Through such steps, healers and physicians were coming to understand each other better and were learning to coordinate their efforts. The practitioners often respected each other's abilities even if they did not hold the same beliefs about health and healing. Western medical practitioners were more likely than before to see some value in traditional healing, even if they could explain it only in psychotherapeutic terms. In return, many healers acknowledged that Western medicine offered some real benefits, but they usually did not accept physicians' explanations about disease. "They tell me [that tuberculosis] is inflicted by a person coughing in your face," said Begay. "Right away I disagree with it. A person should not be that weak to be susceptible to a man's cough. We have a definite point in mind and know of how a man gets to be afflicted with tuberculosis. One is the ceremony about the Wind Chant. If something goes wrong with that, it is tuberculosis and, if lightning strikes you, tuberculosis is the result." As Sam Yazzie indicated, healers tended to categorize their power as different but complementary to Western medicine's power:

> I have great respect for white doctors; there are things they can do that we cannot. For example, they can remove an appendix, they can take out a gall bladder, or treat a urinary tract infection. . . . There are certain sicknesses that a doctor can never cure that we can—lizard illness, for example—or an illness that comes from one of those small green worms you sometimes find on an ear of corn. Sickness might last over a long time and it might be a lingering illness. No white doctor can cure an illness of that type, only a medicine man can cure such patients.

Because their powers differed, the best solution, as far as Yazzie was concerned, was to combine them. "In any situation when a patient isn't getting better," he argued, "then I, or any other medicine man who knows his business, should allow the patient to go to the hospital and have his x-rays and other treatment there. Then he can come back and have the rest of the sing in the hogan."[28]

Of course, some physicians wanted nothing to do with the traditional healers; some healers responded in kind. In 1956, for example, an older physician told one of his colleagues that he had no respect for the healers. It remained for him a zero-sum game. "The fact that Navajo medicine men came to me for treatment," he contended, "proves that they are fakers and do not have confidence in their own methods." If an individual chose not to breach cross-cultural barriers, they were still not compelled to do so.[29]

The Navajo Tribal Council

The Navajo leadership's role in health care continued to grow in the 1940s and 1950s. The Tribal Council became more assertive as a government critic and advisor and as a direct sponsor of medical programs. With direction from the tribal Health Committee, Council members became more concerned with specific details of how medical programs functioned and more aware of other possible avenues for reaching their health care goals. The tribal leadership recognized a real need for Western medical services, and also understood that a weakened BIA Medical Division could not be depended on to provide those services in the postwar years. With new oil revenues in hand, the tribe had enough funds available to encourage and aid extragovernmental organizations that were willing to initiate or expand services for the Navajos. The Health Committee also assisted the larger Council in its attempts to influence exactly how limited government medical funds were being spent.

Funding cuts for reservation health care programs were a cause of great concern for tribal leaders. During and after the war, Chee Dodge and Thomas Dodge led a protest against government health care policy. At a meeting in 1943, Thomas Dodge introduced a petition complaining that sick Navajos were being turned away from government hospitals and urging that those facilities be maintained. His father, Chee Dodge, stood before the Council three years later and expressed his disappointment in what had happened to the government medical program he had helped convince his constituents to accept. The hospitals at Fort Defiance and Crownpoint were the only two federal medical facilities he considered worth patronizing. "There are some other hospitals on the reservation," Dodge said, "but they have been neglected for so long that they have become like discarded rags." That same year, Chee Dodge and other tribal leaders went to Washington to voice their concerns to the House Committee on Indian Affairs and to encourage Congress to increase appropriations. They explained how Navajo people had to travel as many as one hundred miles over poor roads to obtain the nearest medical services. "We, like yourselves have sickness and pain," said the Navajo delegates. "We are only asking what you would want for yourselves; good medical aid to relieve our suffering. Good medical service would enable us physically to be of greater service to our nation."[30]

In addition to lobbying Congress for better BIA medical care, the Council began looking for other ways to attain their goals, without much success initially. Given the large number of Navajos who were serving overseas, the Veterans Administration (VA) seemed an obvious source of supplemental medical care. In 1944, the Council unanimously passed a resolution asking the VA to establish a hospital at Gallup, New Mexico. Unfortunately, the facility was not forthcoming. Instead, Navajo veterans found themselves in VA and military facilities as far away as Santa Fe and California. A beleaguered BIA Medical Division turned down veterans' requests to transfer back to the reservation, arguing that they were overtaxed and that the VA and U.S. Navy could do a better job.[31]

The Tribal Council again attempted to improve the medical situation by using its own funds. In 1947, the Council passed a resolution by a vote of forty to one that appropriated up to $10,000 annually to cover burial expenses for indigent Navajos. If the BIA did not have to pay for funerals out of moneys appropriated for health services, they thought, perhaps more federal funds would be available for medical care. The Council also contributed $500 in 1949 to pay for radio advertisements encouraging Navajo women to go to nursing school, and a year later, the tribe appropriated $1,000 to establish an operation intended to make eyeglasses available to Navajos at wholesale prices, supplementing an insufficient distribution program sponsored by the American Red Cross.[32]

The Council was not as unified when it came to traditional healing and the Native American Church. In 1942, J. C. Morgan and Scott Preston pushed for a resolution mandating a reduction in the number of ceremonies to be conducted in a year to no more than one-quarter of the annual average, ostensibly "in order to conserve food, automobile tires and gasoline for our country." No doubt, Morgan saw this option as doubly satisfying, but Preston, a singer, believed that the Diné had to prepare themselves and their country for "the dangers existing ahead of them." Preston reassured them that he did not want ceremonies to be stopped all together. After all, he argued, the Navajo population continued to grow only because the people kept a strong faith in their ceremonies.[33]

In opposition to the bill, one Council delegate argued that ordering people to stop having sings would hurt the war effort by damaging morale. Paul Begay also pointed out that most sings were done "in case of emergency" and he worried that there would be insufficient time for people to seek permission. Most Council delegates agreed that people had to conserve resources, but the Council rejected the resolution by a vote of thirty to fourteen. Those who favored it and those who opposed it were not necessarily divided on Christian-traditionalist lines, indicating that many were intensely concerned about the war and the hard times it might bring to the people, but also that the majority believed that the ceremonies were too precious to sacrifice. No one, not even J. C. Morgan, spoke out directly against ceremonialism.[34]

In 1954, the Tribal Council reaffirmed its desire to protect and preserve the traditional healing system when Father Berard Haile presented them with a proposition. The friar had recently compiled a detailed account of the Blessingway ceremony from a few healers who recognized him as a friend and were therefore willing to share the sacred knowledge. Haile understood that these things were sacred, but he hoped the tribe would pay to publish it as a teaching guide for young Navajos who wished to perform the ceremony. In spite of his compelling arguments, Manuelito Begay and Grey Valentine argued that publishing the ceremony would be both dangerous and disrespectful, that such things were not to be talked about. Bizahalani Bekis shared their concern. "If you want to give all the holy things—to give it out, it is up to you," he told his fellow Council members. "I am definitely not that type. I want to hold on to the old traditions and not to be too liberal with it."[35]

Chairman Sam Ahkeah led those who favored Haile's proposal. Ahkeah and others argued that the tribe should take advantage of the opportunity to help preserve the traditional ceremonies. Again, all of those who spoke demonstrated a dedication to the traditional ways. They simply disagreed about how tradition should be maintained. The Council approved Haile's request by a vote of fifty to eighteen, and gave him $30,000 to carry out his work. But Haile could not gain proper approval from the U.S. secretary of the interior at the time, and failed to convince the tribe to reapprove his proposal at a later date. The book was not published until 1970.[36]

The Native American Church remained far more controversial than Western medicine or traditional healing. Despite its prohibition on the reservation in 1940, the number of peyotists continued to grow to as many as 14 percent of all Navajos. Anti-NAC fervor increased as well, and in the late 1940s, the religion's opponents conducted a number of raids on peyote meetings. Frustrated by the BIA's unwillingness to help enforce the Navajo law, the tribal government instructed the tribal police to do the best they could to apprehend and prosecute offenders. Missionaries commended the Council for staying the course against peyotism. Salsbury made public statements against the religion while at Ganado and after his retirement.[37]

The NAC proponents responded to these assaults with increased sophistication, taking advantage of non-Navajo allies and formulating clear counterarguments. Collier, Aberle, anthropologists Weston LaBarre and Omer Stewart, and a variety of newspaper columnists offered support, labeling the substance harmless and speaking of the religion's social and individual benefits. Hola Tso, David Clark, and other NAC members defended peyotism vigorously in the Tribal Council. Clark saw nothing foreign or insidious about the NAC, pointing out that peyote rituals were even used to pray for the well-being of Navajo and other American troops overseas.[38]

After thirteen arrests in 1954, peyotists asked the Council to reconsider the 1940 resolution. They received support from David Aberle and a pharmacologist who were present at the government's request, and a few Council delegates stood by them. Most tribal politicians, however, still opposed the religion for the same reasons that were given in 1940. The Council did not overturn the 1940 resolution, but the issue proved divisive enough that members were not willing to officially reaffirm the earlier decision. Navajos involved with the Native American Church had new hope for the future, but the religion had far to go before most tribal members would recognize it as a nonthreatening and legitimate form of spirituality and healing.[39]

Prior to 1950, Chee Dodge and Thomas Dodge had helped the Navajo tribal government establish itself as a force in Navajo health care. At mid-century, another Dodge stepped to the forefront: Annie, youngest of four children in the Dodge family, born in 1910 near Sawmill, Arizona. She grew up with great interest in health care, education, and leadership. As a boarding school student at Fort Defiance, she witnessed influenza and trachoma epidemics firsthand and always remembered what those diseases had done to her friends. Annie Dodge came away from her school experiences with a strong commitment to education and a deep concern about her people's health. In her thirties and now married, Annie Dodge Wauneka had a close relationship with her father, who again served as tribal chairman from 1944 to 1947. From her father, she learned that understanding both the Navajo and non-Indian worlds would help her become an effective tribal leader. In 1951, Annie Dodge Wauneka earned a seat on the Tribal Council and soon thereafter, she became chairperson of the Health Committee (officially known at the time as the Health and Welfare Committee).[40]

Wauneka, along with Paul Jones and other tribal leaders, worked diligently to turn the Health and Welfare Committee into a well-informed and influential body. The committee served as the ideal mediator among Western medical providers, the Tribal Council and Navajo patients because it fostered simple, straightforward communication. Wauneka had learned well from her father the power and necessity of communication and instilled that principle in the Health Committee. "The Navajo haven't been deliberately resistant to modern health methods," she explained. "It's just that they didn't understand, and you've got to throw yourself into explaining things. That wasn't done enough in the past, in the health field."[41]

Supplementing her words with action, Wauneka made annual visits to the three hundred or more Navajo patients in off-reservation sanatoriums. All they needed, she discovered, was for someone to listen to their concerns and speak to them clearly. She reported back to the Council that Navajo patients often deserted the medical facilities prematurely because they did not understand how long it took for the treatments to work. They assumed that a cure would take only a few days, and no one had told them otherwise, not until Annie Wauneka sat down with them. Council delegates and physicians were impressed that, after her visits, patients no longer left the sanatoriums.[42]

Wauneka and other tribal leaders also demonstrated a desire to maintain close relations with the health care providers. Frequently disappointed by government policies made with little regard to their concerns, they wanted to be heard. Peter had helped develop a communicative relationship with the Tribal Council, but the turmoil of war and his departure had been disruptive. Things changed for the better when Deuschle and McDermott arrived in Navajo country.

McDermott, Deuschle, and Wauneka worked well together. Deuschle opened the Fort Defiance sanatorium to a Cornell team, led by McDermott, then working with new tuberculosis therapies on the reservation, and used the facility to hold meetings with Wauneka and the Tribal Council Advisory Committee. Billy Becenti, Frank Bradley, and Howard Gorman were invited to study the tuberculosis bacilli under a microscope, and McDermott carefully explained how the new drug treatments worked. He also candidly expressed the reason for his presence, admitting that the Navajo project served as an initial test for broader national tuberculosis campaigns, but assuring the Council that they were not carelessly "experimenting." For good reason, Navajo leaders were wary about inexperienced physicians "practicing" on Diné patients and they appreciated McDermott's candor. In recognition of the Cornell team's good work, Council members donated $10,000 in tribal funds to the project, and after two years they were sufficiently impressed with the results that, without a request, they unanimously approved another $10,000.[43]

Enter the U.S. Public Health Service

Political shifts on the national level meant significant changes for Navajo health care in the 1950s. Special programs for American Indians came under assault after the war as American politics and economics took a conservative swing. With Collier's resignation in 1945, and a Republican Party victory in Congress in 1946, federal Indian policy shifted. Because Congress viewed the BIA as the epitome of government paternalism and inefficiency, it targeted the agency for elimination. "Termination policy," as the Indian policy came to be known, preached that American Indians were ready for complete assimilation and should be free from government authority and special privilege.[44]

For a few tribes, the policy meant the total dissolution of federal services and legal protection, with disastrous results. For most, including the Navajos, termination came in another form. Congress planned to chip away at the BIA by withdrawing education, health, and certain economic functions from its control. The federal trust responsibility for Indian programs would dissolve as those programs were absorbed by and diluted

Dr. Warner Watkins, Annie Wauneka, and Dr. Clarence Salsbury, ca. 1950.
Courtesy of Arizona State Library, Archives and Public Records, Archives
Division, Phoenix, no. 93-9900.

into other government agencies. In the case of Indian health care, terminationists pushed for a transfer of medical programs from the BIA to the U.S. Public Health Service (PHS). This course of action had been laid out in 1948 by the Hoover Commission, which studied possible ways to reorganize and streamline the executive branch of the U.S. government. The commission recommended the transfer, arguing that the PHS could deal with Indian health care more effectively and efficiently.[45]

The PHS had been involved with Indian health care at times previously, but always in a supplementary role to the BIA. The service had no connection to American Indian health care when President John Adams created it in 1798 to treat American sailors (originally called the U.S. Marine Hospital Service [MHS]). Gradually, the service's scope and size increased. In the 1870s it began enforcing quarantine laws and initiated epidemic control services nationwide. To carry out these duties, Congress established the Commissioned Officer Corps in 1889, giving MHS physicians wages and titles corresponding to Navy grades, although they were not officially part of the military. In 1912, Congress redesignated the MHS as the Public Health Service and gave it the added duty of studying disease "and the propagation and spread thereof." In 1930, the National Institutes of Health were added to the PHS to conduct research, and in 1946 the agency took over the newly established Centers for Disease Control. Since that time, the PHS had also taken on an increasingly important role in the planning and administration of the nation's hospitals, although it was directly responsible for only a few federal facilities.[46]

For those dissatisfied with the BIA's handling of Indian health care and for those who simply wished to weaken that agency by abolishing its medical arm, the PHS represented the ideal alternative. The PHS had access to a great wealth of medical knowledge as well as its large and well-qualified Commissioned Officer Corps. Most Indian health problems were related to communicable diseases, and the PHS specialized in that area. Perhaps, therefore, it could quickly put American Indians on par with the rest of the nation medically, thereby eliminating the need for special services.

The PHS transfer must be understood in this "terminationist" context, but many who wanted the PHS to take over from the BIA Medical Division were genuinely concerned about Indian health. During the late 1940s and early 1950s public awareness of a growing Indian health crisis heightened, and pressure fell upon the federal government to remedy the situation. These public demands dovetailed with the terminationists' plans to withdraw health care responsibilities from the BIA. The transfer occurred because a coalition developed between those advocating termination and those who believed that the PHS could provide better care to American Indians.[47]

The Department of Health, Education and Welfare (DHEW), which oversaw the PHS, was hesitant to take on Indian health care, arguing that splitting up the BIA programs would lead to greater inefficiency. The Bureau of the Budget agreed with DHEW's assessment, but protransfer sentiment grew in Congress. In 1953, bills were submitted in both the U.S. House and Senate. In addition to proposing the transfer, House Resolution 303 specified that the DHEW would be authorized to contract Indian health care facilities and duties out to state and local agencies whenever and wherever Indian health needs could be better met. If tribal governments approved, services could be further passed on to nongovernmental organizations.[48]

The transfer issue led to heated debate in both the House and Senate, with Republicans tending to favor the move and Democrats opposing. Senator Arthur Watkins of Utah, a strong advocate of termination policy, led those who supported the bill. To appeal to congressmen and constituents opposed to or less motivated by termination policy, the senator argued that the transfer would improve medical care for American Indians. The PHS's better training facilities and organizational structure, he argued, would enable young doctors to stay in touch with developments in the medical world. Watkins also pointed to the Doctor-Dentist Draft program as a key issue. The draft, begun during the Korean War, allowed medical doctors to choose service in the PHS rather than the military. This gave the PHS a decided advantage over the BIA in recruiting physicians. Moreover, because those physicians served two-year terms, Watkins claimed, they would not have sufficient time to become disgruntled in their work.[49]

Other transfer supporters were probably more genuinely concerned about Indian health care. Senator Barry Goldwater of Arizona favored small government, but his main concern was that Navajos and other Native Americans in his state had suffered from the BIA's incompetence. Goldwater brought detailed reports on health conditions on every Indian reservation in Arizona to the Senate debates. He spoke of high infant mortality rates among the Hopi, Hulapai, Pima, and Havasupai, and especially the Papago (Tohono O'odham), among whom one out of four infants died before reaching the age of one. But he relied most heavily on the Navajos to provide evidence for his case. Goldwater entered into the record a table that demonstrated the desperate health situation existing among the Navajos. It showed that tuberculosis mortality rates were nine times higher on the Navajo reservation than in the United States as a whole, while dysentery and gastroenteritis mortality rates were thirteen and twenty-five times higher, respectively. Goldwater argued that the BIA hospitals had never been able to provide proper care for Navajos, and he had his own response for critics who said the transfer might be too hasty: "In answer to the question of the junior Senator [Dennis Chávez] from New Mexico as to when is the proper time [for the transfer], let me say that the time is any time when we are not providing adequate health service to any of the people of the country, whether they be whites or Indians."[50]

Both sides in the congressional debate had support from Indian tribal governments. The All Pueblo Council and many tribes in Oklahoma opposed the transfer, while the Intertribal Council of the Sioux Nation and the Navajos supported it. Division within the Navajo Tribal Council may help explain this larger American Indian ambivalence. In a vote in June 1954, the Council agreed to send a telegram to the chairman of the Committee of Interior and Insular Affairs supporting House Resolution 303 by a margin of thirty-six to twenty-three.[51]

Those Navajos who were unwilling to support the transfer and the Pueblos and Oklahoma tribes who openly opposed the bill suspected its actual intent. The atmosphere of termination and closing of smaller hospitals during the war gave them good reason to believe that the transfer could signal an end to government-sponsored medical programs upon which they now relied. Those who supported the idea did so for two main reasons. As Frank Bradley's statements in the Navajo Tribal Council exemplified, their distaste for the BIA may have outweighed uncertainties about the Public Health Service. Bradley blamed the BIA for failing to supply field nurses for people in his area and believed that the PHS would send one. He also accused the BIA of "experimenting" on Navajo patients in the past. His statement and past rumors about BIA conspiracies to kill and sterilize Navajo children with vaccines were indicative of the Navajos' strong distrust of the federal Indian agency.[52]

Annie Wauneka, Sam Ahkeah, Roger Davis, and other Navajo leaders who had been actively involved in health care issues, favored the PHS transfer because of specifically defined medical arguments. Davis and Ahkeah agreed with the American Medical Association and congressional transfer advocates who argued that the BIA had done a poor job recruiting quality physicians and that the PHS could rectify that problem. The legacy of cooperation between the Navajo Tribal Council and the Cornell medical team may have also influenced their decisions. The team had invited Ahkeah and other leaders to visit the New York hospital, and the Navajo politicians had been very impressed. They may have thought that if the Cornell team could outshine the BIA Medical Division, perhaps the PHS could do so as well. Wauneka had also been very impressed with Kurt Deuschle, a PHS physician.[53]

Navajo Agency Superintendent Warren Spaulding failed to sway the Council's opinion against the transfer. In 1954, he explained that the health program was difficult to operate and claimed, somewhat sarcastically, that he would be more than happy if the PHS "took it off my shoulders," but Spaulding stressed the fact that the PHS did not even want the responsibility. How, he asked, could anyone expect the PHS to do a better job than the BIA had done if they were not committed to the cause? The superintendent admitted that the PHS had been better at recruiting physicians, but this advantage would evaporate with the eventual conclusion of the Doctor-Dentist Draft.[54]

Spaulding's arguments did not persuade Wauneka or the majority of Tribal Council members, but they had merit. The BIA Medical Division pointed out that Congress had forced the bureau into a difficult position. The BIA did not have the funding to pay its physicians as well as did the PHS and did not have access to its own conscription program because Congress had not provided the agency with such power. The transfer advocates criticized the BIA for failing to provide proper public health programs, and the opposition argued that the PHS was less prepared to operate hospitals. In reality, the BIA had worked on public health programs but watched them dwindle during the war. Nonetheless, since Congress proved unwilling to revive the BIA Medical Division, Wauneka and other tribal leaders opted in favor of the transfer.[55]

The transfer gained the necessary support for passage in both houses of Congress when the House agreed to a Senate amendment to postpone the transfer until the fiscal year beginning 1 July 1955. The bill passed with a sound majority in the Senate and House, and President Dwight Eisenhower signed it as Public Law 568 on 5 August 1954. The Navajos had been promised, and surely expected, that the transfer would mean better and more accessible care. Whether the PHS could live up to these expectations remained to be seen.[56]

· 4 ·

A NEW PROVIDER,
1955–69

When the Bureau of Indian Affairs Medical Division handed control of the government's Indian health care program to the Public Health Service in the summer of 1955, Annie Wauneka, Paul Jones, Billy Becenti, and other tribal leaders had high hopes for what this transfer would mean for Navajo health. The U.S. Congress and scores of medical experts had promised that the Public Health Service would help American Indians enjoy all the benefits that Western medicine had to offer. The Navajos had been told that the transfer would yield increased medical appropriations and more qualified physicians.

The transfer did not lead to a federal withdrawal from responsibility for American Indian health care as terminationists had anticipated. The transfer neither destroyed the BIA nor reduced the federal presence on Indian lands. Rather, it created a massive new federal agency related to Indian affairs that would expand as a result of changing political currents in the 1960s. The Kennedy and Johnson administrations and increased Democratic power in Congress opened the way for increased social spending. Funding for the Public Health Service's new Division of Indian Health (later called the Indian Health Service—IHS) grew, probably to a greater extent and over a longer period of time than many advocates of the transfer had anticipated. In 1968, the total federal budget for Indian programs reached $448,390,000, with $249,719,000 allocated to the BIA and $103,552,000 allocated to the IHS.[1]

The IHS used these funds to expand its staff and facilities and to establish a more comprehensive health care system than the BIA had been able

73

to muster, combining primary clinical care with sanitation, health education, and other services. The IHS made positive strides on the reservation,
but it did not perform miracles, in part because health care services, no
matter the quality and quantity, were limited in what they could do to
guarantee healthy individuals. Nonetheless, Congress and the Navajo
Tribe expected great things from the new agency.

The Public Health Service's Introduction to the Navajo Reservation

To handle its new duties, the Public Health Service created the Indian
Health Service as a subagency. The IHS divided the United States into six
(and later eight) area offices and assigned a director in each to supervise further subdivisions called service units. The Albuquerque Area Office served
many Indian communities in addition to the Navajo reservation, but a field
office in Window Rock, Arizona, acted as a liaison between the area office
and eight Navajo service units. In order to finance this reorganization and
deliver on the promise to improve Native American health, Congress
increased appropriations for Indian medical care by nearly 50 percent, from
$24,549,112 in 1955 to $34,816,000 in 1956. Between 1955 and 1957, the
operating expenditures for medical activities on the Navajo reservation rose
from $4,300,000 to $5,890,000. The IHS set aside an additional $3,641,000
for new construction projects on the reservation in 1957.[2]

The IHS also inherited the Navajo-Hopi Long-Range Rehabilitation
funds. By the end of fiscal year 1954, $2,710,000 of the original
$4,750,000 had been spent to complete a 75-bed hospital at Tuba City.
The remaining $2,040,000 was earmarked to finish a 75-bed Shiprock
hospital and to plan a 200-bed replacement hospital for the aging Fort
Defiance Medical Center.[3]

Because the BIA had been criticized for favoring primary care over preventive programs, the IHS tried to establish a more comprehensive system
that would combine these approaches. The agency planned to expand
reservation primary care facilities, to supplement its own services by contracting with nonfederal providers, and to create an extensive preventive
health program.[4]

In its first five years, the IHS's Navajo Field Office, which was headed by
Dr. James Shaw, created an elaborate medical network extending from hospitals to hogans. The network included public health nurses who served

patients in their homes and who could refer them to health centers and hospitals. New health centers had permanent staffs: a physician and dentist as well as nurses and ancillary employees. The IHS also attempted to achieve a broader coverage of the Navajo reservation with field stations, which were smaller facilities operated on a part-time basis. By 1959, the IHS completed health centers at Tohatchi, Chinle, and Kayenta, and added field stations at Cornfields, Piñon, Round Rock, White Cone, and Pueblo Pintado.[5]

The IHS expanded its overall staff numbers as well. From twenty-three physicians and a total of 400 employees under the BIA in 1954, the government medical staff increased to more than 670 in 1960, including forty-three physicians and seventeen dentists. Completion of the 200-bed Gallup Indian Medical Center in 1961 added nearly 300 more employees to this total. In addition to creating some new programs and staff positions, the IHS rebuilt the field nursing program, now called public health nursing, increasing the staff from the eight that served the reservation in 1950 to twenty-eight in 1960. A new nutrition and dietetics branch of the IHS provided a nutrition and dietetics officer at Window Rock and other dieticians at Shiprock and Fort Defiance. The IHS also made health education a key component of its preventive efforts, initiating the Long-Range Health Education Program in 1957 with a staff of thirteen. Through cooperation with the Tribal Health Committee, the education program used visual aids and instructional clinics to teach about hygiene, disease contagion, and infant care.[6]

Sanitation engineering efforts became a part of the IHS program as well, when Public Law 86-121 amended the Transfer Act in 1959, giving the IHS responsibility for constructing sanitation, sewage, and water supply systems on Indian reservations. Congress also included funds for the acquisition of lands necessary to carry out these projects and allowed the IHS to transfer these facilities to state, territorial, or tribal control after their construction. These sanitation projects were central to improving health in rural reservation environments. By 1960, $550,000 had been allocated to the Navajo Field Office to complete eight projects, including a water supply and waste disposal system for 3,000 households in seven communities. Between 1959 and 1961, over $1,525,000 in tribal expenditures, combined with over $200,000 from the IHS, allowed for the development of 650 new wells. The environmental health staff, including sanitarians and Navajo sanitarian aides, also worked with the tribe to establish sanitary codes, control rabies, and construct privies on the reservation.[7]

The Navajo-Cornell Field Health Research Project

As part of the IHS's commitment to redefine the scope and nature of health care on the reservation, the agency entered into a contract with the Department of Public Health and Preventive Medicine at Cornell University. Cornell agreed to set up a clinic as part of a five-year study on the Navajo reservation to determine what type of medical delivery system would be best suited for that environment. The U.S. government provided nearly $1 million with other funds coming from the Russell Sage and Fleishman Foundations, the Navajo Tribal Council, and a variety of smaller, private contributors.[8]

Cornell seemed more capable of conducting such a study than the IHS. The arrangement allowed for a more innovative approach, because team members were not bound by bureaucratic guidelines. And Cornell had already established an amiable and productive relationship with the tribe during its antituberculosis study in the early 1950s.[9]

Cornell's Department of Public Health and Preventive Medicine, of which Dr. Walsh McDermott was now chairman, saw the project as a way to enhance its study of global health care delivery. The faculty saw a correlation between health conditions on the Navajo reservation and those in impoverished regions of the world, and working with Navajo patients would help familiarize them with the language and cultural challenges they would face overseas. McDermott led the project and recruited other physicians and social scientists for the team. Dr. Kurt Deuschle agreed to cooperate. John Adair, from the Cornell Sociology-Anthropology Department, accepted a position as the team's lead anthropologist, and his colleague, Tom Sasaki, signed on to conduct various demographic studies of the selected area.[10]

The Navajo-Cornell Field Health Research Project, as the study came to be known, applied a specific philosophy on cross-cultural health care delivery. The Cornell team hoped to find ways of applying modern medicine across a "formidable cultural and linguistic barrier" without compromising "essential medical standards in the process." Success depended on cultural awareness and tolerance, and upon clear communication at all times between the medical providers and recipients. The team argued that the recipient community should always be incorporated into the decision-making process. If the community viewed a technological innovation as an imposition rather than perceiving it as a joint venture with specific benefits, the team counseled, members in that community would reject it.[11]

With help from Annie Wauneka and Council member Seth Begay, the

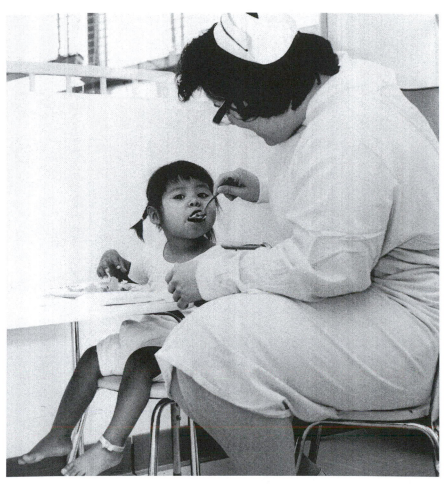

Barbara Watkins, staff nurse in pediatrics, feeds patient Ramona King at the Gallup Indian Medical Center, ca. 1965. Courtesy of Virginia Brown, Ida Bahl, and Lillian Watson Collection, Cline Library, Northern Arizona University, NAU.PH.92.14.51.

team selected the Many Farms-Rough Rock district as the site for its clinic. Located in Arizona, a few miles north and west of Canyon de Chelly at the base of Black Mesa, the area offered a central location and an age and gender distribution close to reservation averages.[12]

From 1956 to 1961, the clinic served the Many Farms-Rough Rock residents. With a staff of eighteen, including two physicians, the clinic provided all of the services that could be found in IHS outpatient facilities at the time. It had an x-ray machine, a laboratory, and even a medical library. Although the primary care services were well received by Navajo patients, the Cornell project's greatest innovations came in field health, particularly in the use of local community members as field medical workers. Team members believed that Western medicine could more efficiently reach Navajo camps if Navajos were recruited to assist the small staff of field physicians and public health nurses. Navajo assistants could also serve invaluably as cultural mediators and interpreters.[13]

Free from Civil Service restraints, the Cornell team could recruit anyone who met their standards and train them as they saw fit. Soon after establishing the clinic, a small number of Navajos, known as "health visitors," were selected to serve as medical assistants and interpreters. Ex-tuberculosis patients such as Frank George and Ruth Anderson were chosen because they had past experience with the medical team, had faith in Western medicine, and were bilingual. Over a period of six months, the recruits learned about basic first aid, nursing procedures, record keeping, and anatomy. Although the traditional Navajo taboo associated with dead bodies limited the students' previous knowledge of human anatomy, dissected sheep proved an effective instructional alternative. After completing their training, the visitors served both in the clinic and in the field. They worked as mediators, interpreters, and technicians in the clinic and went out to Navajo homes to give drug treatments, administer medical tests, and refer patients to Many Farms.[14]

The visitors initially ran into some unanticipated obstacles. In the clinic, Navajo patients accepted the visitors as assistants to the white physicians and nurses. Alone in the field, the visitors dealt with reluctant patients who were suspicious of other Navajos asking personal medical questions and administering medicine without a physician present. Some were especially reluctant to give urine samples or personal information to Navajos they did not know because they were concerned about witchcraft and had not come to identify these people as medical professionals. The visitors eventually overcame these obstacles as people came to know and trust them.[15]

The Cornell team functioned efficiently in a large geographic area and broke through many of the language and cultural barriers that had often frustrated other medical practitioners. The project achieved some medical success as well, reducing the spread of certain infectious diseases, including otitis media. Perhaps because of the x-ray and laboratory facilities, the health visitors, and the development of new antituberculosis therapies, Cornell also noted a decline in tuberculosis deaths in the area. Other diseases, however, seemed unaffected by the clinic's presence, including pneumonia-diarrhea complex, which remained the number one killer of Rough Rock residents.[16]

A primary system of health care did not answer the needs of the relatively isolated and impoverished area, the Cornell team concluded. Even a well-organized system of primary care could not conquer diseases that spread as a result of poor sanitary conditions. On a reservation where the vast majority of families had no running water or waste disposal system, these afflictions continued to be major problems. The Cornell team decided that a "community" approach with an emphasis on hygiene, sanitation, and health education, and joined with primary care, would be more successful. This proved to be one of the most important lessons the Cornell project offered to the incoming IHS.

The Many Farms project's greatest success came in winning the support and respect of community members and the Tribal Council. The Navajo community responded positively to the clinic at Many Farms. Between 1956 and 1961, the team estimated, approximately 90 percent of the district's population used the clinic at least once, and two-thirds used it many times. The Cornell team successfully integrated itself into Navajo politics and managed to steer clear of controversy. Throughout the project, team members were ubiquitous at both local gatherings and Tribal Council meetings. As Cornell had hoped, the Navajo Tribe viewed the Many Farms project as a joint effort rather than an imposition. The tribe donated $10,000 annually to the project and frequently requested that it be extended beyond its end date.[17]

Ironically, the success of the Many Farms project overshadowed its chief benefactor. Even though the IHS initiated the project and provided the bulk of its funds, it did not reap the benefits of the clinic's good reputation. As early as the summer of 1956, Tribal Chairman Paul Jones informed the IHS that its services paled in comparison to the university project and that the government was wasting a good opportunity:

Public Health Service has a model experimental program in operation at the Many Farms Clinic. The Navajos have co-operated wholeheartedly with Cornell Medical School staff there. Yet this marked success has little or no impact on Public Health planning or operations elsewhere. The model is without value. Why? Is it because the Many Farms Clinic was planned in careful consultation with Navajo leaders and the community, and was built to meet medical needs as Navajos saw them? We urge the building of more Many Farms type clinics, and fewer field health stations, in spite of the opinions of Public Health Experts.[18]

But the IHS had only had a short time to respond to the team's findings. IHS officials did learn from the Cornell project and adopted some of its methods, but slowly. To some degree, this delay occurred because the Cornell team had to wait until the five-year period had passed to compile and evaluate its data. Although it communicated with the IHS throughout its run, the team did not make its findings public until a series of articles were published in the early 1960s and a book, *The People's Health*, in 1970. As Cornell later claimed, the IHS had difficulty applying these lessons because it had to deal with bureaucratic regulations that delayed the innovative process. The health visitor model also proved difficult for the IHS to adopt initially because public health nurses did not react positively to the idea; many of them were uneasy about the notion of giving considerable medical responsibilities to people who had not gone through years of specialized training.[19]

Early Tribal–IHS Relations

Tribal leaders did not receive the IHS as positively as Dr. James Shaw and other administrators had hoped. Tribal Chairman Paul Jones and Annie Wauneka were less than enthusiastic about the IHS in the first years after the transfer. While Wauneka and other Council delegates expressed pleasure with certain aspects of the medical program, including the sanitation efforts, they had misgivings about the IHS. Despite Shaw's efforts to maintain solid relations, Navajo leaders were concerned that political and bureaucratic changes affecting the massive Indian health care program were beyond the tribe's control.[20]

A well-educated and well-spoken man, Jones had served as an interpreter for the BIA before his election as chairman in 1955. In that capacity, he worked closely with Annie Wauneka and the Tribal Council Health Committee. Soon after the transfer, Jones began to worry that the tribe had been misled by protransfer arguments. He heard of patients being turned away from overcrowded hospitals and of continuing staff shortages. Jones thought recent changes were counterproductive, and that the new funds were being misused. "Somebody is undoing the job that we have done for many years to get away from the primitive way of healing practices to the modern way," he argued. "We have made a big inroad, and someone is trying to undo that and is undoing it to a great extent."[21]

Chairman Jones complained in particular about the IHS's failure to consult the tribal leadership. At a meeting between the BIA and IHS in Denver in May 1955, the IHS promised that the chief medical officers at area offices would welcome input from the tribes relative to the type of medical care they would receive. "We naturally assumed this pronouncement to mean that full consultation would be developed," said Jones:

We have discarded that assumption. It proved erroneous. There has been no consultation. There is no framework visible within [the] Public Health Service where effective consultation can occur. The planning of this vast health program has been conducted within a rampart of silence, so far as the Navajo people are concerned. . . . [W]e know well the dangers of a unilateral approach to our problems by so-called experts. Grandiose plans for us by someone else are nothing new. But experience warns us that the mistakes can also be grandiose. The health of our people is too important for us to stand by and allow this to happen.

Jones insisted that the Health Committee and Tribal Council play a role in determining how to direct the large influx of new funding. He urged the IHS to cooperate more with the states and the Cornell team to find a cure for reservation tuberculosis. The IHS, Jones claimed, should also address the alcoholism problem, a growing concern on the reservation that the medical program had seemingly ignored.[22]

Surgeon General Dr. L. E. Burney replied with a point-by-point rebuttal to Jones's complaints, arguing that Shaw had delivered detailed reports to the Council and that other administrators had spoken at chapter meetings (chapters were local-level governing units within the Navajo political system). But Jones and Burney defined communication differently. Jones cared most about the tribe's perceived inability to communicate their wishes to the IHS. Indeed, the bureaucratic structure made the kind of cooperation the tribe had experienced with the Cornell team difficult to duplicate with the IHS. Because the Navajos were not assigned a separate area office, the medical director, Dr. Henry Kassel, had to divide his attention among multiple tribes.[23]

Conversely, IHS administrators were often frustrated by the tribe's seeming unwillingness to acknowledge that significant changes in medical programs and disease rates could take years to realize; and that Western medicine, no matter its quality and quantity, could not be expected to eliminate certain morbidity and mortality threats. Speaking before Jones and other Navajo leaders at a Gallup meeting in 1956, David R. L. Duncan, one of Shaw's subordinates at the Navajo Field Office, acknowledged the air of uneasiness surrounding the recent transfer. "I know many people at the moment, are very, very unhappy, that is, that the actual concrete things that they thought they were going to see are still in the form of sand and water instead of concrete," he said. "We do have a lot of plans, but as with everything of this type, and the magnitude of it, it is going to take quite a long while before these things actually become a reality."[24]

The Tribal Council Health Committee worked diligently to be heard in the late 1950s. Wauneka, Howard McKinley, Albert Tsosie, John Mason, and other Health Committee members both expressed thanks for increasing medical services and were straightforward critics when they perceived problems. In addition to representing patients and medical employees to the IHS, tribal leaders sent letters and telegrams to congressional members in Arizona, New Mexico, and Utah whenever Indian health budgets were on the agenda. In 1958, the Health Committee also presented a list of concerns at a congressional hearing about the Long-Range Rehabilitation program. The tribal delegation requested better roads, more health care workers, and the swift completion of the new Shiprock hospital to replace the present "shack" in which people were then hospitalized.[25]

The IHS made a concerted effort to establish better communication with the tribal leadership in the 1960s. Information flowed more freely from the IHS to the tribal government through Dr. Charles McCammon, assigned to Window Rock as the chief medical officer for the Navajo Field Office. Dr. George Bock, who replaced McCammon in

1966, frequently used phrases like "your program" in an effort to fight the IHS's image as an alien presence on the reservation. Bock and the Tribal Council Health Committee together developed a "plan of action" in order to "improve communications" and encourage a "mutual understanding" between the agency and the tribe. They recommended that each Health Committee member be given responsibilities for a specific service unit on the reservation. Each Navajo chapter within the service unit elected a representative to form a service unit committee that reported to the local service unit officer, thereby fostering better communication between the grassroots and the IHS. Relations with the tribe also improved after 1 July 1967 when, upon recommendations

Minnie Platt, R.N., examines a Navajo woman at a government medical facility, ca. 1955. Courtesy of Virginia Brown, Ida Bahl, and Lillian Watson Collection, Cline Library, Northern Arizona University, NAU.PH.92.14.15.

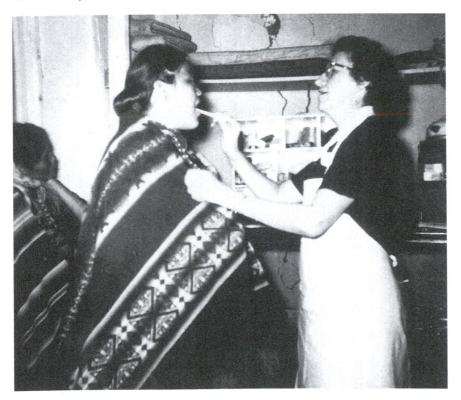

from Bock and Tribal Chairman Raymond Nakai, the IHS gave the
Navajos their own area office in Window Rock.[26]

The IHS and Navajo Health Patterns

The rise of the IHS did not end the discrepancy between Navajo and national health patterns. The Navajo reservation's rugged environment and
dispersed population limited the IHS's ability to significantly influence
reservation health patterns over a short period of time. But, given this
reality, the IHS's effort to provide more preventive care seems to have
been an appropriate response. It is unlikely, then, that any Western medical system with similar funding could have achieved the level of success
that the U.S. government had promised to the Navajos.

Life on the Navajo reservation in the postwar era encompassed both
the persistence of tradition and dramatic change. For the vast majority of
Navajos in the late 1950s, living on the reservation still entailed a rural
existence without the amenities most Americans took for granted. Many
Navajos lived in hogans; few homes had indoor plumbing, electricity, or
telephones. Long-Range Rehabilitation funds had added 291 miles of
paved highways and 360 miles of gravel road across Navajo country, but
many Navajos still braved washboard-surface dirt roads on horseback and
on foot. When it rained, even trucks were stymied by endless miles of
hashklish, mud deep enough to block the way to the nearest trading post,
school, or hospital. New wage-work opportunities arose, but thousands of
Navajos continued to make a living in the traditional ways.[27]

Nonetheless, the IHS found itself as a transitional agency in a transitional
time for the Navajos. Important changes were taking place, especially in the
eastern portion of the reservation. By the 1960s, large numbers worked for
wages in coal mines or industries relocated to the reservation and many
supplemented their incomes with federal social programs. Others worked directly for the government in reservation schools and hospitals. Non–Indian-
style houses became more common, and even those who lived in hogans
were less likely to migrate seasonally with their flocks, as fences and small
urban communities slashed and dotted the reservation. Young people were
especially likely to move to Shiprock, Window Rock, Tuba City, or off-reservation cities such as Farmington and Gallup to be closer to their jobs and
modern services. In addition, by the early 1970s, approximately half of
Navajo households had automobiles or pickup trucks.[28]

Sam Tsosie, a driver interpreter for the Winslow Service Unit public health nursing staff, is welcomed at a Navajo family's hogan in 1961. Courtesy of Virginia Brown, Ida Bahl, and Lillian Watson Collection, Cline Library, Northern Arizona University, NAU.PH.92.14.33.

In the 1960s, the Navajo reservation's health profile began to change as well. During the BIA's tenure, infectious diseases and high infant mortality were the most common causes of death on the reservation. As seen in table 4.1, infant mortality was still high by the time of the transfer. Infant mortality rates and infectious diseases were nonetheless falling, while chronic illnesses and accidental deaths were on the rise.[29]

Table 4.1   Infant Mortality Rates: Navajo, All Indian, and United States, 1955–75 (per 1,000 Live Births)

Year	Navajo	All Indian	United States
1955	87.8	62.5	26.4
1960	71.1	50.3	26.0
1965	46.2	39.0	24.7
1970	31.2	—	20.0
1975	27.8	21.8	16.1

Source: U.S. Department of Health, Education, and Welfare, U.S. Public Health Service, Indian Health Trends and Services, 1970 Edition (Washington, D.C.: GPO, 1971), 14.[30]

Living up to high expectations hinged on the IHS's ability to display statistical improvements in this health environment. Federal government officials and tribal leaders therefore used the infant mortality rate as a key measure of the agency's performance. The IHS's focus on combining clinical with preventive care seems to have been an appropriate, if insufficient, response to this long-term crisis. High Navajo birth rates and the growing willingness on the part of Navajo mothers to have their children in hospitals overwhelmed IHS facilities with maternity cases in the 1960s. More than 4,000 Navajos were delivered every year, and the IHS estimated that the proportion born in hospitals rose from about 88 percent in 1955 to 97 percent by 1968. Handling maternity cases took up a large portion of the IHS hospital beds and taxed the growing but still inadequate staff of obstetricians and nurses. Even if they drew resources away from other aspects of the medical program, these efforts seemed to pay off. Relatively low infant death rates occurring in the first few weeks after birth in the 1950s and 1960s seems to have been associated with the improving quality and acceptance of hospital care.[31]

It proved more difficult for the medical program to care for babies after they left the hospitals. The majority of Navajo infants who did not survive past their first year died in the postneonatal stage, occurring after the first twenty-eight days. During this period of life, infants were highly susceptible to poor sanitation and housing conditions, malnutrition, and a variety of social and economic factors. Both the Many Farms team and the IHS found that Navajo women were much less likely to take advantage of prenatal and postneonatal services than they were to give birth in a hospital, but the medical program did try to make inroads. IHS nurses worked closely with many expectant and recent Navajo mothers, especially in terms of health education. Public health nurses conducted well-baby clinics, as the BIA had once done, and they used slide presentations, films, and pamphlets prepared by the IHS health education staff. IHS sanitation engineers also affected infant health by providing safer sources of water and better sewage disposal.[32]

The IHS campaign to reduce infant deaths on the Navajo and other Indian reservations may have been its greatest accomplishment in its first fifteen years. In 1970, Senator Paul Fannin of Arizona hailed a decline of 48 percent in Indian infant mortality rates between 1955 and 1967 relative to the general population. IHS services alone had not caused the falling rates, but the agency had played a major role in the effort. Yet with Navajo infant death rates occurring 1.5 times more often than infant deaths on average in the United States, the IHS could not claim total victory.[33]

There were other promising signs in regard to Navajo health by the end of the 1960s. New drug therapies, higher hospital utilization rates, and a joint effort among the tribe, Cornell, and the federal government helped push tuberculosis death rates down considerably. Between 1955 and 1959 alone, Navajo tuberculosis death rates fell from roughly sixty-four per 100,000 to about forty-one, and by the mid-1960s, these rates had been cut another 50 percent. Adult deaths from influenza and pneumonia also dropped from an approximate rate of 118 per 100,000 in 1955 to ninety-nine in 1959. As with tuberculosis, death rates from these diseases were significantly reduced during the 1960s.[34]

As encouraging as these signs were for the Navajos and Western medical providers, infectious diseases and ailments spread by unsanitary conditions were still far more common on the Navajo reservation than among the average U.S. population (see table 4.2). Epidemic outbreaks of meningitis, hepatitis, and typhoid swept through reservation boarding schools in 1957 and 1958, infecting hundreds of students. Gastrointestinal mortality rates decreased dramatically during the 1960s, but those rates remained drastically higher on the Navajo reservation and other Indian reservations than among the general population. The Navajos also faced other diseases virtually unheard of elsewhere in the United States, such as bubonic and pneumonic plague.[35]

Navajos also confronted a variety of infectious diseases that threatened their quality of life. At least 2,000 Navajos in 1968 suffered from syphilis,

Table 4.2   Crude Death Rate and Ten Leading Causes of Death:
Navajo and All Indian, 1965–67 Average, and United States, 1966
(per 100,000 Population)

Cause of Death	Navajo	All Indian	United States
All causes	763.9	881.8	951.3
Accidents	175.1	180.8	58.0
Influenza and pneumonia (excluding infants)	61.9	61.0	32.5
Cancers	56.6	69.8	155.1
Coronary diseases	49.7	138.9	371.2
Gastritis, etc.	42.8	18.2	3.9
Tuberculosis	20.6	17.4	3.9
Strokes	19.1	48.5	104.6
Congenital malformations	18.8	15.2	9.3
Cirrhosis of the liver	14.1	36.5	13.6

Source: U.S. Department of Health, Education, and Welfare, U.S. Public Health Service, *Indian Health Trends and Services, 1970 Edition,* 28.[36]

gonorrhea, and other venereal diseases. Otitis media did not occur at a high enough rate among non-Indians to allow a comparison in 1968, but IHS records showed 11,823 Navajos with that disease of the middle ear, which left hundreds of children with serious hearing problems. And as the scourge of tuberculosis began to fade, another old Navajo enemy returned in force. Trachoma had never been totally eradicated on the reservation, and a faltering medical system during World War II had allowed it to revive, especially among school children. By 1968, more than 1,600 Navajos suffered from the disease.[37]

The IHS attacked infectious diseases on multiple fronts, but it could only do so much with limited funds. Throughout the 1960s, sanitation and water projects were high priorities for the IHS and the Navajo tribal leadership. Yet enthusiasm about what was being accomplished in the fight against waterborne disease was tempered by the knowledge that there was still far to go. Dehydration remained a serious problem for infants, and Navajo families tended to spread diseases by sharing wash basins and eating from the same bowls to conserve water. Many Navajos were also at risk from these diseases when they took water from irrigation ditches. Without massive expenditures, the IHS water projects reached only a minority of the Navajo population in the 1950s and 1960s. Although more and more people had access to wells and other, safer water sources, as late as the mid-1970s only 27.6 percent of Navajo homes had indoor plumbing.[38]

In addition to clinical care and water projects, the IHS used health education to address infectious disease. Public health workers distributed illustrated pamphlets informing people to use personal towels and wash basins to avoid trachoma. Another pamphlet warned of the danger of contracting plague from prairie dogs. The IHS also conducted health education clinics at schools, field stations, and health centers. Health educators took advantage of large gatherings as well, including fairs and Indian rodeos, such as the Gallup intertribal ceremonial.[39]

When particularly fierce epidemics struck, the IHS called in assistance from the Centers for Disease Control (CDC). CDC employees, for instance, came to the Navajo reservation during a hepatitis epidemic in 1957. Ten years later, the CDC assigned Dr. Elwin Bennington to Window Rock to direct a special plague program for the reservation and contracted with two non-CDC eye specialists and a group of nurses to start a new campaign against trachoma.[40]

Noninfectious diseases also threatened the Navajos and taxed the IHS's limited resources. The Navajos were once thought to be relatively free from chronic illnesses that killed other Americans in high numbers. Although cancer and heart disease mortality rates in the 1960s remained lower among the Navajos than in the general U.S. population, they were increasing. These lower rates partially reflected different lifestyles and different dietary habits on the reservation, but statistics here can be misleading. As can be seen in table 4.2, Navajo mortality rates from these diseases were so low in comparison to the general population in the mid-1960s that the Navajos had a lower overall crude death rate. Navajos were not healthier, however, because the statistics are not adjusted for age. Cancer, heart disease, and stroke are more likely to kill those who are older and the Navajos were, on average, a younger population because of the high birth rate and lower life expectancy. As infant death and infectious diseases were slowly beginning to kill fewer on the reservation, these chronic ailments were beginning to kill more.[41]

Alcoholism was a particularly serious social and medical problem on the reservation. Statistics showed that few Navajos consumed alcoholic beverages in comparison to the national average, but those who did drink were more likely to do so in excess. Navajos in the postwar years commonly cited alcohol abuse as the most serious problem facing the Diné, and the Tribal Council devoted a great deal of time to discussing the problem. Council delegates were concerned both about the ill effects alcohol had on those Navajos who drank heavily and about the tendency on the part of non-Navajos to stereotype all of the Diné based on their observations of alcohol abuse in border towns such as Gallup.[42]

Scholars have disagreed about the causes underlying American Indian alcoholism. A variety of explanations have been presented, including ones based on biology, social conditions, and historical processes. Stephen Kunitz and Jerrold Levy have argued that the Navajo problem with alcohol can be perceived as more of a regional problem than a racial one. They found that rural non-Indians living around the reservation were just as likely to suffer from alcohol-related cirrhosis as Navajos. According to Kunitz and Levy, Navajos were relatively unaffected by alcohol before the 1930s because few could afford to purchase it from Anglo and Mexican bootleggers. Those who began drinking, they argue, were influenced by non-Indians who tended to binge drink. During the Great Depression, livestock reduction put cash into the hands of more reservation residents and alcohol consumption became more prevalent. It became even more of a problem in the postwar era, especially after 1953, when the federal government ended prohibition on the sale of liquor to American Indians. Because the Navajo government retained prohibition on the reservation, those who did drink congregated in border towns where they could obtain alcohol, perhaps perpetuating the trend toward problem drinking. Regardless of the underlying cause, alcohol-related cirrhosis became the tenth leading cause of death among the Navajos by the late 1960s. Alcohol also contributed to the increase in motor vehicle accidents, and may have had an influence on rising suicide and homicide rates.[43]

The IHS responded slowly to the alcoholism problem, but by 1968 the IHS referred to Indian alcohol abuse as a "high-priority health problem" and argued that it demanded an "attack on many fronts." The IHS contracted with the New Mexico Commission on Alcohol to accept Navajos and other American Indians at the Turquoise Lodge in Albuquerque for treatment. It also allotted a limited number of beds in its hospitals for patients to receive drug therapy with Antabuse, a drug that caused nausea and vomiting when used along with liquor, and which medical experts at the time hoped would be a miracle cure for alcoholism. Meanwhile, Alcoholics Anonymous, the Office of Navajo Economic Opportunity, and various state agencies began reservation programs to combat the problem.[44]

Partially related to alcohol abuse, accidents were the leading causes of death on the Navajo reservation, and their numbers escalated rapidly after the war. The IHS proved relatively impotent against accidental deaths, although it did improve emergency room care and increased the availability of ambulances. Highway collisions and automobile accidents involving pedestrians were especially problematic. Of all accidental deaths occurring between November 1966 and October 1967, half involved motor vehicles.[45]

The IHS estimated that about half of all motor vehicle deaths were alcohol related. But other factors were equally influential. During the 1950s and 1960s, the reservation road network expanded and more Navajos had access to automobiles. Driving conditions were less than ideal. Navajo vehicles were often poorly maintained, and narrow roads with blind curves and steep declines in the mountainous regions of the reservation made driving treacherous. About half of the fatalities involved pickup trucks, which provided little protection to Navajo children and others who frequently rode in truck beds. Moreover, it has been estimated that, as late as the 1970s, 33 percent of Navajo drivers had invalid operator licenses. When accidents did occur, fatalities were more common on the Navajo reservation than in metropolitan areas where medical facilities were more accessible.[46]

Not all accidents involved motor vehicles. Large numbers of Navajos were injured or killed every year in falls, suffocations, and drownings, and children were especially susceptible to burns and poisonings. Many Navajo homes still relied on open fires for heat and cooking, and parents had difficulty keeping dangerous substances away from small children in the one-room hogans. For such problems, the IHS could do little more than to provide health education and emergency services. New hospitals were unable to provide miracle solutions for these and many other Navajo health dilemmas. Although the agency had made some notable strides on the reservation at the end of its first decade and a half of service, the terminationists' hopes that the IHS would resolve the Indian health care crisis remained unfulfilled.[47]

State and Local Involvement in Navajo Health Care

Terminationists may have believed that states and localities could assume health care responsibilities for American Indians, but while the federal effort increased significantly through the late 1950s and 1960s, states and counties were only minimally involved in Navajo health care. States were not willing to relieve the federal government of Indian health care responsibilities, especially since the scope, scale, and expense of those services increased dramatically after the IHS took control.

The Navajo reservation straddled three states: Arizona, New Mexico, and Utah. Of the three, Utah was the most willing and Arizona the least willing to extend medical programs to Navajos and other American Indians. These attitudes reflected the number of Indians who resided in each state. Utah had the smallest Native population of the three, approximately 5,000 in 1955, compared to Arizona's 70,000 and New Mexico's 55,000 Indian residents. Arizona also spent less per capita on health care for all of its residents than the other states, while Utah's expenditures on health care were relatively high in comparison to the rest of the country. Not surprisingly, in 1955 Arizona led the Southwestern states in infant mortality, tuberculosis, and venereal disease rates, while Utah claimed a healthier population than Arizona, New Mexico, Nevada, or Colorado.[48]

Utah, Arizona, and New Mexico all offered limited medical services to needy state residents. All had disabled children services, disease control programs, public health nurses, and laboratory services in addition to other programs, such as Arizona's tuberculosis control activity. Theoretically, Navajos and other Native Americans residing in those states were eligible for these services if they had limited incomes. But other than contributing medicine and staff members to epidemic control efforts on the reservations, states and counties had no specific programs aimed at American Indians.[49]

In general, New Mexico honored its obligation to off-reservation Native Americans with low incomes. The state also paid for medical laboratory work done for Indians referred to them by the IHS, and helped individuals find employment after receiving treatment for alcoholism in the government hospitals. Utah did comparatively more for Indian health care. Its Crippled Children Division actively sought out disabled Indian children and even conducted clinics on the Navajo reservation from time to time. The IHS referred disabled Indian children to private hospitals in Salt Lake City that cared for them free of charge. Arizona's record with Native patients paled in comparison. The Arizona Department of Health

and other related agencies occasionally worked with the federal government on epidemic control and helped compile vital statistics, including
those for Indians. County hospitals and medical programs in the state,
however, frequently denied access to Indian patients, arguing that Indian
health care was entirely a federal responsibility established by past
treaties. New Mexico state medical providers frequently used the same argument when challenged by the IHS or Navajos to fulfill their obligations
to Indian patients.[50]

IHS administrators and Navajo tribal leaders were particularly dis-
pleased when states denied their obligation to Navajos living off the reservation. In 1963, for instance, Annie Wauneka criticized New Mexico for
failing to care for Navajos residing in an area known as the Checkerboard,
off the southeastern edge of the reservation. "The Public Health Service
doesn't actually go in there; it is not their responsibility," she argued. "It
belongs to the State of New Mexico's Health Department, but they just
don't seem to do anything about it."[51]

States became more involved with Navajo health care, largely against
their will, through the Medicaid program established by the federal government in 1965 in conjunction with Medicare. Under Medicaid the federal and state governments contributed matching funds to provide health
care for the poor. The program at first had only a limited effect on Navajo
medical care. The IHS could not bill Medicaid for services rendered in its
hospitals, and Arizona legislators refused to implement Medicaid at all,
fearing that it would encourage American Indians to use nonfederal
medical facilities at the state's expense. But Navajos could access
Medicaid through some missionary providers on the reservation and private practitioners.[52]

Although state interaction with the IHS was thus limited, the agency
did cooperate with county and city governments through its contracting
program. The IHS relied heavily on contracting to keep up with the growing American Indian population, finding it cheaper to pay nonfederal
hospitals and physicians to handle referrals than to construct an adequate
number of medical facilities on the reservations. Local government enthusiasm about IHS contracting did not necessarily reflect a high level of
concern for Indian health. Instead, county and city officials often saw it as
a means to support facilities for non-Indian residents. For instance, in
1952 Bernalillo County (New Mexico) arranged for the federal government to help fund a new hospital in Albuquerque in exchange for making

The Gallup Indian Medical Center in Gallup, New Mexico, still under construction, ca. 1960–61. This off-reservation facility served as the hub for IHS medical services to the Navajos, replacing the aging Fort Defiance hospital in Arizona. Courtesy of Virginia Brown, Ida Bahl, and Lillian Watson Collection, Cline Library, Northern Arizona University, NAU.PH.92.14.69.

at least 100 beds available to American Indian patients. Completed at the time of the transfer, the Bernalillo County Indian Hospital was used by the IHS as a referral center for Pueblos, Apaches, and Navajos, but many of the beds served non-Indians.[53]

Contracting made modern hospital facilities more accessible to the Navajos than the IHS could have afforded to provide otherwise, but the arrangement had serious drawbacks. Navajos did not always feel welcome in towns surrounding the reservation and might not be pleased about being referred to such places. American Indians commonly faced racial discrimination off the reservation. Some stores in Gallup denied access to Indian customers, and many private physicians who contracted with the IHS tended to favor their non-Indian patients.[54]

Navajo reservation border towns such as Farmington, Gallup, and Winslow also urged the IHS to build new facilities off the reservation. Mayors, city council members, and chamber of commerce and medical society members hoped that new IHS hospitals could open up new economic opportunities. The Navajo Tribal Council, not surprisingly, opposed such measures.[55]

The Navajo leaders prevailed over the city of Farmington when Congress placed a new IHS hospital in Shiprock. But, after the IHS transfer, Congress chose to place a new medical center in Gallup instead of renovating the one in Fort Defiance, in effect moving the Navajos' medical hub off the reservation. Against the tribe's will, Congress opted for Gallup over Fort Defiance, because the former, they claimed, would be better able to provide utility service for a large hospital and housing for employees.[56]

The new hospital at Gallup became the referral hub for all of the surrounding IHS hospitals, including those serving Zunis and other American Indian groups nearby. The medical center provided needed beds and modern medical equipment, but Navajo patients with serious ailments were now compelled to leave the reservation. There was at least one other problem with the medical center. The city of Gallup had promised to provide enough affordable housing for the hospital's nearly 300 employees as part of its bid. Soon before the facility's completion in 1961, the IHS discovered that Gallup had not lived up to its part of the bargain. The agency could not house many of its staff members because housing and apartment developers had been slow to build the needed units. As a result, the hospital was severely understaffed in its first year.[57]

The new Gallup Indian Medical Center symbolized much about the IHS in its first fifteen years. A state-of-the-art medical facility that rivaled or bettered hospitals available to non-Indians in the region, it represented improvements in the quantity and technical quality of Western medical services available to the Navajos. The medical center served as a reminder of a stronger federal commitment to Indian health care. At the same time, however, it contributed to a general sense among Navajo leaders and patients that they had insufficient say in how the government medical program functioned. A relatively tall building, modern looking for its day, the medical center also appeared monolithic and foreboding, rising up from an off-reservation location where Navajos were treated as outsiders.

· 5 ·

MEDICAL SELF-DETERMINATION, 1955–69

The first decade and a half following the introduction of the Indian Health Service to the Navajo reservation also witnessed a flurry of Navajo efforts to shape and broaden their healing options. With encouragement and assistance from the U.S. government and the medical missionaries who once hoped to overwhelm Navajo sovereignty and tradition, the tribe (which referred to itself as the "Navajo Nation" beginning in 1969 to assert its autonomy) made major strides toward determining its own medical care. That larger effort for self-determination included a striving to preserve traditional healing and a continuing struggle by a growing minority of Navajos to protect the rights of Native American Church members.

Tribal Government and Western Medicine

In its first fifteen years after the transfer, the IHS continued to rely heavily on the Navajo tribal government to encourage people to seek medical care. Perhaps Annie Wauneka fulfilled this role better than any other tribal leader. Since her days touring off-reservation sanatoriums comforting Navajo patients in the early 1950s, Wauneka continued to speak on their behalf to the IHS and the contract hospitals, and she encouraged others suffering from tuberculosis and other ailments to seek care. Wauneka also offered a weekly radio program on KGAK in which she delivered health education messages in the Navajo language. Dr. James Shaw credited her radio program and her other activities for helping win Navajo confidence in sanatorium care after the war.[1]

Not all Navajos shared Wauneka's or the tribal government's enthusiasm about Western medicine. In particular, many Navajos suffering from tuberculosis still refused institutionalized care or left the facilities before their treatment had been completed. In the late 1950s and 1960s, the IHS relied heavily on off-reservation contracting to deal with tuberculosis. As incidence of the disease declined nationwide, many sanatorium beds became vacant and thus available to the IHS at a much lower cost than if the agency had built new sanatoriums. Navajos were more willing to use the facilities than they had been in the past, but the long stays away from the reservation remained stressful for many patients. Desertion rates at the sanatoriums gradually declined, but the IHS and Wauneka estimated in 1959 that about 235 Navajos on the reservation and in surrounding towns were aware that they were contagious and refused to seek Western medical care.[2]

Wauneka's patience with these holdouts wore thin because she and other Council delegates believed that they threatened the health of others. She and the Tribal Council reacted with drastic measures, showing how deeply tribal leaders were concerned about reservation health matters. But their methods also reveal that the tribal government, while a champion of medical self-determination for its people, could, at times, be as overbearing as the federal government and missionaries.

Health Committee members tried unsuccessfully to track down those who refused sanatorium care. One woman gave Wauneka an alias and slipped away when the Health Committee chairperson came to her door. Frustrated by such behavior, Council delegates, encouraged by Wauneka, proposed in 1959 that the IHS cooperate with the tribe on procedures for involuntary commitment of reservation residents with dangerous contagious diseases. Wauneka understood that Council delegates were reluctant to use force on their Navajo constituents and knew that it would be easier politically to do nothing, but she spoke adamantly in the Council chambers. "If we leave these cases, they will be happy and it will save the Tribe money," she admitted. "But, we have found it is a contagious disease and we are trying to pre[v]ent your children from getting it. That is all we are asking for."[3]

As Wauneka anticipated, the involuntary commitment proposal sparked debate in the Council chambers. Although other leaders shared Wauneka's concern about tuberculosis, some balked at forceful tactics. Hoskie Cronemeyer, Paul Begay, and Sevier Vaughn believed that Navajo carriers would listen to reason if Council delegates sat down and spoke with them. They argued, however, that the tribe did not have the authority to force people to tend to their own health. "Why should we say that we should have to use force or use the courts to commit our people to the hospitals?" asked Vaughn. "I don't believe that's necessary, because when a Navajo is already afflicted with a disease, why should we ask him to pay a penalty?" Vaughn suggested that traditional herbal remedies might be a good alternative if someone suffering from the disease could not be persuaded to use Western medicine.[4]

By a fifty-nine-to-six vote in January 1959, and with Chairman Jones's support, the Tribal Council approved Wauneka's proposal. But hoping to avoid conflict, Council delegates chose to first speak face-to-face with as many of the 235 tuberculosis carriers as they could find and tried to persuade them to go to sanatoriums willingly. They had only limited success. At the end of 1961 the tribe gave its courts the go-ahead to commit those with contagious diseases to hospital care. The patient first had to go to an IHS facility but could then be transferred to an off-reservation contract sanatorium. Patients were guaranteed the right to have a healing ceremony or religious service before commitment. Some Council delegates worried that this allowance might permit the patient to stall the process, but Clifford Beck of Low Mountain insisted upon it, pointing out that ceremonies would help alleviate emotional and psychological strain. "We have seen where medicine men would perform a ceremony before a patient leaves for the hospital, not only for people suffering from tuberculosis but other diseases," he argued. "We have seen how, in a way, it is helpful to the patient in that the patient realizes that everything possible has been done in his own home area, and in that way he is content to be confined to a hospital."[5]

To a large extent, changing national policies during the 1960s encouraged increasingly bold tribal activity in Western medicine. During the decade, the Kennedy, Johnson, and Nixon administrations proved less enthusiastic about the assimilationist goals of the termination policy, and thus helped pave the way for Navajo medical self-determination. While Congress and IHS administrators continued to make most of the key decisions affecting Indian health care, the federal government opened new avenues for tribal participation in the delivery of Western medicine.

One such initiative stemmed from an IHS decision late in the decade to devise a program similar to Cornell's "health visitor" program at Many Farms. The federal government decided to fund Community Health Representative (CHR) programs nationwide that would be administered by tribal bodies. The IHS hoped that the CHRs could serve as vital links between the various service units and the local communities. On 11 December 1968, the Navajo Tribal Council agreed to participate in the program. Chairman Raymond Nakai selected Thomas Todacheeny to oversee thirty-two Navajo CHRs and eight coordinators. Like the "health visitors," the CHRs wore many different hats. They accompanied IHS field health workers and sanitation workers around on their assigned portion of the reservation, serving as medical assistants and translators. CHRs also cared for the sick and disabled in their homes, carrying firewood and water and administering first aid. Occasionally, they were invited to chapter meetings where they reported on the CHR program and medical activity occurring locally.[6]

After their selection, the CHRs spent four weeks training at the Desert Willow Training Center in Tucson, Arizona, where they were instructed in communication skills, cross-cultural educational techniques, environmental health, home nursing, first aid, and defensive driving. Following completion of the course, each CHR spent two to six weeks training with various health professionals and officials in his or her local area to become familiar with the medical situation.[7]

The CHRs spent much of their first year trying to "sell" the program to skeptics and those who were indifferent to them in the Navajo communities. With termination policy still fresh in their memories, some Navajos worried that the program might be an excuse for the government to reduce its services. And, according to Dr. George Bock, others perceived the CHR program as just another War on Poverty effort to employ Indians. Todacheeny rallied his CHRs, reminding them that they were doing an important job and that many people in the tribe and the government medical program supported them. The CHR program overcame its obstacles and endured through the coming decades, continuing to give Navajos valuable experience as both medical providers and administrators.[8]

President Lyndon Johnson's Office of Economic Opportunity (OEO) also facilitated tribal involvement in health care. OEO offered federal funding to encourage Community Action Programs in which low-income Americans would administer their own community revitalization efforts. The Navajos accepted the program in 1964, set up the Office of Navajo Economic Opportunity (ONEO), and appointed Peter MacDonald as its director.[9]

ONEO became involved with health care in different ways. In 1965, its employees canvassed the reservation and helped register the elderly for Medicare. ONEO also became the tribe's main arm for attacking alcoholism. The Tribal Council had addressed alcohol abuse in the early 1960s by setting up a special committee on alcoholism under Wilson Halona and encouraging local communities to set up Alcoholics Anonymous (AA) groups. Later during the 1960s, ONEO worked in conjunction with the IHS, chapter officials, and local AA groups in erecting a cooperative alcoholism treatment network. After the IHS administered Antabuse treatments in the hospitals, Community Alcoholism Workers (CAWs) from ONEO conducted follow-ups with the patients and helped them find employment and establish community support networks composed of friends, family, and a CAW.[10]

Other Navajo initiatives in Western medical delivery were funded internally. In addition to donations to medical missions and wages for members of the Health Committee, the Tribal Council appropriated over $100,000 annually to its own medical service programs. The Navajo Nation left clinical care duties to the IHS but paid for a variety of medical appliance programs. In 1963, the Council appropriated $136,000 to supply eyeglasses, hearing aids, dentures, wheelchairs, and infant layettes for needy Navajos. The IHS also tried to convince the tribe to establish a nursing home for the reservation using the old Tuba City Hospital. The Council did not act on that proposal, but in 1968, it approved a lease for a private, nonprofit organization, Diné Bitsiis Baa Aha Yaa, to establish a nursing home at Chinle.[11]

The Decline of the Medical Mission

Missionary medical services continued to play significant roles on the reservation in the 1950s and 1960s, but those services changed dramatically in form by the end of that time period. In the late 1950s and early 1960s, the Seventh Day Adventists, members of the Christian Reformed Church, and Presbyterians all constructed new hospitals on or near the reservation. Yet even while expanding their activity, the medical missions were being forced to come to terms with a changing health care profession and the expansion of IHS programs. The prolonged personal communication and individual focus required by the evangelical process proved difficult to maintain in the modern medical environment. Missionaries had to devote more energy to finding new funding sources and to coordinating their efforts with a larger referral network involving federal hospitals. These forces of change compelled church mission boards to rethink the utility of the medical mission in the late 1960s. By the end of that decade, unwilling to continue operating the facilities, some of the missionaries encouraged local Navajo communities to take over their hospitals, thus offering rare opportunities for grassroots involvement in Western medicine.

Despite the new challenges, medical missionaries had reason to be optimistic about Navajo reactions to their services. Navajos often favored missionary facilities over IHS hospitals and clinics even when they had to travel farther to reach them. More Navajos were Christians after World War II than in the early days of the medical mission, but the generally positive attitude toward these hospitals probably had more to do with confidence in the medical services provided. Paul Jones, in a 1957 address to the College of Medical Evangelists, spoke highly of the medical missions. He based his support for sectarian physicians on his pragmatic concern about consistent and accessible care, arguing that missionary doctors were more likely to remain on the reservation than were government doctors. Local residents became familiar with the missionaries and often trusted them more than government medical workers, who tended to be young and came and went at a rapid pace. Tribal Councilman Jack Tinhorn shared Jones's admiration for the medical missionaries, comparing service at mission hospitals favorably in comparison to the bureaucratic hassle and indifference many patients found at government facilities. "When that happens, these people then seek other help," explained Tinhorn.

> They go to other hospitals, usually those operated by the missions like the one located at Ganado and the one at Gouldings [Monument Valley]. There, the minute you open the door, there is someone to receive you, a nurse or somebody that is interested in your welfare; and that person asks what is wrong and you indicate what is wrong with you. Without further questions, you get this attention. They don't have to ask you an endless array of questions and have you wait. They see to it that you get some relief immediately.[12]

Through the late 1950s, the Seventh Day Adventists still believed that the medical mission could thrive on the reservation in the postwar era. Marvin and Gwen Walter were pleased with their progress among

Navajos living around Monument Valley on the Utah-Arizona border. They believed that they had established positive relations with local healers, thereby winning confidence in their effort and displacing the traditional healing ways. The couple had asked healers to call them as soon as they were consulted by a patient with a serious illness. Gwen Walter felt that the healers had accepted the relationship and the efficacy of modern medical care and believed that they too would eventually discard traditional ways. According to her, the higher admissions reflected the patients' waning connection to the traditional healing ways. "Harry [Goulding] tells us that nowadays he sells very little material for sings—that people come to us instead," she said. In response to their positive reports, the church approved plans for a new, fifteen-bed facility for the area. The Monument Valley Hospital opened its doors in 1961, after obtaining a $10,000 grant from the Navajo Tribal Council.[13]

The Presbyterians also viewed the future of medical missionary work optimistically. In 1962, the Board of National Missions of the United Presbyterian Church planned a new, forty-bed hospital for Ganado. Sage Memorial had been serving Navajos in the center of the reservation for more than thirty years and could no longer handle the large patient loads. In 1961 alone, Sage delivered 458 babies, admitted 2,111 patients, and treated 13,157 outpatients. The Board estimated that Sage Memorial's replacement facility would cost approximately $500,000 and asked the Tribal Council to contribute $50,000. Chairman Jones urged support for a $25,000 donation, even though he expressed concern that missionaries would never stop asking for money now that the Seventh Day Adventists and Presbyterians had succeeded in doing so. "Ganado Hospital has performed outstanding service to the Navajos when we did not have Public Health facilities available on the Navajo Reservation," said Jones. "They have done tremendous work among the Navajos; for the Navajos, in fact, they made a record for themselves. So, people from remote areas disregarded the other hospitals and came a long distance to visit the hospital at Ganado." The donation resolution passed by a vote of sixty to zero.[14]

But as medical mission hospitals expanded during the early 1960s, the evangelical fervor behind them began to fade. The hospitals had won the trust of many Navajos, but operating those facilities after World War II proved expensive and complicated. More and more time had to be devoted to securing adequate funding and other administrative concerns, leaving less time to focus on the gospel.[15]

Entrance to the old Tuba City Hospital during the winter, ca. 1960. Courtesy of Virginia Brown, Ida Bahl, and Lillian Watson Collection, Cline Library, Northern Arizona University, NAU.PH.92.14.16.

Of the three major medical missions on the reservation, the Christian Reformed Church program in Rehoboth may have been the most outdated by the early 1960s. Located near Gallup, the Rehoboth facility was now eclipsed by the new IHS Medical Center, and gradually the Rehoboth medical program began to stray from its original purpose. In 1960, the Christian Reformed Church moved away from its focus on Indian groups and began to serve all residents of the Gallup area. And in 1965, the Christian Reformed Church severed its direct link to the hospital, placing it under the direction of the board of governors of the Rehoboth Christian Hospital Association. Christian Reformed health care professionals linked to the Luke Society continued to run the facility. The church then opted to merge with an aging hospital in Gallup run by a Catholic group, the Sisters of Perpetual Adoration. In 1968, using forty acres and $400,000 donated by the Christian Reformed Church, federal funds, and $25,000 donated by the tribe, the two missionary groups built the seventy-five-bed Rehoboth-McKinley Hospital.[16]

Ostensibly, the merger that gave rise to the new hospital came in response to increased demand for medical services which the small facilities could not meet on their own. The old Rehoboth facility commonly reported utilization increases of 6 percent per year in the 1960s. Although patients were asked to pay according to their ability, far too few did so given the rising cost of medical care in the United States. Even after the merger, the Christian Reformed Church and St. Mary's had to turn to new funding sources. IHS reimbursements, private insurance, Medicare, and Medicaid became staple resources for them and other missionary hospital operations, but these new funds came with strings attached, intruding on the hospital's autonomy. As Raymond Estrada, an employee at Rehoboth-McKinley in later years, pointed out, "Medicaid dictates to you now what you need to do."[17]

The Christian Reformed Church insisted that the new McKinley Hospital maintain a mission statement and the Christian designation, but the missionaries no longer controlled its administration. Instead, the official administrative body for the facility was made up of Navajo and non-Navajo community representatives from the Rehoboth-Gallup area. "I think the Christian part of it comes from each of us," said Estrada in 1993, but the older medical mission model no longer existed in Gallup after the 1960s.

The Presbyterians found themselves in a similar financial situation, and like the Christian Reformed Church, opted to turn their facility over to community administration. In 1969, they left Sage Memorial to Project HOPE on the understanding that the hospital would pass to local administration after a six-year transition period. Project HOPE (which stands for Health Opportunity for People Everywhere) had been established in 1958 to deliver medical care to needy populations overseas. In the 1960s, the organization decided to "turn some of its talent and expertise inward and work among our own minority groups in an effort to give them the hope and confidence to survive and progress in our society," and they viewed Ganado as a perfect opportunity to begin work in the United States. While continuing to operate the hospital, HOPE planned to use Sage Memorial as a base for training Navajos as nurses, technicians, and administrators so that the community could take over at the end of the transition period.[18]

According to John King of Sage Memorial, the Presbyterians pulled out of Ganado in order to contribute more funds to inner-city projects. This shifting focus to other economically depressed groups drew funding and interest away from the Navajos. As a result, both the reservation hospital and education programs were canceled. Reverend David Watermulder explained the Presbyterians' decision to leave Sage Memorial, saying that "a half century ago, dedicated Christians responded to needs, and we have responded to different ones." Whereas Sage originally met the medical needs of the reservation, "now, health problems require the special expertise that Project HOPE possesses. And the training aspect carries out our conviction that Navajo self-determination is essential."[19]

Traditional Healing

By the 1960s, many Navajos believed that the traditional healing ways would not survive. It is impossible to quantify the number of traditional healers who served the reservation after World War II or the number of ceremonies they knew. Many Navajo elders, however, judged ceremonialism to be in decline, and there is every reason for scholars to agree with that assessment. But Navajos continued to value the old ways and to demand sings, and some of those who were most worried about the decline took action to preserve the ceremonies.

Traditional healers, older Navajos, and other observers commonly referred to a decreasing number of singers and a loss of respect for traditional ways. "I have been acquainted with several medicine men who have recently died who were not able to teach ceremonies they knew to their grandchildren or anyone else," said Yazzie Begay, a Navajo educator. "Today their sacred instruments sit unused." For Begay and others, this situation endangered more than Navajo health. "The Navajo ceremonial system has given our lives meaning, our personalities dignity, and has been the reason our people and land have increased," said Begay. "We believe that, if the harmony and beauty that are part of the Navajo way are lost through the deaths of medicine men, then we as people are lost and have no future."[20]

Surveys conducted by the Cornell team during the 1970s suggested that ceremonialism remained central to Navajo life. In fact, the team estimated that well over half of the Navajos around Rough Rock and Many Farms used both Western medicine and traditional healing and that many combined these ways with other forms of healing, including the Native American Church.[21]

Nevertheless, Navajo elders were intensely concerned that future generations would no longer be able to practice the traditional ways. Interviews conducted by the University of New Mexico and Navajo Community College (later known as Diné College) in the 1960s and early 1970s of respected elders provide some sense of how older Navajos viewed traditional healing. The Navajo respondents generally did not attribute the loss of traditional healing practices to Western medicine's influence on Diné society; only a few of the Navajos even spoke of Western medicine in the same context with traditional healing. They were more likely to view Christianity, economics, education, and broad contact with the non-Navajo world as the real threats to Diné healing.[22]

For many elders, changing religious beliefs topped the list of threats to Navajo ceremonialism. By the 1970s, approximately 60,000 Navajos, or a little less than half of the population, identified themselves as members of Christian denominations. Not all Navajos who converted to Christianity gave up traditional healing. Some Catholic and Episcopalian missionaries were lenient about their congregants attending traditional ceremonies. In addition, many Christians continued to have ceremonies conducted on their behalf in times of illness. According to Garrick and Roberta Bailey, some older Navajos claimed that even J. C. Morgan, the Navajo missionary, had a ceremony performed for him late in his life. But a growing number of Navajos belonged to evangelical Protestant churches that were outspoken against Navajo traditional ceremonialism and the Native American Church.[23]

Evangelical Protestant churches, sometimes led by Diné ministers, drew hundreds of Navajos into their revival camps during the 1960s, and sometimes offered faith healing as an alternative to, rather than supplement to, traditional healing. The churches' success concerned Navajos such as Deescheeny Nez Tracy, who believed in the traditional ways. "This helps to make them turn away from the Navajo religion; even some of our medicine men cast their healing paraphernalia aside to join the Christians, and most young people have little interest in the long and tedious task of learning ceremonies," Tracy said. He worried that young people were finding it easier to be Christians than to learn to be singers. Whereas it took years of hard work to become a singer, said Tracy, "To become a Christian takes only a short time—a few lessons and prayers, and you are converted." Charlie Brown and John Dick also emphasized the dichotomy between traditional healing and Christianity. "Today there are many religious denominations on the Reservation," said Brown. "I seem to be confused at times, and I still choose the Navajo ceremonies because I believe in the medicine men who have corn pollen of which to partake," he continued. "I want the Navajo singing and prayers. I want the corn pollen and the Navajo medicines. That, I think, is the right way."[24]

Older Navajos were also disturbed by influences that corrupted the ceremonies, including the availability of alcohol at traditional dances and sings. Such corruptions, elders believed, threatened the whole tribe, for if used properly, ceremonies were powerful sources of healing, but if abused, they could bring harm to the individual and the larger community. It particularly upset Tracy that people were no longer acting with proper respect while attending ceremonies. "The squaw dance is a healing ceremony, NOT a Navajo social dance, as some call it, where people drink and make up stupid songs to amuse themselves with."[25]

Some elders worried that a few contemporary traditional healers played a role in the corruption of Navajo ways. "The medicine man, too, must perform his ceremony to the best of his ability and knowledge," said Thomas Clani. "We hear or see where some medicine men have become careless, even drinking during the act of duty." Financial concerns also lay behind the changes in the ceremonies. Howard Gorman believed that a whole class of ceremonies that had traditionally been conducted without compensation for the healers had disappeared, presumably because singers had no interest in learning them in the modern economy. Tom Ration, like many others, believed that too many people had become healers for

the wrong reasons. "Some medicine men have great respect for our ceremonies," said Ration. "Others do it only for the money and do not really
care to help the people. I am quite aware of the statement often heard,
'Nothing is holy now.' We who still have faith in our religion know that
EVERYTHING is holy. How else can we be alive?"[26]

Healers in the 1950s and 1960s may have been more likely to use shorter
ceremonies, and Frank Mitchell viewed such alterations as a sign of laziness
and suggested that some singers were using "made-up" ceremonies. He also
lamented that singers no longer demonstrated a commitment to their patients by staying with them until the illness passed, as had been the custom.
"Now many singers do not bother about that anymore," said Mitchell.
"They may sing for three or two days, and then they begin to say, 'Well, I'm
out of voice, I'm getting hoarse.' They start making excuses."[27]

Navajo elders, including traditional healers, also worried about how
modern society had affected the young people responsible for carrying on
the traditional ways. Younger people relied on wage work and went away
to school more than in the past, and this absence made it difficult for them
to find the time and money to commit themselves to years of apprenticeship with a traditional healer. Under the livestock economy, families
could support a young person while he or she studied to become a singer,
but the wage economy made it more challenging to do so. Some healers in
the 1960s also believed that people returning from off-reservation schools
did not want to become singers because they had not been sufficiently exposed to traditional culture. Many of these students also came back to the
reservation unable to speak Navajo, and this made it difficult for them to
follow the traditional ways.[28]

Modern technology also appeared to distract younger Navajos. Tape
recorders and radios filled up their leisure time and steered them away
from the traditional teachings. In many ways, these changes were no different from those occurring among non-Navajos in the 1950s, 1960s, and
1970s. But such trends may have been particularly disturbing to Navajos
because elders had to pass on essential ceremonial information orally, and
they required attentive audiences. Tracy considered Navajo youths disrespectful and unfocused, and he lamented that they were headed down the
wrong path:

In the homes the refrigerators are full of pop and Kool-Aid. Our children sit in front of the TV and consume gallons of pop into all hours

of the nights. When morning comes they want to sleep until noon. That is life to them. We seldom hear about a person running at dawn yelling at the top of his voice, or the screams that come from taking an ice-cold plunge or rolling in the snow. We hear only the screaming of the radios and stereo players. Who is to blame? The white man made the inventions.[29]

John Dick did not blame just the young people or non-Indian influence. Dick believed that the elders themselves had failed to instill the proper values in the children and did not work hard enough to pass on the traditional stories and ceremonies. "Our elders should have continued to tell their stories," he said, "then our religion would have been made stronger and we still would have enough medicine men to serve our people where they are needed." Yet, according to Dick, the children were to blame for failing to be attentive when the elders did speak to them. "Such talks 'bug' them," said Dick, "and they do not listen."[30]

Less frequently Navajo people commented on the influence Western medicine had on traditional healing. They seemed most concerned about the effect hospitals had on herbalism. "Most of these medicine herbs are being forgotten just because of the hospital," said Tom Joe. "A hospital is a good thing to have but then at the same time there are a lot of good things in the line of herbs, medicine herbs that our Navajo used to use for different kinds of sickness." Eighty-eight-year-old Jack Johnson saw the passing of many herbal remedies. "Mostly all these old medicine way of doing is just passing away because the hospital has more other kinds of medicine that they use for curing," said Johnson.[31]

Joe's and Johnson's emphasis on the competition between Western medicine and Navajo herbalism may have been related to the tendency for Navajos to see herbalists and physicians on the same level. Both Western medicine and herbalism were generally categorized as symptomatic treatments rather than cures, and neither could substitute for ceremonies. In 1967, Dr. Bock claimed that IHS physicians were often shocked to find out that Navajos tended to rank them below traditional healers along with herbalists, Hopi healers, and Christian faith healers. Whether most Navajo people actually thought in those terms, they were more likely to view medical drugs and herbs as being in competition because they performed similar functions.[32]

Cornell team reports add scholarly insight to supplement elders' statements. Through interviews in their study area, the team found that sixty-six diagnosticians and forty-nine traditional singers served a population of approximately 1,000, and they estimated that about 1,350 ceremonies had been conducted there in 1961. Healers Adair and Sasaki spoke to did not believe that the number of ceremonies they performed yearly had declined.[33]

Nonetheless, the Cornell team did find evidence that the traditional ways might be endangered in the future. Of the singers they located, 90 percent were over the age of fifty. Healers who spoke to Adair and Sasaki did not necessarily believe that people were less reliant on them than they had been in the past, but they were concerned that apprentices were harder to find than before. They knew of only six people then studying to be healers. Similar studies showed a declining ratio of singers to the Navajo population, with about half as many singers to the population in the 1950s as there were in the late 1930s. None of the Cornell respondents, however, said Western medicine had caused the decline or saw it in conflict with traditional healing. Forty-two of the healers had used the Many Farms clinic themselves at least once, and one-third of them said they frequently referred patients to see the physicians. The healers attributed the problem mainly to economic changes. They noted that many young people could not afford to pay for lessons or to obtain a medicine bundle and could not coordinate wage work with the apprenticeship process.[34]

Many Navajos who worried what the future held for Navajo healing took action to preserve the traditional ways. Some healers, such as Hosteen Klah and Frank Mitchell, were willing to share their knowledge with outsiders and allowed themselves to be recorded, believing that this would preserve the prayers and chants for posterity. Deescheeny Nez Tracy, who also approved of such actions, said, "Gathering all of the information that is vital and keeping it on records or tapes, or printing it in books, can be our Bible, like the white man has." Others, as Howard Gorman explained, were cautious about recording their knowledge, because revealing such information, especially at the wrong times, could bring about illness or other harm.[35]

Some healers also looked for ways to provide institutional support for apprentices and their teachers. In 1962, a group of traditional healers approached the Tribal Council and asked them to establish a training program for Navajo singers. The Council did not act on the suggestion at the time, but the idea stayed alive, and in the late 1960s, a group of psychiatrists, educators, and singers came together to turn the concept into reality.

Navajo-controlled education played a key role in this process. During the 1960s, the tribal government and local communities focused energy on taking control of education by administering their own schools, free from BIA influence. The effort led to the establishment of Navajo Community College in 1968 and a variety of community schools by the end of the decade, including Rough Rock Demonstration School in 1966. These new institutions made Navajo history and culture an official part of their curriculum and provided a possible support base for initiatives focused on training new healers. Robert Roessel, an educator from Arizona State University who helped establish both the college and demonstration school, took a personal interest in traditional healing. In 1967, he and others at the Rough Rock school, in conjunction with some traditional healers, decided to establish a training program for singers.[36]

Rough Rock found funding for what became known as the Navajo Mental Health Program through a grant from the PHS's National Institute of Mental Health, lasting from 1968 to 1983. It seemed natural for funding to come through an agency related to mental health. For a long time, psychiatrists such as the Leightons were more interested in Navajo healing than other medical doctors because they considered it to be psychotherapeutic. Psychiatrists in the 1960s, including Dr. Karl Menninger from Kansas, and Dr. Robert Bergman, a Public Health Service psychiatrist assigned to Window Rock, continued to show an interest in Navajo healing. Bergman quickly came to understand the power of Navajo healing as more than mental and later argued that scholars did it a disservice by trying to define it scientifically. Menninger and Bergman's support helped win funding from the Institute and both played roles as advisors to the Navajo Mental Health Program.[37]

Under the direction of John Dick and Frank Harvey, the project selected six healers to receive stipends through the Rough Rock Demonstration School to teach twelve apprentices. The school also supported the apprentices with a smaller stipend to help them through the long program. Actual instruction went on outside the classroom, often in the healers' homes, just as it had traditionally. The IHS agreed to take part in the program by sending physicians over from Gallup every other Monday for discussion sessions with the healers and apprentices. At those meetings, healers and physicians shared information about their practices and agreed to formalize procedures for referrals. Bergman gave lectures on these occasions during which he explained the use of x-rays and other medical technology and answered questions from the healers and apprentices, and the Diné participants responded positively to what he and other physicians told them. A number of healers who were not officially part of the project were interested enough in the proceedings to attend.[38]

Although the program had institutional roots, the Rough Rock staff emphasized the need for training to follow the traditional pattern. Apprentices were not rushed through the learning process but allowed to go at a pace they and their teachers set. This meant that the first group did not finish until 1972, but it ensured that the new singers were fully prepared to carry on the ceremonies. The healers taught their apprentices the complex chants and prayers, a process non-Navajo observers compared to learning how to recite a Wagnerian Opera or the New Testament from memory. Most of the first twelve apprentices were older, averaging about fifty-five, while the healers averaged in the eighties. Apprentices that followed them in the early 1970s were younger, averaging closer to forty years old.[39]

Rough Rock Demonstration School and Navajo Community College aided traditional healers in other ways as well, collecting biographical information from older Navajos and preparing texts dealing with Diné history, religion, and culture. By helping children to respect and understand their culture, these efforts provided promise for the future of traditional healing and reinforced Navajo identity. "Our adaptation to transition from the old life to the new one should help our people in the future," said Hoke Denetsosie, looking back on his involvement with Rough Rock and Navajo Community College in the late 1960s. "In the final analysis it is our Navajo heritage and the significance of our Navajo beliefs which bind our people—the Diné—together through our traditional ceremonialism which helps to make us a great and unique tribe."[40]

The Native American Church

IHS activity and opposition from other Navajos did not stop people on the Diné Bikéyah from participating in the Native American Church (NAC) in the 1950s and 1960s. The peyote religion grew rapidly on the reservation after World War II; David Aberle has estimated that between 35 and 40 percent of all Navajos in 1965 took part in NAC meetings during this time period. The peyote religion appealed to thousands who faced the pressures of modern life and personal struggles with alcoholism and to those who were less than satisfied with other forms of spirituality and healing. New converts were also likely to have inherited their faith from relatives who were already members. The pan-Indian religion had gained so many converts on the reservation that the Navajos had more practicing members than did any other Native American tribe by the 1960s. Even while the federal government cracked down on drug use nationwide, it permitted NAC members to use peyote. Although the Food and Drug Administration established stricter drug laws, including the prohibition of peyote, NAC members remained exempt because of constitutional religious freedom guarantees. Yet it concerned non-Navajo peyotists like Frank Takes Gun, a Crow leader of the NAC, as well as Navajo members, that the large body of practicing Diné peyotists still had to operate against tribal and state laws.[41]

State laws regulating peyote use, which varied across the country, were some of the most serious challenges to the NAC in the 1960s. New Mexico had legalized peyote use for NAC members in 1959. Colorado and Utah were slower to accept the rights of NAC members to use peyote, but finally did so at the end of the 1960s. Arizona's legal statutes proved the least tolerant of the NAC in the Four Corners states (Arizona, Colorado, New Mexico, and Utah), but the courts tended to be relatively lenient. Navajo NAC members faced the greatest danger from legal prosecution in other states, such as California, where some moved to seek wage work. In 1962, three Navajos working for the Santa Fe Railway were arrested in Needles, California, for having a peyote ritual in a hogan they had constructed from railroad ties. New hope arose for peyotists when the American Civil Liberties Union stepped in to defend the three men. The Supreme Court of California overturned the convictions in 1964, arguing that their religious rights had been violated.[42]

For the majority of Navajo NAC members living on the reservation, the 1940 tribal law against peyote continued to be their greatest obstacle. Opposition to the NAC remained strong on the reservation, and many Navajo elders, healers, and Christians continued to view the NAC as a corruptive and alien influence. Missionaries were also likely to lash out against the NAC, even more so perhaps than against traditional healing. But as the number of Navajos joining the NAC grew in the 1960s and anxious rumors about it had time to run their course, general opposition to peyote use declined.[43]

One source of hope for peyotists came from Raymond Nakai, a Catholic who ran against Paul Jones for tribal chairman in 1963. Nakai recognized that large numbers of Navajos were taking part in the NAC and were looking for someone to help them gain legal acceptance on the reservation. He ran on a platform of religious tolerance and seems to have won considerable support from NAC members. Nakai may have won without support from Navajo peyotists, but many on the reservation, including Frank Mitchell, did not believe so:

> I do not know why the majority of the People voted for this new leader, because he was never among us over here. . . . The People all around who belonged to the new leader's Peyote church believed that he would repeal the law which had been passed limiting the use of peyote on the reservation. Of course, all of the People belonging to that group wanted that and so they voted for him.

Peyote remained illegal in 1963, but Nakai's administration took a more lenient stance, and this may have helped him secure reelection in 1966, perhaps indicating that reservation residents viewed the NAC more favorably by the middle of that decade. Attitudes had changed enough on the reservation by 1967 that the Tribal Council finally legalized peyote use for NAC members. By a narrow margin of twenty-nine to twenty-six votes, the Council passed CO-65-67, which allowed peyote use on the reservation in the name of religious freedom—a step that made it easier for Navajos to access the peyote religion's healing power as a supplement to growing Western medical services and their enduring traditional ceremonialism.[44]

· 6 ·

PATIENTS AND
MEDICAL PROVIDERS,
1955–79

Although some tribal leaders had extensive experience with Western medicine and the bureaucratic and political issues tied to it, most Navajos experienced modern medicine solely as patients. The thousands of patients who came to accept IHS and missionary medical services in the postwar era judged Western medicine's strengths and weaknesses on a personal level. Similarly, most IHS employees had little influence over politics or policy, and they did not necessarily agree or act in full accordance with decisions made from above. Their personal attitudes and individual actions, and those of missionary medical employees, therefore, had a great deal to do with Western medicine's successes and failures among the Navajos. Most IHS and missionary employees, no doubt, performed their jobs to the best of their ability and were proud of the services they offered to the Navajo Nation. Likewise, many patients were satisfied with IHS and missionary care, or were at least so reliant upon those services that they continued to use them despite certain misgivings. But both providers and patients were challenged to cope with the effects of underfunded and understaffed medical programs, language barriers, and cross-cultural tensions that complicated the hospital and clinic experience.

Patient Attitudes About Primary Care

"Our records show that there has been a tremendous increase in the use of our Navajo hospitals and clinics during the past ten years," proclaimed Area Director George Bock in 1967. "We hope and feel that this increased demand for service shows an ever increasing acceptance of modern medical practices by the Navajo people." Bock could support his statement with statistics. Between 1959 and 1968, IHS hospital admission rates had risen from 9,884 annually to 17,020 and outpatient visits rose from 163,041 to 295,425. Clearly, Navajos were accessing government medical services in large numbers and had been doing so for quite some time. But the growing rates through the 1960s were not simply signs of patient satisfaction. They reflected the still poor status of Navajo health in comparison to the U.S. average, and were also the result of an increasing Navajo population, which, by the 1970s, included over 130,000 people on the reservation and thousands of others off the reservation.[1]

As encouraging as high utilization rates may have been to Bock, other indicators in the 1960s and 1970s suggested that Navajos were less than satisfied with the care they received. Many still went out of their way to avoid the IHS, even if they readily accepted the need for Western medicine. Many favored Sage Memorial and other nonfederal reservation hospitals over the government facilities, and a growing number of Navajos chose to pay for care from off-reservation private practitioners. One study estimated that as many as 40 percent of Navajo patients went to private physicians in certain portions of the reservation. They did not give in and go to an IHS facility, the study claimed, "until their money ran out." Other patients may have used the IHS for minor medical problems while paying for services in more serious cases. Navajo veterans sometimes exercised their right to use Veterans Administration (VA) hospitals, even if they had to travel great distances to do so. Billy Tochin, for instance, always traveled to a VA hospital in Albuquerque rather than going to the Gallup Indian Medical Center, because he believed that "a lot of people die" at the Gallup facility.[2]

Of course, there were still substantial numbers, but probably a minority, of Navajos who refused to use Western medicine at all or who did so very sparingly. Although many Native American Church members practiced multiple forms of healing, some held Western medicine in low esteem. And more than a few Navajos took advantage of traditional healing exclusively. Some questioned Western medicine's utility or viewed it as counter to the traditional ways. Asdzani, an elderly Navajo woman an Anglo nurse named Ida Bahl met in the 1950s, held such attitudes. Asdzani refused to allow Bahl to take her grandson to a hospital for a hip operation because she believed that doing so would offend the

Holy People. After Bahl convinced her to allow the procedure, the boy's condition improved, but Asdzani still denied the efficacy of Western medicine and attributed the result to the traditional care he had received.[3]

While some avoided the hospitals and clinics at all times, others accepted care in those facilities, but did so reluctantly. In the 1970s, studies looked into Navajo patient reactions to the care they received in IHS hospitals and clinics and uncovered a great deal of dissatisfaction. Early in the decade, Robert Kane, a physician and former service unit director at Shiprock, and his wife Rosalie devised a survey and employed Navajo Community Health Representatives to distribute it to people in their hogans and at trading posts on the reservation. Meanwhile, Richard Bozof conducted a smaller survey of twenty-five outpatients at the Shiprock hospital. Responses to the surveys revealed a wide variety of complaints, some of which might have been heard from patients anywhere in the

The old IHS hospital at Shiprock, now administered by the Department of Behavioral Health under the Navajo Nation's Division of Health. Photograph by author.

United States, and some of which were linked to specific IHS policies and cross-cultural tensions.[4]

Survey respondents commonly complained about the excessive length of time they had to wait to be treated in the IHS hospitals, which were overcrowded and understaffed. Overwhelmed staff members were unable and sometimes unwilling to devote proper attention to their patients. Patient loads frequently exceeded official hospital capacities, and it became common to find patients on mattresses in hallways and two babies squeezed together in a single bassinet. Other patients, some of whom had traveled fifty miles or more to reach the hospital or clinic, were forced to sit for hours in crowded waiting rooms without food, coffee, or any kind of entertainment. "I waited too long for the doctor," wrote one woman in the Kane survey, "waiting in line, lobby, hallway, in office, and for medicine. Just waiting all the way." Many blamed the waiting on the many "coffee breaks" that the staff seemed to take. Compared to the intense attention Navajos were used to receiving from singers and family members during traditional ceremonies, IHS treatment seemed uncaring. As one man put it, many felt as though they were "sheep being put through the sheep dip."[5]

These complaints may differ little from those offered by non-Indians about their own medical experiences, but cultural barriers between Navajos and non-Indian health care workers made the IHS experience especially difficult for some Navajo patients. Such conflicts did not necessarily stem from IHS policies. The IHS had not officially condemned traditional beliefs about health and healing in its early years of service to the Navajos. In fact, during the 1960s, certain hospitals, such as the one at Tuba City, were very receptive to patients who requested healing ceremonies inside the facility. And beginning in the 1970s, the IHS officially supported Navajo healing's coexistence with Western medicine. In the clinics and hospitals, however, cross-cultural coexistence depended on employee knowledge and attitudes rather than policy statements—and personal attitudes varied greatly. Dr. James Shaw, Dr. George Bock, and other IHS officials displayed respect for Navajo healers, and many physicians were very understanding of patients who wished to consult singers and herbalists. But some IHS physicians still tried to dissuade their patients from having healing ceremonies and tried to prohibit singers from entering the facilities.[6]

Language differences also caused tension and misunderstandings. A large number of patients spoke only Navajo, or were not comfortable enough with English to speak it with the physicians. Others may have avoided conversing in English out of scorn for the doctors or because they felt uncomfortable about personal questioning. Traditional diagnosticians and healers appeared confident and respectful when they told patients why they were ill. They did not often need to ask awkward questions because they already knew a great deal about the personal lives of the patients and their families and could converse with them comfortably. Physicians, in contrast, often appeared indecisive, incompetent, or rude when they asked blunt questions about a patient's habits and history. These cross-cultural problems were only exacerbated when the physician could not understand the patient. Language barriers placed greater responsibilities on physicians and nurses to determine causes for illness and methods of treatment, often with detrimental results for the patients who had difficulty protecting themselves from the effects of mistranslations.[7]

Despite the decades that Navajos had struggled with language barriers, the government had never established an official program for training people as interpreters. Linguist Robert Young recalled that the BIA physicians, prior to 1955, "latched" on to any bilingual Navajo who could mediate between the health professionals and patients. Many of these interpreters were ancillary staff, including custodians and nursing aides known as "blue girls." These workers often lacked sufficient command of English or Navajo, or the medical background necessary to do the job well. Poor communication could sometimes be worse than no communication. One Navajo patient with a thyroid tumor hastily fled a hospital after an interpreter told him that the doctor would "slit his throat."[8]

The IHS did only a slightly better job than the BIA dealing with the language barrier. Neither a 1957 field report from Alexander Leighton and Donald Kennedy, which stressed the crucial role trained interpreters could play, nor the success Cornell enjoyed with its health visitors, prompted the IHS to adequately address language problems. Occasionally hospital and Service Unit staffs set up voluntary seminars in interpreting for their medical employees. Navajo Area IHS pharmacists also proved particularly innovative, developing a system of symbols to replace written directions on prescription drugs. Yet, while the IHS admitted that a problem existed, the only employed interpreters were driver-interpreters who accompanied the field health staff. Hospital and clinic staffs had to rely on their own devices.[9]

It might seem that the increasing number of Navajo IHS employees after the transfer would have helped ease the cross-cultural tension and overcome the language barrier, making the hospitals seem less alien to patients; this was no doubt true, but not always so. Conflicts between Navajo health care providers and patients occasionally occurred. One patient explained to the Kanes that the Navajo "[n]urse's aide did not interpret what my problem really was to the doctor. She was mean to me." Another criticized Navajo employees for their lack of proper Diné "manners and respect."[10]

Always assuming that tension between a Navajo provider and patient resulted from the provider's loss of traditional knowledge and practices ignores the fact that many conflicts occurred between individuals who were both very aware of tradition. Status issues and personal tension between neighbors or clan members were common sources of tension. But some Navajo employees did find themselves caught between two cultures. Some of them may have seemed less than sympathetic to their patients because they were placed in a difficult position. As Robert Kane and P. Douglas McConatha noted, a job at a hospital or clinic provided a steady source of income in times of high unemployment. Many Navajo health care providers therefore found their loyalties split between their patients and their employers, upon whom they depended for their livelihood. Those Navajos who did become nurses and paramedics had to go through training programs that rarely stressed the importance of Navajo culture and occasionally condemned it. In the Sage Memorial School of Nursing, the primary source of Navajo nurses in the mid-twentieth century, students were heavily influenced by the missionary message. Jennie Joe, a Navajo nurse, educator, and tribal leader, observed that nursing students at Sage "were more indoctrinated to the religion part of that training and so they were not very strong advocates when it came to traditional medicine." These factors did not preclude Navajo medical workers from retaining their Diné and clan identities, and they did not compromise their professional abilities, but they did make it harder for those workers to serve as cross-cultural mediators.[11]

Patient-provider tension could arise from personal appearance as well as from spoken words and cultural attitudes. Maintaining a positive appearance for its patients proved troublesome for the IHS. Patients wanted providers and an environment that looked professional and consistent, but if the IHS, through its facilities and employees, presented itself as a monolithic government agency, patients might feel alienated. In 1963, the IHS reversed its generally relaxed attitude on attire and ordered commissioned officers into uniform (IHS physicians were either civil servants or commissioned officers, and the latter had official uniforms that resembled Navy dress). IHS officials were concerned about the tendency for many physicians who came to the IHS through the Doctor-Dentist Draft program to wear long hair and sandals. Such personal appearances often made Indian patients question their credentials. "During the '60s, most of the doctors wearing their hair long or wearing sandals were not really viewed as being doctors, or serious doctors," recalled Jennie Joe. "Most communities wanted someone who looked older or seasoned. They had a lot more confidence in that kind of person." While the IHS could take credit for responding to these concerns with its 1963 directive, it may have made the problem worse by doing so. In their Navy-like uniforms, the physicians looked more like military officers than doctors. This contributed to an image of the IHS as an imposing institution that, as Joe says "wasn't theirs."[12]

Whether a Navajo patient responded positively to the IHS probably had more to do with individual physicians and nurses than with the overall institution. "We need a good doctor just like they have in town," said one respondent to the Kane's survey, "because lots of these doctors at Shiprock were not very good and not kind to the Indian people[,] especially the older people." "Well, while being hospitalized," said another, "I feel like I am hated by all the nurses because I call for help every time I need assistance. I wish there were nurses who can be more friendly." Patients rarely took any recourse against practitioners they disliked, but they did try to avoid them when possible. On the other hand, "when a doctor is well liked in the community," said Jennie Joe, "it is very visible because the patients will come in and ask for that physician." Unfortunately, for reasons discussed below, a patient could rarely count on seeing the same physician or nurse on subsequent visits.[13]

Concerns about the quality of IHS medical providers were frequently transparent when Navajo tribal leaders, patients, and even Navajo ancillary staff members in the IHS hospitals referred to physicians as "interns." Patients complained of physicians "practicing on them" and one argued that a hospital "should not be a training school, we need real doctors." These comments frustrated IHS health administrators and physicians, and they quickly pointed out that their staff was fully qualified and that their "doctors" did indeed have their medical degrees. Chief Medical Officer for the Navajo Area Charles McCammon found himself explaining this matter to Tribal Council delegates repeatedly in the early 1960s. But, although IHS physicians had completed internships, most had not completed their residencies and were fresh out of medical school. Many were well trained, committed physicians, but their youth and relative inexperience gave Navajo patients a cause for concern. Maybe some Navajos were not aware of how IHS physicians were trained or what internships were, but others probably knew what the term "intern" meant and intentionally used it to express their misgivings about certain IHS physicians.[14]

Some Navajos expressed negative views toward IHS health care workers through the use of humor. For instance, Annie Wauneka evoked some laughs from fellow Council delegates by telling the story of a physician who chastised an elderly Navajo patient for being "dirty." "How many times does the doctor take a bath in a week?" the patient asked in response. "Almost every day I take a bath," said the physician. "I guess you are dirtier than I am because you have to take a bath every day," replied the patient. Editorial cartoons in the tribal newspaper, the *Navajo Times*, occasionally depicted physicians and nurses in a less than flattering light. One marked the IHS's decision to put its commissioned officers in uniform by showing a Navajo man cowering behind a table while a sinister, long-armed man in military dress beckons him to come closer. Another depicted a blond-haired nurse striking a recumbent patient with a fist. Richard Mike's "SuperNavajo" comic strip in the alternative Navajo newspaper, *Diné Baa-Hani*, featured Dr. Meanie and some poignant plots about the IHS. In one strip, Dr. Meanie reluctantly agrees to interrupt his music listening to treat Yazzie Manykids, thanks only to SuperNavajo's cajoling. Then, when SuperNavajo suggests that the government find physicians who would stay on the reservation long term instead of sending interns to practice on them, Meanie erupts, "Interns! We're not interns! Their [sic] are no interns out here!" "Yeah!!" responds SuperNavajo. "Well nobody out here has started residence either! You've just finished internship! Most of these nurses know more than you!!"[15]

Few advocates stood up for Navajo patients' rights before the 1970s. For the most part, the IHS could and did ignore problems with physicians or nurses unless their colleagues or Tribal Council delegates lodged complaints. As Wauneka commented in 1975, most Navajo patients assumed that their leaders would address these issues. She tried to make them understand that they were "entitled" to better care and had a right to ask for it. But few patients had Wauneka's power to elicit a response from the government.[16]

Employee Reactions to the IHS

IHS employees were aware of deficiencies in Indian health care, and many were devoted to changing the situation for the better and were willing to work long hours to do so. Disgruntled employees, however, also became part of the dilemma for Navajo patients. A cyclical problem developed in which IHS employees became frustrated with bureaucratic red tape and negative patient attitudes and displayed that frustration, contributing to more negative attitudes around them. Employee dissatisfaction also contributed to high staff turnover rates, which hindered Navajo patients from developing long-term relationships with physicians.

Most IHS physicians and registered nurses were non-Indian, and they often found it frustrating when they could not understand how their patients were responding. Some had problems dealing with patients reluctant to answer personal questions and who did not effusively thank them for their care. Such responses ran counter to traditional Navajo social practices. Dr. R. L. Gorrell, a visiting physician in Lukachukai, Arizona, during the 1970s found it unsettling to deal with Navajo patients who did not respond with physical and emotional expressions similar to those of non-Indian patients. "To look into the Navajo eyes is to look into blackness, a dark well at midnight, an opaqueness that reveals nothing," Gorrell told Sister Celestine, a Navajo nurse. "So you wonder if they are understanding what you are trying to tell them," she replied. "Exactly," responded Gorrell. "I feel uneasy as I try to explain health and illness to such eyes." Even with someone to interpret for them, Gorrell and other physicians found it difficult to diagnose and treat patients who did not respond in the expected fashion. Conversely, many physicians and nurses who chose to stay on the Navajo reservation as a career, or who maintained open minds and optimistic attitudes, found working with Navajo patients to be rewarding. Indeed, most of the nurses and physicians who responded to a survey sent to them by Ida Bahl, asking about their experiences on the reservation between 1930 and the early 1970s, said that they had been happy to work among the Navajos.[17]

*Annie Wauneka, members of the National Indian Health Advisory Committee,
and others. Front row, left to right: Frances Satterthwaite, Wauneka, Susie
Yellowtail, Dr. Thomas Points. Back row, left to right: Lloyd Sutton, Dr. Ernest
Siegfried, Dr. Charles McCammon (former IHS chief medical officer for the
Navajo Field Office), and Dr. Emery Johnson (IHS director), ca. 1970.
Courtesy of Labriola National American Indian Data Center, Arizona State
University Libraries, CTH 2128.*

Yet even some who enjoyed their patients and the reservation found it
difficult to remain in the IHS. Frequently changing employee assignments
under the BIA and then the IHS made it difficult for the government
medical workers to maintain continuity in Indian health care at the
provider-patient level. The IHS occasionally moved its employees from
area to area and often shuffled staff members to various service units, making it difficult for communities to form relationships with them, especially
when employees were isolated in special housing units erected near the
hospitals. Some BIA and IHS nurses served as many as a dozen different
reservations before they finally retired.[18]

The problem of retaining medical professionals proved even more disruptive to continuity than did relocating them. The Doctor-Dentist Draft
supplied the IHS with large numbers of physicians, but it led to high

annual turnover rates. Since 1950 the draft had brought a group of young physicians to the reservation who had chosen IHS duty over military obligation. By 1962 McCammon estimated that 90 percent of all IHS physicians on the reservation were "serving their military time." The "two-year" physicians, as the Kanes called them, brought with them the youth, vigor, and modern medical training that most of the older physicians lacked. Many of them were more familiar with psychiatry and anthropology than their predecessors, and they were often more open to Navajo perspectives on health; but most of them left as soon as their obligations were complete. As a result, some patients and staff members longed for the BIA doctors of the past. Barbara Munn, an IHS employee, recalled that many of the people in the Navajo community did not feel as comfortable with these younger physicians. Even though the BIA physicians who preceded them had not measured up to the IHS conscripts in terms of modern medical knowledge and enthusiasm, many had devoted years to the reservation and had earned the admiration and trust of their patients.[19]

Many of the "two-year" physicians left at the end of their terms because they wished to pursue more lucrative careers and desired familiar environments. Others left at the insistence of their spouses or to find off-reservation schooling for their children. As Dr. Steven Borowsky suggests, however, many of these physicians may have left because the IHS showed little interest in keeping them, even if they were highly qualified and well liked. Borowsky served on the Cheyenne River Reservation in South Dakota in the early 1970s. He found it to be a very positive experience, but he also noted the stress high turnover placed on incoming employees. When Borowsky arrived at Cheyenne River, he found that only one of the four physicians there had served in the IHS the year before. As long as one person could be there to mentor incoming physicians, the IHS did not seem to care about turnover. The situation placed a great burden on each successive staff to adapt to or even remake the medical program.[20]

The Navajo Nation witnessed similar dilemmas. While the IHS may have been satisfied to have anyone to staff a position, Navajos worried about the effects the revolving-door approach had on patients. In 1973, for instance, Tribal Chairman Peter MacDonald complained that the excessive physician turnover rate precluded doctors from having the "commitment and the dedication necessary for rendering an effective service to the people."[21]

Although they were not part of the Doctor-Dentist Draft, registered nurses also had a high turnover rate in the 1960s and 1970s, compounding a long-term problem the IHS had in staffing qualified nurses. A study by University of New Mexico graduate students in 1972 found annual nursing turnover rates in Navajo Area IHS hospitals ranging from 25 to 55 percent. These percentages actually represented improvements over those experienced two years before. Between 1969 and 1970, the Gallup Indian Medical Center lost 80 percent of its nurses. This statistic partially reflected the IHS's willingness to hire nurses for one-year commitments, but the problem also stemmed from the nurses' dissatisfaction with the IHS. Nurses at Gallup complained about being overworked, and they claimed they were required to do menial tasks that did not utilize their education and training. Another survey conducted by an IHS employee in 1979 revealed a similar situation in Shiprock; the hospital there experienced a 100-percent registered nurse turnover between October 1978 and July 1979. Shiprock nurses believed that administrators had ignored their concerns and given them an insufficient orientation. They also complained that the IHS had failed to bring in new nurses to fill vacancies, thus demonstrating its disregard for those who remained.[22]

Employees and patients had good cause to complain about the staff shortages, insufficient resources, and inadequate facilities. As late as 1975, the Navajo Nation averaged only ninety physicians per 100,000 patients compared to 163 for the rest of the United States. The Navajo Nation also had a lower hospital bed/population ratio, with 4.4 per 1,000 versus a U.S. general average of 7.8.[23]

In 1974, a physician at Winslow (unnamed here) reached the end of his tether. He wrote a letter to Senator Henry Jackson of the State of Washington to ask for help. The physician's reaction was no doubt extreme in comparison to those of other employees, but his letter summed up the general dissatisfaction many of his colleagues felt. He opted to serve in the IHS after the Doctor-Dentist Draft had ended, and he found many aspects of his job to be "fascinating, challenging, and fulfilling." He claimed, however, that "equipment and staff shortages have compounded small problems, making them into almost insurmountable obstacles." Worst of all, the physician understood why patients were upset about waiting four to five hours to be seen, but he could not endure taking the blame:

For a full month, I was in the hospital day and night. I hardly saw my wife and kid. At the same time, patients were screaming at *me* for making them wait. They told me I was a lousy doctor. . . . I'm tired of working an average of 80–90 hours a week under these conditions. I'm tired of lying to people. I'm tired of not seeing my wife who's threatened divorce, not out of lack of love, but out of lack of visual contact with me. To put it quite bluntly, the government has to fund the program, provide equipment and staff or get out. . . . I'd like to stay here. If things don't change, I'll leave, just like so many other dedicated people have left because of the "system" and the shortages.[24]

IHS administrators heard and understood the complaints they received from employees and made some attempts to address those concerns in the 1960s and 1970s. In the late 1960s, they established the Division of Indian Health Training Center in Tucson, where they planned to train incoming employees to handle cross-cultural situations. The IHS also prepared an orientation guide specifically for employees on the Navajo reservation that included information on traditional healing and tribal culture. Theoretically, employee concerns could be voiced through formal channels extending from service unit directors to the area offices. Yet, in spite of these efforts, many IHS employees did not believe that they had sufficient guidance and support, and morale often suffered.[25]

·7·

CONTROVERSY
AND NEW OPPORTUNITIES,
1970S

Taylor McKenzie perceived no conflict between his role as a medical doctor and his identity as a Navajo. The first Navajo ever to earn an M.D., McKenzie played a major role in Navajo health care in the 1970s. Beginning in 1964, he served as an Indian Health Service physician and administrator and later helped to direct tribal health initiatives. At the same time, he maintained a deep respect for Navajo traditional healing and a strong commitment to tribal self-determination. A dedicated provider of Western medicine, McKenzie was not satisfied with the health care services available to the Navajos. "It is ironic," he said in 1975, "that after decades of bringing our people and modern medicine to a common meeting ground that we should be giving our sick inadequate care."[1]

Even though the Indian Health Service had succeeded in establishing comprehensive health care on Indian reservations and had made significant strides against infectious disease, many Native people regarded it and other Western medical providers with mistrust, and were not satisfied with their health status. In the early 1970s, a number of health care controversies, some directly involving the IHS, helped convince Navajos that their efforts toward medical self-determination were as necessary as ever. In the past, Navajo concerns about government health care had usually been channeled through members of the Tribal Council. Now, published studies, tribal newspapers, and young American Indian activists supplied other avenues for Navajos to voice their concerns about the health dangers contact with the non-Indian world posed, and about the need for more control over their bodies.

As the 1970s was a time of controversy, it was also an era in which tribal-federal cooperation spawned new opportunities for Navajo medical self-determination. Disputes involving the IHS, coupled with that agency's continuing efforts to improve its services and relations with the tribe, contributed to changing federal policies. The Indian Self-Determination and Education Assistance Act in 1975 and the Indian Health Care Improvement Act in 1976 were influenced by those processes. Through this legislation, the federal government encouraged American Indians to administer and staff IHS health programs and injected sorely needed funds into reservation medical care.

Inspired both by its dissatisfaction with government medical care and by this positive legislation, the Navajo Nation pushed on with its own medical efforts. Local Navajo communities also proved their willingness to take Western health care into their own hands by administering their own medical facilities. And although most Navajo employees were relegated to ancillary positions in the IHS, Taylor McKenzie and others began to take on critical roles within the bureaucratic structure. At the same time, Navajo healers worked to preserve the traditional ways and Native American Church membership blossomed across the reservation. Out of a time of controversy, cooperation, and tribal initiative, came the promise of a brighter future for Navajo health care.

Health Controversies

The early 1970s were a time of social tension and activism. Given this national social environment, it is not surprising that American Indians were more likely than ever to stand up publicly for their medical rights. American Indian activists, disgruntled employees, and a few concerned health providers and politicians drew attention to deficiencies in Indian health care, perceived malpractice in the IHS, and new health threats brought to Native peoples through the economic exploitation of their land.

Young urban Indian activists in the late 1960s and 1970s forced many non-Indians to turn their attention to Native Americans for the first time in decades. They made better health care an important part of their agenda. Activists generally referred to the Indian Health Service in negative terms, but their criticisms focused less on the institution than on the federal government's failure to adequately fund Indian health care programs. For example, the "Indians of All Tribes" who occupied Alcatraz Island in 1969 referred specifically to a lack of proper medical services and sanitation in their famous Proclamation. In his widely read "Indian Manifesto," *Custer Died for Your Sins*, Vine Deloria, Jr. included the Indian Health Service in his list of mismanaged and underfunded federal agencies, but he spared the agency the strong criticism he directed toward the BIA.[2]

The IHS did not get caught up in highly publicized confrontations with the American Indian Movement (AIM) or other Native American activist groups in the late 1960s and early 1970s. But a few minor AIM takeovers of IHS facilities were threatened in 1973, including one at Cheyenne River by members on their way to Wounded Knee. Early that same year the Gallup Indian Medical Center (GIMC) became a target. Victor Cutnose, a Cheyenne who worked in the GIMC's housekeeping division, had witnessed many of the problems patients and workers faced in IHS hospitals. Prompted by his belief that he and his wife had been mistreated by the GIMC following an accident, Cutnose, his brother John, two Navajo men, Michael Upshaw and Woody Foster, and two freelance reporters from the American Indian Press Association, Samuel Fletcher Jr. and Richard Giron, chose to take dramatic action.[3]

At 11:00 P.M. on 28 January 1973, the six men entered the hospital armed with rifles and a briefcase fashioned to look like a bomb, and informed the administrator in charge that they had taken control of the facility. The men identified themselves as AIM members, criticized the IHS for "inadequate" care, and insisted that they would stay until the agency met their demands. Cutnose explained to reporters that the hospital should be "six times as big to adequately care for the Indians in this area" and that extra funds were sorely needed. Based on Cutnose's experiences as a GIMC employee, the group also demanded that a number of hospital officials be dismissed, although they did not reveal their names to the press. As their final demand, the men insisted that the IHS do something to alter the "disrespectful" attitudes of its physicians. Failing to achieve their goals, the group ended the occupation without a physical struggle after negotiating with the Federal Bureau of Investigation and the local district attorney.[4]

Many Navajos, no doubt, agreed with the GIMC occupiers' arguments but disagreed with their actions. Ellouise DeGroat remembered an ambivalent community reaction to the episode: "Some of them thought, 'well good,

The Northern Navajo Medical Center (IHS) in Shiprock, New Mexico. Built in the 1990s, this hospital housed modern medical technology as well as paintings and sculptures by Navajo artists. It symbolized cooperative federal, tribal, and community efforts to plan and administer Western medical facilities. Photograph by author.

somebody is going to do something,' but as to the way the AIM were dressed with the long hair, and how they were rowdy—this was not Navajo."[5]

A longer-lasting and higher profile controversy hit the Navajo Area IHS (NAIHS) at the end of 1974. In December, two nurses, Valerie Koster and Sandra Kramer, wrote a highly critical letter about the Shiprock hospital to a number of U.S. senators and to the *Navajo Times*. The two criticized the hospital for being unsanitary and claimed that workers focused their activity on "filling out forms, doing the least possible work with the least possible effort and just getting by." They also criticized a Shiprock physician for failing to respond to an elderly man who fell out of his bed and argued that improper medications had been administered to patients.[6]

Soon after the letter, Area Director Marlene Haffner reassigned Koster and Kramer away from the Navajo reservation. When the nurses refused to report for their new duties, IHS Director Emery Johnson terminated them. By that time, the case had sparked a controversy that eventually caused a great deal of distress for Haffner, Koster, and Kramer. In defense of her actions, Haffner explained that she had not transferred the nurses in response to their letter of protest but because of their use of profanity, "carelessness of dress," and "insufficient attention to duty." Not surprisingly, her denial did not allay suspicions that the IHS administrators had fired the nurses because they had publicly criticized the agency.[7]

The nurses' persistent efforts to retain their positions drew national attention to the dispute. Senators Edward Kennedy of Massachusetts and James Abourezk of South Dakota intervened on the nurses' behalf and demanded that they be reinstated. Abourezk blamed the controversy on the "lack of effective complaint and grievance procedures" within the IHS. Other IHS employees and Navajo patients lent further support to the nurses.[8]

The controversy sullied Haffner's relationship with the Navajo Nation's leadership. In January 1976, Elwood Sagney, chairman of the recently formed Navajo Area Indian Health Advisory Board (discussed below) petitioned IHS Director Johnson for Haffner's removal, citing the Shiprock incident, her lack of "leadership qualities," her "unwillingness to consult with others," and her "apparent indecisiveness." Although a number of tribal leaders apparently agreed with Sagney, Peter MacDonald and others supported Haffner's continuance as area director. Haffner weathered the dispute and went on to build constructive relations with the Navajo Nation, but the controversy contributed to the IHS's image as a mismanaged agency.[9]

Accounts of inadequate services and employee strife in the NAIHS paled in comparison to a national scandal that developed during the 1970s. Dr. Connie Uri (Cherokee) contended in 1974 that IHS physicians across the country were intentionally violating their patients' rights. Indian women Uri interviewed claimed that male physicians had prompted them to have tubal ligations without explaining the long-term results of the operation. For many of the women, sterilization had dire emotional consequences. As scholar Patricia White has argued, "one of the results of the large numbers of forced sterilizations performed on Indian women is that the fundamental link to their identity as life givers had been severely undermined." The findings led many American Indians and concerned non-Indians to believe that the IHS may have been engaging in a program of "genocide" through population control.[10]

It is unclear to what degree the problem existed on the Navajo Nation, but a later study showed that sterilization procedures may have doubled on the reservation between 1972 and 1978. This statistic is particularly alarming given scholar Stephen Kunitz's finding in an unrelated study that Navajo women rarely opted to have ligations or hysterectomies and that they rarely spoke about contraception with anyone except their physicians.[11]

Prompted by Uri's findings and the growing wave of concern among Native Americans, the General Accounting Office (GAO) reported on the problem. The report said nothing of genocide and blamed the problem on mismanagement within the IHS and the agency's failure to hold contract physicians to Department of Health, Education and Welfare (DHEW) guidelines (30 percent of the sterilizations were performed by contract). Physicians frequently were unaware of regulations or misunderstood them, and the GAO found the IHS culpable for failing to adequately orient them and for failing to supply the various area offices with proper forms. It also insisted that IHS sterilization forms include a statement at the top informing patients that federal benefits could not be withdrawn if they refused to consent to the procedure. The report further recommended that the minimum waiting period for the procedure of seventy-two hours be extended. Despite the changes that followed, however, many American Indians believed that the federal government had simply glossed over the problem.[12]

Another controversy made Navajos more aware of the ways that non-Navajos affected their health outside of hospitals, and contributed to their desire for greater control over their land and bodies. In the 1970s, Navajo residents around Grants and Red Rock in New Mexico and Cameron and Tuba City in Arizona, as well as other communities on the western, eastern, and northern ends of the reservation began to recognize the medical costs of industrial development. Uranium mines and mills leased to private companies had provided employment and revenue for the Navajo Nation since the late 1940s. After decades of exposure to radon from the uranium, Navajo miners and local residents began to suffer the consequences. Public Health Service studies at the end of the decade revealed that an extraordinary number of miners were dying from lung cancer. One estimate from the early 1980s showed a lung cancer rate of 148 per 100,000 among Navajo miners as compared to a rate of 1.7 per 100,000 among non-miner men.[13]

As awareness heightened, the miners began to question the actions of their employers. They had assumed that the mining companies would inform them if they were in danger and had therefore taken few precautions to protect themselves. Miners ate and drank in the mines, sometimes quenching their thirst with water that seeped through the rocks, and frequently went home and washed their contaminated clothing with their family's laundry. "When I was on the job," remembered Tommy Dee, an ex-miner suffering from cancer in 1983, "only a white man dressed for safety when he walked down into the tunnel. We did talk about it: 'Maybe it *is* dangerous. Why is he all protective-clothed-up? Why don't they do the same for us?' It never got anywhere. Nothing was ever done for us." In the late 1970s, Navajo miners learned that the Atomic Energy Commission and the Public Health Service had conducted studies demonstrating the dangers of radon-related illness, and still, their employers had not informed them.[14]

Uranium's impact reached beyond the ailing miners. Navajo parents in the 1970s feared for their children who frequently played on the tailings. Others worried about the effects exposure would have on fetuses, and at least one woman felt that her sister had given birth to two disabled children because of the neighboring uranium mills. Likewise, Navajo herders were concerned about their livestock, which were not only in danger of falling into abandoned mine "dog holes" but which also ventured into contaminated areas where they fed and watered.[15]

The issue gained some public recognition in time. In many instances, mine officials began to implement safety standards by the early 1970s, but afflicted residents on the reservation had little relief throughout the decade. Some Navajos attributed the disease to taboos that had been broken in disturbing the land, and many dealt with the disease using traditional healers and even Pentecostal healing services. Musician and artist Vincent Craig created a lasting monument to those who suffered from exposure. Inspired by a real incident in 1979 in which radioactive waste from the mills spilled into the Puerco River, Craig invented "Muttonman," an editorial comic strip featured in the *Navajo Times*. Whereas uranium had killed others, Muttonman gained superhuman powers after eating mutton stew from a sheep that had drunk from the Puerco.[16]

The Self-Determination and Health Care Improvement Acts

Although all-Indian and Navajo death rates continued to fall through the 1970s, controversies involving the IHS and a continuing disparity between Native American mortality statistics and U.S. averages prompted Congress to reassess its Indian health care efforts. In 1975 and 1976, respectively, the Indian Self-Determination Act and Indian Health Care Improvement Act promised better medical service for American Indians and encouraged Native communities to play more active roles in administering federal health care programs.

The Indian Self-Determination and Education Assistance Act (P.L. 93-638), passed in 1975, allowed American Indian tribes to administer federal reservation services, including those related to health care, without losing government financial support. In 1970, President Richard Nixon had called for "self-determination without termination," in an attempt to find a compromise between failed termination policies and federal paternalism. Nixon argued that increased Indian involvement in administering and delivering their own social services would ensure their greater satisfaction while increasing government efficiency.[17]

In 1971, the Nixon administration proposed a bill to transfer government services to tribes along with federal funds, an idea of which, in principle, many tribal groups approved. But many American Indians, including Navajo Chairman Peter MacDonald, suspected that the federal proposal represented another veiled attempt at termination. To ease these concerns, the final version of the legislation allowed tribes to choose which services they wished to, and wished not to, administer. It also left the involved federal agencies with final authority over the extent of those contracts, ostensibly to provide a more secure future for the contracted programs.[18]

The results were often less than desirable and new pitfalls presented by P.L. 93-638 made American Indians question the law's true intent. By 1980, some 370 tribes contracted $200 million worth of federal services. Many of these tribes later discovered that they lacked true self-determination because the BIA and IHS could withdraw the contracts. They were further displeased to find that federal funding requests necessary to keep the services functioning pitted them in bidding duels against other tribes. Nevertheless, self-determination legislation opened new avenues for Indian communities to establish health care systems to meet their needs and desires, and gave them the power to control the pace of change. By 1980, 90 percent of the recognized tribal governments had contracted out at least portions of the IHS services, and 10 percent of all tribes had taken total control over their reservation health programs.[19]

For the Self-Determination Act to succeed in empowering American

Indian groups, contracted federal services needed to be adequate before they were handed over to tribal governments. Led by western Republicans and Democrats, Congress acknowledged that existing health conditions on Indian reservations were still poor and that supplemental legislation had to be passed to provide better federal services. In addition, many members of Congress stressed the need for legislation to aid American Indian tribes in preparing to staff those services with Indian health care professionals. Such legislation would not only serve immediate medical needs in Native communities, but would also aid the smooth transition to Indian control of Western medicine.[20]

Any new efforts to improve Indian health at least had a positive base on which to build. Early in the decade, the IHS appeared to be making medical progress with the 800,000 Native Americans it served, including the Navajos. Infectious disease and infant mortality rates on the Navajo reservation fell considerably from the mid-1960s to the mid-1970s. And tuberculosis rates dipped from twenty-one per 100,000 in 1965 to seven per 100,000 in 1975, while deaths from gastrointestinal disease and infant mortality were cut in half.[21]

As encouraging as falling mortality rates may have been, other statistics reflected negatively on the IHS's ability to address Indian health problems effectively. A GAO report in 1973 revealed "serious unmet needs" in Native American medical care, including the IHS's failure to adequately address problems of otitis media and alcoholism. Next, a U.S. Civil Rights Commission report in 1975 noted a seven-year gap between American Indian and average U.S. life expectancies.[22]

Other statistical data demonstrated inadequacies in the larger IHS network. IHS facilities were often judged ill equipped, understaffed, and unsafe, with only twenty-five of its fifty-one hospitals meeting Joint Commission on Accreditation of Hospitals standards. Only eighteen of the IHS hospitals across the United States maintained 80 percent or more of the standard staffing levels for their facility type. Furthermore, half of the eighty-six health clinics and 300 health stations were staffed below 50 percent of the acceptable level. IHS estimates also indicated that 20,329 necessary surgeries had been deferred in 1975 because of insufficient facility space and staff shortages. Considerable progress had been made in sanitation networks since 1959, but an estimated 54 percent of American Indian families had no running water and 48 percent lacked adequate waste disposal facilities. It was now clear that existing services could not bring Indian health to parity with national averages; that the transfer advocates in the 1950s had overestimated the powers of Western medicine and underestimated the IHS's funding requirements.[23]

Growing concerns about Indian health issues in the 1970s may have been linked to a general sense among American liberals and conservatives alike that increasingly high costs and low accessibility to medical care across the United States had led to a national health care "crisis." With health care reform for the general population on the public's mind, ignoring dismal Indian mortality and health care statistics may have proved more difficult for politicians than in the past. As sociologist Paul Starr has argued in reference to American health policy in the 1970s, "[C]rises make hard decisions seem unavoidable; they change the political agenda and create political opportunities."[24]

In August 1976, the U.S. House of Representatives approved Senate Bill 522, introduced by senators Paul Fannin and Henry Jackson, and President Gerald Ford signed it as P.L. 94-437 on 30 September 1976. Known as the "Indian Health Care Improvement Act," the legislation authorized $480 million to improve medical services for American Indians. The Act represented the most serious federal commitment to American Indian health care to date. It included a strong statement meant to clear up decades of ambiguity left by various treaties, and the Snyder and Transfer Acts. "Federal health services to maintain and improve the health of the Indians," it stated, "are consonant with and required by the Federal Government's historical and unique legal relationship with, and resulting responsibility to, the American Indian people." The Act also clearly articulated a goal to raise Indian health conditions "to the highest possible level," even beyond parity with national averages if that were possible. At the same time, it promised to "maximize the participation of Indians in the planning and management of those services."[25]

The legislation included a number of different titles dealing with a variety of Indian health care issues. Title I addressed staff shortages and the relatively low number of American Indians in professional health care positions by authorizing over $7 million in health care scholarships for Native American students. Title II called for an expansion of key services to eliminate "backlogs" in their current application by authorizing $34 million for patient care and $9 million for field health by 1978. It also increased funds for alcoholism and mental health programs. Title III authorized funds to repair facilities and construct new ones, amounting to nearly $300 million, and set out more money for sanitation projects. In keeping with the self-determination policy, it directed the IHS to favor American Indian construction firms for the new projects. And the Act finally allowed the IHS to access Medicaid and Medicare.[26]

House legislation that originally accompanied the Senate bill had promised a number of improvements in the Navajo Area Indian Health Service. But reduced authorizations in the final Act and discrepancies between those authorizations and actual expenditures allowed a slower expansion of NAIHS services than the Navajo Area administrators and tribal members had expected. In May 1975, prior to P.L. 94-437, Tuba City received a 125-bed facility and, between 1974 and 1976, the NAIHS staff increased from 1,380 to 1,659. After the 1976 legislation, new facility projects went into the planning stages. Fort Defiance received a new clinic in 1977, and Shiprock, a 210-bed replacement hospital in 1978, but other parts of the reservation had to wait years for the new hospitals Congress promised. Staffing shortages and budget constraints also led to reductions in the initially planned bed capacities in those facilities. A new hospital in Chinle finally opened in 1982 at a cost of $22 million, but it included 60 rather than the originally proposed 125 beds. Crownpoint residents also had to wait until the early 1980s before their demands for a new hospital were answered. Despite the wait and unmet expectations, however, the Act yielded significant improvements in the quality and availability of Western medical services on the reservation.[27]

Navajo Health-Related Agencies

Peter MacDonald's election as Tribal Council chairman in 1970 promised increased tribal control of all resources and services, including health care. Under his administration, the Navajo government erected a complex network of medical-related agencies to supplement the functions of a newly restructured tribal Health, Alcoholism, and Welfare Committee (HAW). Building on past tribal actions, these new agencies initiated bold actions in the 1970s intended to guide the Navajo Nation toward complete medical autonomy.[28]

The tribal government did not yet wish to take over administration of a massive NAIHS medical network involving more than one thousand employees, six large hospitals, and ten health centers. But with the IHS's encouragement, the Navajo Nation stepped up efforts to guide those services in an advisory role. On 12 May 1970, Vice Chairman Nelson Damon certified Council Resolution CMY-57-70 establishing the Navajo Area Indian Health Advisory Board. The resolution stipulated that the board would meet "at least quarterly" with the NAIHS director "to participate in the development and improvement of a comprehensive health program for the Navajo Indian people." Its membership included tribal HAW members and community health representatives selected from each of the eight NAIHS service units. In June 1972, the Navajo Tribal Council expanded its single board into eight separate service unit health boards with the unanimous passage of CJN-62-72. These health boards were composed of members elected by local chapter governments and were intended to provide communication links between IHS facilities and the surrounding communities. As a result, residents were given a body of their own government through which they requested better services, relayed criticisms, and sometimes complimented programs and individuals they liked; but these boards lacked administrative power. Their influence depended on the various NAIHS Service Unit directors, who had final say over how medical programs would be operated.[29]

On 2 June 1972, the Navajo Nation took another step toward self-determined health care by forming the Navajo Health Authority (NHA). Tribal Council Resolution CJN-44-72 directed the NHA to "foster, guide, and assist in the planning, development, operation and evaluation of a health service system for the Navajo people which will be exemplary and a model for the American Indian community." The Council also instructed the NHA to gather data about Navajo health and establish programs aimed at increasing the number of Navajo medical professionals. In the preamble to its 1973 "Statement of Goals, Functions and Philosophy," the NHA claimed that "the Nation is at a turning point. Its leaders recognize the need for planning and the opportunity to build a new society for The People— one which borrows from the science and technology of the non-Indian culture those skills which can be merged with the essential elements of Navajo culture." With these goals in mind, the NHA collected information on Navajo traditional healing and looked for ways to incorporate those traditional ways into modern medical practices on the reservation.[30]

To guarantee the administrative freedom necessary to succeed in its duties, the Tribal Council established the NHA as a separate nonprofit organization. Although the organization served at the Tribal Council's pleasure, its independent status allowed it to apply for additional funding outside the Navajo government—a task it performed quite well. Because the NHA focused on Western and Navajo healing, its board members were drawn from a variety of cultural and professional backgrounds. Members included Navajo Vice Chairman Wilson Skeet and a variety of Navajos who understood both forms of healing well, including Annie Wauneka, Taylor McKenzie, Louise Hubbard, and Jennie Joe. Traditional healers were represented by David Clah and Jack Yazzie. Non-Navajos were also invited to sit on the NHA board, including John Schaefer, the president of the University of Arizona, and Dr. Robert Bucher, the dean of the University of South Alabama College of Medicine.[31]

To carry on the traditional aspects of its mission, the NHA created an Office of Native Healing Sciences under the guidance of Carl Gorman. Gorman served both as a researcher and as a liaison between the two forms of healing. He also oversaw a project, beginning in 1972, to compile a directory of singers on the reservation and the ceremonies they could perform, hoping that better knowledge of traditional healing's status would help Navajos to preserve it. The NHA also advocated NAIHS recognition of Navajo healing and advised the government agency on everything from facilities management to possible sanitation projects. At the same time, it stepped up its role in the Western side of medical care. With federal funding assistance, the NHA ran the Emergency Medical Services Program, which provided ambulances to the reservation and assisted in the training of emergency medical technicians. It also operated the Office of Health Education to reach the community on various health issues.[32]

Through the NHA, the Navajo Nation became involved with a nationwide trend toward health planning. Initially, the NHA established the Navajo Comprehensive Planning Agency to incorporate Navajo consumers into the process. Two pieces of federal legislation encouraged further tribal health planning in the mid-1970s. In an effort to reform American health care, the National Health Planning and Resource Development Act (P.L. 93-641) divided the country into health systems agencies—consumer-based groups that regulated local hospital construction and advised the federal government on health expenditures. The Navajo Nation took advantage of the legislation to create its own Navajo Health Systems Agency (NHSA) in 1975; it was the only American Indian group to do so. P.L. 93-641 did not allow HSAs to review certain federal programs, including the IHS. The Indian Health Care Improvement Act, however, had given Native Americans that power through its Tribal Specific Health Plans. By drawing from both pieces of legislation, the NHSA, in cooperation with the IHS, developed the Navajo Nation's first Master Health Plan in 1979. In this plan, the NHSA stressed hospital and clinical services, alcoholism treatment, nutrition, sanitation, community health nursing, and health education as the tribe's highest medical priorities.[33]

In order to centralize leadership over the tribe's blossoming health care activities, Peter MacDonald pushed for the creation of the Department of Health Improvement Services (DHIS) as an official arm of the tribal government. Beginning in 1977 this body worked alongside other Navajo health-related groups and took over responsibilities for administering services contracted out to the tribe through P.L. 93-638, including the CHR, emergency medical technician, social hygiene, tuberculosis, and streptococcal programs. The DHIS also oversaw various nutritional and educational services, such as Women, Infants and Children (WIC), funded by the U.S. Department of Agriculture through the state of Arizona. Altogether, by 1982 the DHIS administered programs totaling some $19 million in state, tribal, and federal funding.[34]

This burgeoning network of Navajo-controlled health agencies contributed to a somewhat confusing web of federal, state, tribal, and private groups involved in administering health care on the reservation, and their roles occasionally overlapped. The Navajo agencies underscored the tribe's commitment to assert its authority over that network of medical services and gave the tribe at least limited power to form those services to meet its needs and desires. In the process, dozens of Navajos earned valuable experience as administrators and health planners.

Navajo Health Care Workers

True medical self-determination depended on increasing the number of Navajos involved in Western medicine as health care professionals and medical administrators. During the 1970s, the Navajo tribal leadership actively tried to break down barriers separating young people from medical careers, hoping that Navajo health care professionals would make Western medicine more responsive to Diné patients. In addition to encouraging students to obtain Western medical training, the NHA looked for ways to teach them respect for their traditional culture and healing ways.

For decades, Navajos had made up a significant portion of the BIA and IHS medical employees. By 1968, 48 percent of the IHS workers on the reservation were Navajo and 14 percent were from other American Indian groups; but almost all of these employees were in support roles, including housekeepers, driver-interpreters, and medical technicians. Comparatively few Navajos were registered nurses, administrators, or physicians. In 1976, the NAIHS and other medical facilities on the reservation employed approximately 350 registered nurses, of which only 18 percent were Indian, while 139 out of 140 of the practical nurses were Indian. A similar paucity of Native American medical professionals existed nationwide. In 1973, only thirty-nine physicians, one dentist, one pharmacist, and two veterinarians were American Indian, out of an Indian population of over 800,000.[35]

Years of racial discrimination, poverty, and substandard education had

A Community Health Representative (CHR) vehicle. Conceived by the federal government, but administered by tribes, the CHR program helped American Indians play greater roles in the delivery of Western medicine. Photograph by author.

prevented Indian men and women from undertaking professional medical careers. Young American Indians rarely grew up believing that they could become doctors, because they had not seen Native people in those roles. As one Indian student explained in 1976, "I thought doctors should be very tall, authoritative, overbearing. In other words, Anglo. Since I didn't fit the mold, I thought I should study something else."[36]

In keeping with the spirit of self-determination, the Indian Health Service took steps in the 1970s to incorporate more Native Americans into its higher delivery and administrative levels. In addition to establishing a scholarship program, the Indian Health Care Improvement Act granted $4 million to tribal organizations like the NHA to recruit Indians into medical careers. The IHS also looked to give American Indians more active roles in medical decision making. Beginning in 1971, Navajos who had experience as military medics or had worked as hospital nurses or technicians were provided an opportunity to train at the Phoenix Indian Medical Center and the Gallup Indian Medical Center as physician assistants (also known as community health medics). These employees helped ease problems with understaffing by taking care of outpatients and less serious emergency cases. Taylor McKenzie, Marie Allen, and Mike Lincoln were also among a growing group of Navajos who took on upper-level administrative roles within the NAIHS. McKenzie served as the Shiprock service unit director, Allen served as assistant area director under Marlene Haffner, and Lincoln replaced Haffner as area director in the 1980s.[37]

But the Navajo Nation did not wish to leave it up to the federal government to control the flow of Diné people into health careers. Through its Office of Student Affairs headed by Jack Jackson, and aided by a grant from the Kellogg Foundation, the NHA offered scholarships to American Indian students interested in medical careers. The NHA supported approximately five hundred Navajo and other Indian students by 1980, of which fifty-three became nurses, twenty-three earned their medical degrees, three became dentists, and dozens of others earned other degrees related to health care. As a tribute to the NHA's effort to convince Indian providers to serve Indian patients, 94 percent of these graduates chose to work for the IHS or other groups involved with Native Americans. Among the Navajos who received financial assistance through the NHA were men and women who played key roles in Navajo health care in the 1970s, 1980s, and 1990s: Marie Allen, Ellouise DeGroat (NHA board member and NAIHS tribal relations director in the 1990s), Mike Lincoln, and Orville McKinley (one of the next three Navajo physicians who followed Taylor McKenzie). In addition to these scholarship and support activities, the Health Authority's Office of Nursing Education, directed by Lydia Pourier, cooperated with Navajo Community College to train Navajos as registered nurses.[38]

As the centerpiece of its Indian health manpower efforts, the NHA planned to establish an American Indian School of Medicine (AISOM) that would eventually allow Native American instructors to train Native medical students. In a specially designed environment, AISOM could offer excellent medical training, geared toward reservation environments, while familiarizing students with traditional healing. The Navajo Nation hoped that AISOM graduates would seek employment through the IHS, thereby helping resolve high turnover problems and infusing the agency with Native cultural perspectives. The NHA also planned to make AISOM the central feature of an American Healing Sciences Education Center that would house the NHA's health planning division, a medical library, and various community meeting rooms.[39]

Under Taylor McKenzie's direction, the NHA tried to find financial support for AISOM and succeeded in convincing the IHS and the University of Northern Arizona in Flagstaff to help train the students. Because the NHA presented AISOM as a pan-Indian initiative, the National Congress of American Indians and the newly formed Association of American Indian Physicians wrote documents in support. McKenzie also established contact with western-state congressmen in an effort to secure government funds for the school, which the NHA estimated would cost $30 million to build and $5.2 million annually to operate.[40]

In 1975, AISOM succeeded in securing an old civic center belonging to Shiprock Chapter, where it established its offices and library. It looked as though the NHA's vision would become a reality. But AISOM did not go further because it could not secure the necessary funds to construct and operate the school. Congressional leaders, including Paul Fannin, believed that existing medical schools could do the job at a much lower price. According to McKenzie, private benefactors were unwilling to go ahead with the project when they discovered that federal funds were not forthcoming. The Navajo Nation had already pulled back from the project by the end of the decade because tribal leaders were concerned that AISOM might draw federal funds away from existing services on the reservation. In addition, because the Navajo Nation had led the development process and planned to provide the land for the school, many tribal leaders felt that it should be designated as a "Navajo medical school" and that it should focus on Navajo issues. They wanted the traditional healing practices and beliefs incorporated into the curriculum to be Navajo. Of course, other Native American groups and benefactors would have had trouble agreeing to that. "If it were going to succeed," said McKenzie, "you would have a kind of pan-Indian participation not only at the executive level but at the governing body level as well. I'm not sure that the Navajos would have accepted that."[41]

Despite its eventual demise, the AISOM effort marked a milestone in Navajo health care. The tribe had shown a willingness and ability to administer large medical initiatives and had gained valuable experience in the process. The AISOM effort had revealed that different Native American groups were willing to work together to reach certain goals in health care, even though it failed to break through some of the obstacles such an approach presented. Together with the Association of American Indian Physicians, founded in 1971, and Indians Into Medicine, founded in 1973, AISOM demonstrated that Native Americans desired to exercise greater control over Western medicine by encouraging Indians to become practitioners. As did the NHA, the abovementioned groups worked to recruit and support Native American students interested in health careers and provided forums for Indian physicians to discuss shared goals and problems.[42]

In part because of these groups and scholarship programs, young Navajo men and women began pursuing careers as physicians in greater numbers during the 1970s. Following the example of those who came before them, including McKenzie and Beryl Blue Spruce—a San Juan-Laguna Pueblo man who graduated from the University of Southern California in 1964— Orville McKinley, Ervin Lewis, and Roger Greyeyes earned their medical degrees in the late 1970s. Another group took advantage of tribal and federal scholarships to enter medical school later in the decade.[43]

Even with financial assistance and guidance from the Navajo Nation, these aspiring Diné physicians had much to overcome. As had other Navajo health care workers in the past, Navajo medical students often experienced difficulties reconciling their cultural beliefs with their Western medical training, but they found ways to do so. For instance, Navajo students who had always been taught to avoid contact with dead bodies were often uneasy about taking part in animal and human dissection. At an NHA seminar for Indian medical students in Albuquerque in 1976, some Navajo students explained how they overcame those concerns without rejecting traditional beliefs. "When I found out that the people who give up their bodies actually sign their names to have something like that done to their bodies, I decided that I didn't think their spirit or anyone else could complain," said one student. "For me it was a quest. I had to use the world of the dead to gain knowledge to help my people. Others have this bridge to cross."[44]

Navajo Community Efforts

Local Navajo communities also looked for ways to exercise more control over Western medical services in the 1970s. Dissatisfaction with the relative inaccessibility and deteriorating quality of health care in certain parts of the reservation prompted chapter governments to request more attention from Congress and the IHS. Two communities, Rough Rock and Ganado, went a step further and administered their own health care services, showing that they did not have to depend entirely on tribal leaders to attain medical autonomy.[45]

Rough Rock and Ganado had an advantage over other Navajo communities at the time because both had institutional bases from which to build— Rough Rock Demonstration School in the first case and Sage Memorial Hospital in the latter. Both community efforts attempted to wed traditional healing and Western medical practices, and in their quest to do so, they confronted funding obstacles that seemed insurmountable. By struggling to overcome those difficulties, these two community initiatives served as examples to other communities, the Navajo Nation, and other tribes.

Rough Rock became part of the Chinle Service Unit under the IHS structure, but community members discovered that the arrangement did not serve them well. They had access to the Many Farms clinic in the south, but after the Cornell team left, the IHS ran the facility only once per week. As Robert Roessel commented, "[T]his proved unsatisfactory since it meant that you had to get sick on schedule." Any other day of the week, residents in the Rough Rock vicinity had to travel twenty-five miles or more to the Chinle health center—a difficult prospect for the more than half of those Navajos who had no motorized transportation. In 1968, the IHS agreed to send a physician to conduct a clinic in Rough Rock once per week, but this did not satisfy community residents, so in 1971, they convinced a retired nurse in Cape Cod, Massachusetts, Ruth Roberts, to take a position at the Demonstration School. In 1975, Rough Rock residents interviewed possible physicians to assist Roberts and eventually decided to hire Dr. Donald Gatch, a physician who had previously served underprivileged communities and who focused on preventive medicine.[46]

The community-sponsored clinical services provided a unique opportunity to intertwine Western and Navajo healing practices because the Demonstration School continued to train traditional healers. Roessel, and other people involved with the Demonstration School, naturally assumed that the healers and the small medical staff would work together to serve community members. In 1972, the Navajo Mental Health Program graduated its first four healers: Jim Hatathle, Mae Hatathle, Dan Yazzie, and Billy Conn. By that time, the training project had earned national attention, with both the *Wall Street Journal* and the *New York Times* running feature articles about the school.[47]

The small clinic won the trust of local residents in Rough Rock and surrounding communities such as Kitsilee, but long-term success depended on procuring funding. Because Congress had promised to encourage such initiatives in the recently passed Self-Determination Act, Gatch, Roberts, and the school director Ethelou Yazzie assumed that the IHS would provide the necessary assistance. Instead, they were disturbed to find resistance from both the IHS and the Navajo Nation.[48]

In 1976, Yazzie and attorney Jerry Davich convinced the IHS to provide $110,000 in contract funds to aid the clinic, but they quickly became embroiled in tribal and bureaucratic politics. Peter MacDonald apparently opposed the IHS contract because the Rough Rock effort functioned outside the network of tribal health agencies. This may have concerned MacDonald because he viewed federal funding as a zero-sum game and believed that $110,000 for Rough Rock would have meant a decrease in funding for other medical programs. Yazzie also found Area Director Marlene Haffner to be reluctant because she believed that the IHS's limited funds could be better used elsewhere on the reservation. Eventually, Haffner agreed to provide a $30,000 loan.[49]

Yazzie and Gatch considered the IHS loan insufficient, and also objected to specific provisions written into the contract that compelled Gatch to divide his time between Rough Rock and a clinic at Rock Point. While Ruth Roberts tried to persuade Ambassador William Scranton at the United Nations to designate Rough Rock as a "Third World Area," and thereby give it access to U.N. funds, Kitsilee, Rock Point, and Rough

Rock community leaders drew up petitions of protest over the IHS's contract stipulations and its failures to release the funds in a timely manner. Frustrated by the process, Yazzie wrote a letter to Haffner arguing that "it is your obligation to provide support for this sort of community program under the terms of the Self-Determination Act. The law was enacted to force people within bureaucracies to help, not hinder, community progress in these areas."[50]

The clinic weathered its financial difficulties in 1976 and found relief a year later when the National Institute of Mental Health gave the Demonstration School a grant to establish new offices for its traditional healer training program. Rather than losing the clinic, the healers and clinic staff chose to cooperate and occupied the new building together.[51]

In 1974, Project HOPE handed Sage Memorial and its outlying clinics over to the Navajo Nation Health Foundation (NNHF), a community-administered organization in Ganado. Because they now possessed a functioning hospital, the NNHF effort seemed to have a better chance for success than did the Rough Rock endeavor. Like Rough Rock, Ganado also had the advantage of strong leadership and a dedicated staff. Led by Medical Director Dr. Wallace Mulligan, the foundation was able to persuade Taylor McKenzie and Annie Wauneka to join its board of directors. At the same time, the NNHF could be truly called a community-based Navajo effort because most of its board members were Navajos from the surrounding area. Its physicians and medical director were non-Indians, but Navajos led the nursing staff and headed some departments.[52]

In addition to operating the forty-five–bed Sage Memorial Hospital, the NNHF ran a family health clinic at Wide Ruins, conducted outreach services through its Navajo health aides, and offered dental and maternal clinics. Maintaining such a comprehensive medical system proved difficult, but the NNHF showed its enthusiasm in an attack on its understaffing problem. In 1965, the hospital had only two physicians, but the foundation discovered innovative ways to increase that number. It established a voluntary medical program that allowed enthusiastic eastern-state physicians to spend time at Ganado as visiting practitioners and made similar arrangements with IHS doctors. These measures helped meet Sage's needs until more physicians could be hired later in the decade. The NNHF also buttressed its nursing staff and cemented its relationship with the larger Navajo Nation by accepting trainees from the Navajo Community College nursing program.[53]

Mulligan hailed the NNHF medical program as the "nation's first and only comprehensive health care program run by American Indians." This contention was debatable given the influence non-Indians still had in the operation, but the NNHF could easily claim to have addressed Navajo health in a variety of ways, and clearly Navajo beliefs, concerns, and cooperation were central to its program. While maintaining Sage Memorial's reputation as an excellent Western medical hospital, the NNHF stressed prevention and placed a great deal of emphasis on the need to incorporate traditional Navajo healing. In line with this philosophy, physicians frequently worked in rooms next door to Navajo traditional practitioners who agreed to meet with patients in the hospital.[54]

Because of Sage's strong reputation, the foundation found it easier to procure funds than did Rough Rock. A contract with the IHS brought in over $800,000 annually, and the Navajo Nation donated a grant of $250,000. To a lesser degree the Presbyterian Church continued to assist the medical program. Even with this outside support, the foundation still operated as a community-based venture, as local chapters proved by donating as much as $1,000 from their limited treasuries. Nevertheless, the foundation faced serious financial challenges in its first years. Both the NNHF and the Rough Rock clinic operated on fee-for-service bases, but provided free care to those who could not afford to pay; most of their patients fell into the latter category. Despite large donations from multiple sources, the NNHF's operating expenses of over $1.6 million annually exceeded its revenues, and it was forced to raise its outpatient fees. The fee increase caused utilization rates to drop, but the added revenue of $1,600 a month helped Sage to persevere.[55]

The NNHF survived its first decade and continued to expand its services in the 1980s and 1990s, even adding a new addition, Poncell Hall, in 1990. By 1990, the foundation's operating cost exceeded $8 million annually, yet it occasionally ran a financial surplus. In 1992, Sage Memorial's director of development, John E. King Jr., could say with confidence that Ganado area residents were satisfied with their foundation and favored its services over the NAIHS. King argued that the NNHF had an edge because it had established itself in the community's eyes as a facility that truly belonged to them.[56]

Traditional Healers and Self-Determination

Building on the Rough Rock Navajo Mental Health Program's momentum, Navajo healers continued to look for ways to preserve the traditional ways in the 1970s. In general, Navajo healers found a more receptive audience among non-Indian medical providers in those years. The IHS occasionally invited Buck Austin, Robert Fulton, and other healers to address groups of medical employees, and the mental health workers were particularly interested in working with them. Robert Roessel, Robert Bergman, Karl Menninger, and a few other non-Indians who had assisted in the Rough Rock training program, continued to encourage cross-cultural accommodation in the 1970s, and as a sign of increasing cooperation between Western medicine and Navajo healing, fifteen healers met with twenty physicians at a seminar at the University of New Mexico School of Medicine in 1978 to discuss cancer treatments.[57]

As encouraging as these trends may have been to those healers who wished to combine the powers of traditional healing with those of Western medicine, serious challenges remained. No one knew for sure how many traditional practitioners were left on the reservation in the 1970s, but the registry prepared by the NHA listed just under one thousand singers and under two hundred herbalists in the Chinle, Crownpoint, Fort Defiance, Shiprock, and Tuba City areas in 1979. These were low numbers for a rapidly growing population. The Rough Rock program helped, but the classes were small. Estimates of the number of Rough Rock graduates by 1980 ranged from about 90 to 178. Meanwhile, some non-Indians were still antagonistic to the traditional healing system. Pentecostal ministers were especially confrontational toward traditional healing; some of them even told Navajo parishioners to help them destroy medicine bundles.[58]

Encouraged by the NHA's Office of Native Healing Sciences, singers and other concerned Navajos began to consider the need for a tribal-chartered organization to promote traditional healing. In 1973, Carl Gorman, Miller Nez, and fifty healers gathered at the Navajo Nation capital in Window Rock to petition the tribe's assistance in establishing a Medicine Men's Association to preserve traditional healing. Finally, in 1978, the group of healers established Diné Be' Azee Iil'iini' Yee' Ahot'a'. In its plan of operation, the Medicine Men's Association (MMA), as they still referred to the group, committed itself to "develop new health care systems which combine the healing arts and skills of trained Navajo healers and medicine men in conjunction with practitioners of western medical science, and thereby improve the health and well-being of the Navajo people."[59]

Referred to as the Navajo healers' equivalent to the American Medical Association, the MMA sought to encourage and regulate traditional healing. It considered the possibility of establishing certification standards for healers to combat the contamination of the ceremonies by alcohol and improper conduct. The association also hoped that the certification procedures would persuade coal mining companies to pay for their workers to have sings. The MMA offered healing services to prison inmates in New Mexico, and worked cooperatively with the IHS. In addition, the association planned to sponsor future training programs and to establish scholarships for aspiring healers, and it planned to serve as an advocacy group to fight against threats to the traditional ways. In 1977, MMA members helped IHS staff design the new Chinle hospital with greater sensitivity to Navajo culture, encouraging the inclusion of space for traditional ceremonies to be conducted within the facility. In 1978, the MMA succeeded in prompting the tribe to pass a resolution aimed at protecting ceremonial objects. The tribe ejected at least one missionary for violating the law, but the desecrations continued.[60]

Despite its successes, the MMA's unsuccessful attempts to obtain an official charter from the tribe underscored the fact that, while many Navajos still valued traditional healing, they disagreed strongly over the means that should be used to protect it. Obtaining a charter would have helped legitimize the group and allow it to raise funds as a nonprofit organization. In pursuit of a charter, MMA supporters stressed that their organization allowed Navajos to present a united front against outside threats to their healing ways, such as anyone who aided in the destruction or outside sale of ceremonial items. They also tried to assure the Council that none of their bylaws would impinge upon the religious freedom of other Navajos, including healers who did not join the group.[61]

The Council vacillated on the issue, in large part because of the many negative comments they heard about the healers' organization. Some Council delegates worried about the political power a chartered MMA would gain in the tribal government. Opposing traditional healers argued that the group's structure and methods, such as the use of certification, bylaws, and paperwork, were based on non-Navajo organizational models. Opponents also pointed out that the traditional ways had survived for centuries without such a group. They further objected to an MMA proposal that a singer's religious paraphernalia be turned over to the MMA for protection after death, if that singer had not passed it on to another in training. Other concerns included a fear that the organization would reduce the individual autonomy of healers, that its proposal to certify singers was "ridiculous" and might be a means to prevent non-MMA singers from practicing, and that most of its members were associated with the Native American Church (some still worried about the NAC's corrupting influences on traditional healing). The last argument was probably exaggerated (apparently only a few of the founding members were associated with the NAC), but the widespread misgivings were enough to convince the Council to shy away from granting the charter.[62]

The MMA thus struggled with outside opposition, and it was also plagued by internal rivalries and disagreements, but it persevered. Its creation and service to the Navajo Nation demonstrated that many Navajos were ready to try new, and what some would consider to be extreme, means to resolve a long-term and very serious problem.

As traditional healing continued as an alternative and a supplement to Western medicine in the 1970s, so too, did the Native American Church. In spite of those Navajos, both Christian and traditional, who opposed the religion, the critics seemed to make up a smaller portion of the population than previously. The NAC thrived in the decade in part because members no longer feared prosecution from tribal law enforcement. In fact, between 40 and 50 percent of Navajos were estimated to be taking part in peyote rituals in the 1970s. "This would give a range of 60,000 to 80,000 members," David Aberle argued, "figures equal to or larger than the total estimated Protestant, Catholic, and LDS affiliation."[63]

· 8 ·

COOPERATION AND CONTROL,
1980s AND 1990s

The final two decades of the twentieth century revealed signs for both optimism and concern regarding Navajo health care. Navajos were living longer, healthier lives on average than they had for many decades. The Navajo Area Indian Health Service medical system had expanded in size and scope, and medical statistics suggested that its comprehensive model had been quite successful. But many problems remained. New health threats emerged as old ones receded. Limited funding held back improvements in Western medicine on the reservation and made community-based and tribe-sponsored initiatives uncertain propositions. Although the Diné were committed to holding on to their traditional healing practices, dwindling numbers of singers, herbalists, and diagnosticians challenged Navajos to seek new solutions to old problems.

In recognition of what they had gained and what they were losing, Navajos worked harder than ever to preserve the integrity of the healing ways, both Western and traditional, upon which they depended. The IHS offered new forms of assistance to the tribe in this process. Together, the IHS and Navajo Nation looked for ways to maintain, and hopefully to increase, Western medicine's effectiveness on the reservation. Both the IHS and tribal government also cooperated with traditional healers to incorporate traditional ways into the hospital environment. And while cooperating with the IHS, the tribe moved closer toward full control of all forms of healing on the Navajo Nation.

Navajo Health After 1980

By the mid-1980s, Navajo health patterns had improved significantly. Overall mortality rates had changed dramatically, falling from as high as 11 per 1,000 in 1945 to approximately 6.5 per 1,000. In little more than a decade, life expectancy had risen five years for women and eight years for men. Navajo women could now anticipate a lifespan of seventy-seven years, and Navajo men sixty-seven; this compared to a nationwide average of seventy-eight for women and seventy for men. As seen in table 8.1, overall, Navajo health patterns still compared unfavorably to the general American population, but the gaps had narrowed.[1]

Table 8.1 **Age-Adjusted Mortality Rates by Major Causes of Death: Navajo and All IHS Clients, 1986–88, and United States, 1987 (per 100,000 Population)**

Cause of Death	Navajo (rank)	All IHS Clients (rank)	United States, 1987
Accidents, all types	160.7 (1)	102.9 (2)	34.6
Coronary diseases	98.9 (2)	156.1 (1)	169.6
Cancer	85.8 (3)	99.8 (3)	132.9
Influenza and pneumonia	* (4)	18.6*(7)	13.1
Diabetes mellitus	26.5 (5)	29.7 (5)	9.8
Homicide	22.2 (6)	16.9 (9)	8.6
Cerebrovascular disease	19.7 (7)	30.3 (4)	30.3
Suicide	16.3 (8)	17.9 (8)	11.7
Chronic liver disease and cirrhosis	* (9)	28.3*(6)	9.1
Selected diseases of infancy	10.1 (10)	11.1 (10)	10.1
Age-adjusted mortality rate	644.0	665.8	535.5

Source: U.S. Department of Health and Human Services, U.S. Public Health Service, Indian Health Service, *Regional Differences in Indian Health,* 1992 (Washington, D.C.: GPO, 1992).
*Incomplete data or data drawn from alternate sources.[2]

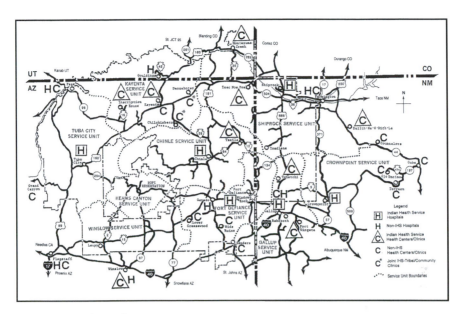

Navajo Health Facilities, 1991

It is difficult to isolate the influence Western medicine had on Navajo health at the end of the century from other contributing factors, such as economic trends and dietary differences, but declining deaths from certain diseases were encouraging signs of medical success. Tuberculosis deaths, already reduced significantly in the 1950s and 1960s, continued to decline in the 1970s. By the mid-1980s, tuberculosis mortality rates had fallen to 5.3 per 100,000, as compared to a U.S. average of 0.5. The Navajos still suffered disproportionately from the ailment, but tuberculosis no longer killed them in great numbers. Similarly, gastrointestinal diseases were no longer among the top ten killers on the reservation, having fallen to a rate of 3.0 per 100,000 as compared to 1.8 for the larger IHS service population and 1.3 for the U.S. average. At least to some degree, these improvements were linked to IHS and tribal drug therapy, health education, and sanitation efforts.[3]

The Navajo infant mortality rate continued to fall as well, reaching parity with the U.S. average by the 1990s. Infant deaths had declined for a variety of reasons, not all of which were directly related to improvements in health care. In part, falling Navajo infant death rates may have resulted from the growing tendency since World War II for Navajos to move to towns and small cities on the reservation where they had greater access to emergency medical services, wage work, indoor plumbing, and other utility services (though many Navajo families on the reservation still lacked indoor plumbing, telephone service, and electricity). But as discussed earlier, it seems evident that improved clinical care had a significant impact.[4]

The degree of success in combating infant death seems even more significant when the Navajo case is compared to rates for non-Indian communities with similar deficiencies in sanitation services and income levels. The author selected a group of non-Indian counties based on their similarities in 1970 to the Navajo reservation in terms of income and utility services, which are conditions linked to infant mortality. In 1950, infant death rates for these counties were less than half as high as Navajo rates, but by 1990, the Navajo rate had fallen below the average for these counties (10.1 compared to 11.3 per 1,000 live births). The IHS's tendency to gauge its medical success or failure by making comparisons to U.S. averages, therefore, may de-emphasize how successful Western medical providers and the tribe had been in dealing with Navajo infant health.[5]

Not all health statistics were so positive as the century came to an end; some medical dilemmas from the past remained. Even in the late 1980s, influenza and pneumonia still caused many deaths among Navajos, especially the very young and the elderly. In addition, epidemic outbreaks of meningitis, hepatitis, hantavirus, and even plague were not uncommon in the 1980s and 1990s. Lower mortality rates also failed to reveal a relatively high incidence of certain infectious diseases that did not normally cause death. For instance, as seen by hospital patient visits listed in table 8.2, otitis media still threatened the quality of life for thousands of Navajos.[6]

A new killer also emerged toward the end of the century. By the late 1980s, Navajo Area Indian Health Service (NAIHS) and tribal health officials estimated that between thirty and 100 Navajos were infected with human immunodeficiency virus (HIV), the pathogen that causes the acquired immunodeficiency syndrome (AIDS). Although these numbers were relatively low, the problem promised to get worse. In 1987, AIDS caused four Navajo deaths, and four more followed by 1992. By 1995 a total of fifty-nine AIDS cases were reported on the reservation.[7]

Deaths from certain chronic diseases, which normally struck older citizens, were still less frequent among the Navajos than the rest of the United States on average, but they were rising as well. As mentioned earlier, the lower than average rates did not necessarily reflect the medical program's

Table 8.2 Navajo Area IHS Outpatient and Inpatient Utilization, 1990

Five Leading Reasons for Outpatient Visits	Visits	Five Leading Causes of Hospitalization	Discharges
Otitis media	68,836	Obstetrical	6,775
Upper respiratory infection	58,490	Respiratory system disease	2,423
Prenatal care	49,079	Digestive system disease	2,024
Well child care	32,266	Injury and poisoning	1,924
Diabetes mellitus	30,541	Genitourinary tract disease	982

Source: U.S. Department of Health and Human Services, U.S. Public Health Service, Navajo Area Indian Health Service, Office of Program Planning and Development, *Navajo Area Indian Health Service, Area Profile, 1992* (Washington, D.C.: GPO, 1992).

success. Navajos were still relatively young on average in comparison to the United States as a whole, and even older Navajos tended to suffer from cancer less often than older non-Navajos for reasons no one fully understood. In part, Navajo habits explained the discrepancy. Relatively few older Navajos drank and very few smoked. But as the Navajo population aged and as dietary habits changed, chronic illnesses became more serious.[8]

Diabetes may have been the most terrible chronic disease afflicting the Navajos and other American Indians late in the century. During the 1960s, approximately one out of six Navajos had been diagnosed with this potentially life-threatening disease. In the 1990s, this figure increased to almost one out of three. As evidence of the increasing problem with the disease, the number of diabetes-related amputations among the Navajos doubled between 1994 and 1998.[9]

Medical professionals did not convincingly explain the causes for the increasing incidence of diabetes among American Indians, but they tended to agree that dietary changes had been involved. Just as contact with non-Indian society once brought infectious diseases, modern industries and modern foods contributed to the rise of diabetes and other chronic ailments. One theory speculated that Navajos and other American Indians adapted to eating low-fat diets and to surviving periods of famine in the centuries before contact with Europeans. Their bodies

Signs such as these can be found next to IHS facilities and across Navajo country. Given the high incidence of auto fatalities and diabetes among the Navajos, health education became one of the IHS and Navajo Nation's major efforts in the late twentieth century. Photographs by author.

were thus less able to handle the introduction of fatty foods and "junk foods" high in sugar. At the very least, many Navajos were convinced that modern supermarkets, convenience stores, and fast food chains, which had sprung up across the reservation as it urbanized, were detrimental to Navajo health. "Until fairly recent years our cornfields were our life-givers," Deescheeny Nez Tracy said in the late 1970s. "In fact, the farm was where most of our food came from—food that made us strong and healthy. But today we have all kinds of useless foods; some are just imitations; many are harmful sweets and candies, pastries, sodas, and so on."[10]

The rising incidence of chronic diseases among the Navajos may also have been linked to a disruption of the traditional exercise patterns. Elders began to worry that young people spent too much time watching television and too little time practicing the traditional endurance rituals. Many Navajos also lost the physical benefits incurred from herding and shepherding on foot. Fewer Navajos were involved in raising livestock, and those who were so engaged often used pickup trucks and other vehicles to herd their animals. Sonya Yazzie, a student at Diné College in the 1990s, recalled that as a young child, she had to push a wheelbarrow many miles to get water and had to chop wood for the family. Electrification and indoor plumbing eliminated such forms of exercise for many people. Modern sports, especially basketball, engaged the interest and energies of the young but did not furnish a full substitute for rural lifestyles that were far more physically demanding.[11]

Federal Indian Health Care Policy and the Navajos

During the 1980s and 1990s, the IHS, tribal providers, and traditional healers all pushed forward in a combined effort to meet Navajo and Indian health care needs. The tribe, often with help from the IHS and sympathetic national politicians, had to fight to obtain funds necessary to maintain medical services and to gain the health care benefits that the federal government had promised.

At first glance, funding levels for Navajo health care at the end of the twentieth century appear to have been favorable. Federal dollars spent on Indian health care increased dramatically after 1970. Indian Health Service expenditures rose from approximately $84 million in 1968 to $690 million in 1980, $1.62 billion in 1991, and to $2.1 billion in 1995. For the Navajo Nation, these figures translated into $60 million for the NAIHS in 1981, $108 million in 1985, and more than $200 million in 1995.[12]

But as IHS funds increased, so did the American Indian population, from approximately 792,370 in 1970 to 1.37 million in 1980, and 1.9 million in 1990. The Navajos accounted for a good proportion of that population increase, with 170,000 tribal members in the mid-1980s, 200,000 by 1990, and more than 220,000 in the mid-1990s. The IHS did not provide care for all of these people, many of whom identified themselves as members of a particular tribe in the census, but were not deemed eligible for federal Indian services. Nonetheless, between 1985 and 1990 alone, the IHS service population grew from a little less than a million to 1.17 million, and the number of people served by the NAIHS rose from 171,097 to 181,330. IHS projections showed those numbers reaching approximately 1.5 million overall and 240,000 for the Navajo Nation by the year 2000.[13]

Even without taking the effects of the population increase into account, IHS expenditures would have still risen rapidly because the average cost of medical care per patient increased dramatically nationwide. Beginning in the 1970s, medical costs in the United States grew at rates exceeding inflation and, between 1970 and 1991, health care spending went from 7.3 to 13.2 percent of the U.S. gross national product. In such an environment, and with such a large service population, the IHS had to fight an uphill battle to maintain, much less increase, its medical programs.[14]

Throughout the 1980s and 1990s, advocates of better Indian health services, including the Navajo Nation, found themselves on the defensive, combating efforts to reduce budget deficits by the reduction of federal programs. Congress approached Indian health care with a crisis mentality, authorizing massive increases when Indian voices of protest and dismal medical statistics reached a crescendo, and then failing to appropriate the full amounts in following years.

Promising to encourage "self-governance" by breaking American Indians free of "excessive regulation and self-perpetuating bureaucracy," and in a larger attempt to decrease federal spending on domestic programs, President Ronald Reagan sought to slash BIA and IHS funding in the early 1980s. Whereas President Jimmy Carter had proposed an IHS budget of $771.8 million before leaving office, Reagan recommended $634.9 million for Indian health care in his first budget. Actual funding for the IHS in 1981 increased to approximately $690 million, but Reagan requested a nearly $43-million cut for fiscal year 1982, setting off a storm of protest from American Indian groups, the IHS, and senators and representatives from states with large Indian populations.[15]

Navajo leaders stood in the forefront of those calling on the federal government to deliver financially on its health care promises to Native peoples. During the winter of 1981, Acting IHS Director Joseph Exendine and Navajo Division of Health (formerly DHIS) Director Ron Wood joined Senator Dennis DeConcini of Arizona and others in opposing the Indian health care funding cuts. At a meeting of the Select Committee on Indian Affairs of the U.S. Senate in Phoenix, Exendine relayed the possible effect of the cuts. For the first time since the IHS's creation, its funds would actually decrease, and it would have even fewer tools with which to attack health problems on Indian reservations. In particular, urban Indian health programs, sanitation projects, and the Community Health Representative program would essentially cease to exist, as would scholarship programs for Indian students. After complaining that Congress had always underfunded Indian health care, Wood expressed his befuddlement as to why the effective CHR and "tremendously successful" sanitation programs were to be curtailed.[16]

Budget cuts in the early 1980s threatened to stop the construction of needed projects for the Navajo Nation. A new hospital at Crownpoint and clinics at Tsaile and Huerfano would be eliminated, and insufficient funds for housing construction threatened to deny a new Chinle facility sufficient staff. Reductions in P.L. 93-638 funding also forced the tribe to reduce appropriations for its Navajo Aging and Behavioral Health Department programs. Limited relief finally came in July 1981 when the House budget increased Indian health funds by $41.3 million over the Reagan proposal, allowing the two clinics and the Crownpoint facility to move toward construction. But the NAIHS lamented that it needed an additional $30 million to maintain its current level of activity with the Navajos.[17]

In 1984 Congress appropriated $824 million for Indian health care, enabling the NAIHS and Navajo Nation to begin "cautious rebuilding" that included renovations for facilities in Shiprock, Tuba City, Winslow, Gallup, and Fort Defiance. But after the president vetoed a reauthorization bill for the Indian Health Care Improvement Act in 1984, prospects for the future of Navajo health care again looked bleak. While Senator Barry Goldwater and other congressional leaders promised to reintroduce it the following year, American Indian groups responded with strong statements of protest—the National Congress of American Indians referring to this and other Reagan policies as "termination by non-appropriation."[18]

Although Congress did reauthorize the Indian Health Care Improvement Act in 1986, and even though IHS funding increased in the late 1980s, IHS costs and American Indian medical demands continued to exceed federal appropriations. During President George Bush's administration, the IHS budget reached $1.62 billion, but area offices nationwide, including the Navajo Area, were still forced to ration medical care, lest they exhaust their funds before the end of each year. This situation prompted Mike Lincoln, a former recipient of Navajo Health Authority support and then director of the NAIHS, to argue that a "serious crisis" existed in the delivery of health care to the Navajo Nation.[19]

In lieu of sufficient and consistent funding, the IHS increasingly turned to assistance from third-party providers in the 1980s and 1990s. The NAIHS began billing private insurance companies in 1981, but so few Navajos had health insurance that the Navajo Area collected only $100,000 annually from private insurance by 1985. Things later improved in this regard. Many Navajos who could afford to purchase health insurance in the late 1980s and 1990s did so, enabling the NAIHS to collect $7 million from insurance companies in 1995. By then, Medicare and Medicaid supplied a much larger share of the NAIHS budget, providing approximately $5 million in 1985 and $42 million ten years later. These infusions provided sorely needed supplemental funds. But dependence upon these programs and insurance also meant that area offices relied on large patient loads to maintain revenues, because such payments were available only on a patient-by-patient basis. Securing funds from third-party sources also required prolonged legal and legislative fights among the IHS, states, and insurance companies.[20]

Albeit reluctantly, states slowly did more to help ease the IHS's burden and assist Navajos in need of medical services. Like Utah and New Mexico, Arizona extended health care services to American Indians in the 1980s and early 1990s to include behavioral health, disabled children, alcohol and drug abuse, and communicable disease prevention programs. Yet as late as 1980, Arizona lacked a Medicaid system because the state hoped to avoid heavy expenditures for its large Native population. Counties eventually found it excessively burdensome to supply medical care to Arizona indigents, thus forcing the state legislature to consider taking part in the system. After the state secured an assurance from the Department of Health and Human Services (formerly DHEW) that the IHS would remain the primary health care provider for American Indians on reservations, the Arizona legislature established its own version of Medicaid in 1981—a prepayment managed care program known as the Arizona Health Care Cost Containment System (AHCCCS).[21]

A dispute soon developed between the federal government and Arizona. From 1982 until 1986, the state, under protest, expended $15 million for Indian patients the IHS sent to contract off-reservation facilities. Worried that this arrangement would "bankrupt AHCCCS," state officials filed suit against the federal government in 1986. IHS Director Everett Rhoades protested, informing AHCCCS that his agency "is not and never has been an entitlement program upon which your agency may rely as a basis for denying benefits to Indian citizens of Arizona." On 12 September 1988, a federal court ruled in favor of Arizona, ordering the IHS to pay for all reservation residents referred to non-IHS facilities.[22]

Although sometimes at odds with the IHS, Arizona did continue to provide aid to the IHS and Navajo Nation. During the 1990s, AHCCCS provided services to off-reservation Indians, including a small number of elderly Native people through its Arizona Long-Term Care Service (ALTCS), and it established a special health plan that helped cover care sought in IHS facilities. Nevertheless, state and other alternate sources of aid to the IHS failed to solve the Navajo Area's long-term budget woes. Throughout the early 1990s, funds available to the NAIHS and other IHS Areas from all sources met only 65 to 70 percent of the estimated needs.[23]

Navajos received at least some signals of hope from Washington in the early 1990s. Recognizing that serious medical deficiencies still existed on reservations and among urban Indian populations, Congress reauthorized the Indian Health Care Improvement Act, with some key amendments. Initiated as Senate Resolution 2481, the new Act authorized another $940 million for Indian health care in fiscal year 1993 and established new mandates. First, it promised that "all persons who are eligible for the health care services provided by the Indian Health Service have access to the same fundamental health care benefits." In other words, no matter whether individuals lived near an IHS hospital or a contract facility, they were guaranteed the same basic package of service benefits. Second, the Act set specific goals aimed at decreasing the prevalence of sixty-one different causes of morbidity and mortality. Known as the "Healthy People 2000" objectives, the guidelines addressed Indian health issues in a comprehensive fashion. The Act, for example, mandated that the IHS reduce the diabetes mortality rate to no greater than sixty-two per 1,000 by the millennium. Based on these IHS guidelines, the NAIHS set its own, dealing with everything from reducing suicide and infant mortality rates to increasing seatbelt use.[24]

Initially, Navajo leaders were also encouraged by President Bill Clinton's Health Security Act proposal. They believed that this effort to deal with a national health care "crisis" would benefit Indian medical care as well. In addition to promising all Americans a "comprehensive package of benefits that can never be taken away," the Clinton plan promised to improve medical services for American Indians. A member of the Clinton administrative team, Philip Lee, claimed that the plan would "strengthen" and "expand" the Indian Health Service, which he lauded for doing "an absolutely outstanding job of providing services to Indian populations with limited resources." The proposal advocated that American Indians be allowed to choose between the IHS and other health plans and ensured that the IHS would provide a comprehensive benefits package equaling those of other health plans. The Clinton plan thus promised to retain and improve the existing IHS system while providing more options to Indian people.[25]

But Navajos had heard such promises before, and realized that bold words were meaningless without the long-term commitment and funding to back them up. Navajo President Peterson Zah approached the administration's health plan with caution, reminding a task force led by Hillary Rodham Clinton that "by ceding our land to the non-Indians, we have already paid our health bill." As massive and imposing as the IHS often appeared, Zah understood from experience that the agency had a tenuous status. He set out basic ground rules for any new policies affecting Indian health. First, he insisted that tribal sovereignty and the Navajo Nation's right to self-determination be respected. Second, the IHS should be preserved and expanded. Third, with off-reservation and urban Native Americans in mind, he argued that Indian people should be able to seek health care anywhere. Zah also stressed the importance of paying attention to cultural differences and concerns, guarding against any policy that would treat all Indian people alike and thereby inequitably.[26]

By early 1994, the Navajo Nation had turned against the Clinton plan. The Clinton administration planned to extend health care benefits universally while reducing federal expenditures simultaneously, in an attempt to find the middle way between conservative and liberal interests in the United States. Therefore, the benefits the administration promised carried along with them new threats. Clinton's Health Security Act had to be viewed in the context of the administration's larger effort to cut back the number of federal employees and overall government spending—objectives that struck at the Indian Health Service. In fact, the president called for a $247 million reduction in IHS expenditures for fiscal year 1995.[27]

Once again, Navajo leaders rose up in protest. In April 1994, Navajo Health and Social Services Chairperson Genevieve Jackson, Navajo Division of Health (NDOH) Director Lydia Hubbard-Pourier, Peterson Zah, and other tribal leaders voiced their concerns about health care reform at a Senate Committee on Indian Affairs hearing in Shiprock. Joined by Republican Senators John McCain (Arizona) and Pete Domenici (New Mexico), the Navajo leadership declared their opposition to proposed cutbacks. "We believed that the promises of this badly needed reform [would] benefit Indian people, up until recently," said Jackson. The Clinton administration's staff reduction plan, claimed Jackson, "has badly shaken our faith in the promises of health care reform." Zah vowed that the United States would be held accountable for breaking past agreements with American Indians and promised that the Navajos would "do whatever we need to do to make the United States fulfill its responsibility toward the Indian people."[28]

The Clinton budget and staffing reductions threatened both Navajo health care and Navajo employment. The Navajo Nation had a shortage of hospital beds, with about one-quarter the national per capita average, and hoped that a new hospital completed at Shiprock (the Northern Navajo Medical Center) would provide limited relief, both in terms of health care and jobs. Yet a proposed federal layoff of 500 to 600 NAIHS employees would have left the facility with only half of the 720 staff members it required to operate at full capacity. It seemed ludicrous to Zah and tribal Vice President Marshall Plummer that the government would cut $10 million and hundreds of employees from the NAIHS after spending $55 million to build a hospital that could not even fulfill its potential. Zah also estimated that the reductions could double waiting times for routine medical care and would preclude patients from receiving necessary specialized care through contract services. Zah also pointed out that the layoffs would impose a financial burden on hundreds of Navajos, who were more likely to be released than "white doctors and nurses."[29]

Navajo leaders allied with McCain, Domenici, Democrat Senator Daniel Inouye (Hawaii), and others to convince the administration and

Peterson Zah, Navajo Nation president during the 1990s. He fought for increased federal funds for the IHS and for Native American Church rights, and encouraged cooperation between Western medical providers and traditional healers, especially during the hantavirus outbreak. Courtesy of Peterson Zah Collection, Labriola National American Indian Data Center, Arizona State University Libraries.

congressional delegates to reverse the cuts. In February 1994, Zah met with Ira Magaziner, Clinton's chief health advisor, and in March, McCain and Inouye urged Mike Lincoln, the new IHS director, to take a strong stand against the cuts. Zah and Plummer also threatened to file suit against the federal government if it went through with the proposed staff and budget reductions. In late April, Clinton agreed to restore $125 million to his proposed budget for the IHS, and the Senate Appropriations Committee urged the increase of that budget figure by another $9.4 million to help staff the Shiprock facility.[30]

Navajos also lobbied the U.S. government to live up to other promises regarding their health and well-being. On 15 October 1990, the Radiation Exposure Compensation Act (RECA) became law and included a promised payment of $100,000 to Navajo uranium miners who suffered from radon-related illnesses. Once again, Navajos had high hopes that the federal government would bring aid to those suffering from disease and, once again, those hopes gave way to despair and frustration in the following years. Many Navajo miners and widows of miners had to go through a dehumanizing application process, only to find years later that their claim had been denied. By 1993, only 380 Navajos had been certified out of 2,700 applicants. Many others had simply abandoned the process or had never bothered to apply in the first place.[31]

RECA was also criticized by many Navajo claimants and their supporters for failing to account for cultural differences. It did not recognize Diné widows who had married miners in Navajo traditional weddings. RECA benefits were denied to men who admitted that they had smoked and therefore had compromised their eligibility on the basis of lung cancer—only, by "smoked" they were often speaking of their participation in traditional ceremonies involving tobacco. Quite often Navajos also had difficulty providing medical evidence for their claims, as it sometimes took months for the IHS to track down their records. To make RECA seem even more inequitable, the Act offered no compensation to uranium millers or widows of millers. Complicating a payment process that had little power to alleviate their pain, even if it had been administered flawlessly, did little to foster Navajo trust in the U.S. government. "To this day they have not realized what they have done to many of us," said Anna Aloysious of Cove, Arizona. "Their so called [RECA] compassionate payment is not justice. Not in our thoughts and deep inside our hearts."[32]

Navajo leaders and victims joined forces in seeking redress. The tribe approved in 1997 a $123,000 donation to the Navajo Uranium Radiation Victims Committee (NURVC), an organization established by community members in Red Valley, New Mexico, to assist mining and milling victims and to bring about changes in RECA. NURVC Director Phil Harrison Jr. believed the original Act failed to close old wounds and opened new ones. "RECA was supposed to bring justice for radiation victims across the country, but the intent of the bill did not work for us," he said. Tribal and community efforts finally convinced New Mexico Republican Representatives Bill Redmond, Steve Schiff, and Joe Skeen to sponsor a new bill that promised to reconstruct RECA, extending coverage to millers, increasing the compensatory payment to $200,000, and making the application process more sensitive to Navajo conditions. The bill died in Congress, but Redmond and a variety of Republican and Democrat members of Congress continued to dedicate energy to the effort the following year.[33]

Western Medical Services

Funding dilemmas continued to plague the IHS and Navajo Nation after 1980, but Western medical services available to the Navajos improved in quality and expanded in scope. Through cooperation, and thanks to help from innovative employees and local communities, the Navajo Area IHS and Navajo Nation were able to make more efficient use of the limited resources at their disposal.

A significant portion of the NAIHS's funds were devoted to establishing better medical facilities for the Navajo Nation. By 1991, the IHS operated six hospitals, seven health centers, and thirteen health stations for the Navajos. Lean budgets left them understaffed, but all six hospitals were able to maintain Joint Commission on the Accreditation of Healthcare Organizations accreditation throughout the 1980s and 1990s. The Gallup Indian Medical Center, with 107 beds and 715 employees, was the largest NAIHS hospital, and one of the two oldest in 1991. Tuba City had the second largest number of beds with eighty-five, and employed 430. The Crownpoint hospital, planned in the early 1960s and completed in 1987, had the smallest staff, with 240, and the fewest beds, with thirty-nine. Chinle received its new hospital in 1982, and Shiprock replaced its antiquated facility in 1995 at a cost of $35 million. As of 1998, only the Fort Defiance facility could trace its roots to the era of Chee Dodge and

W. W. Peter. But plans had been drawn up for a $47-million replacement facility, requiring 536 employees. Workers finally broke ground for Fort Defiance's Tsé Hootsooí Indian Medical Center in January 1999. It would have thirty-eight inpatient beds, and twenty adolescent psychiatric beds, six outpatient clinics, and a dental clinic with twenty-four chairs.[34]

The new facilities certainly improved Navajo health care, but more were needed. The NAIHS hospitals offered only 390 beds to the Navajo Nation by the early 1990s—fewer than the BIA Medical Division had before World War II. New facilities were expanding that number, but the Navajo population continued to grow rapidly. As Genevieve Jackson warned U.S. Senators at the Shiprock hearings in 1994, "[D]o not become sick or be in an accident while you are in Navajo Nation. All the beds may be taken." So, without sufficient space in its own hospitals, the NAIHS continued to rely heavily upon contracting arrangements with off-reservation facilities to provide additional space and specialty services.[35]

Missionary and former missionary hospitals continued to serve the Navajo Nation and cooperate with the IHS. The Navajo Nation Health Foundation's Sage Memorial Hospital in Ganado still operated, as did Rehoboth-McKinley Hospital next to the Gallup Indian Medical Center. In the north, Navajos utilized the Monument Valley Hospital—the last on-reservation hospital owned and operated by missionaries. Twenty years after its founding, the hospital continued to meet the needs of Utah and Arizona Navajos. The Seventh Day Adventists had kept the twenty-bed facility functioning through the 1970s and 1980s by providing $500,000 annually, and supplementing this money through a contract arrangement with the IHS and funds from private donors and foundations. By the mid-1990s, however, annual operating costs reached $5 million and threatened to force its closure. Rather than lose the only hospital in the vicinity, Oljato Chapter residents voted in 1995 to contribute what they could to keep it open. In exchange, the church agreed to share administrative duties with the local community.[36]

While still insufficient in terms of quantity and availability, new NAIHS hospitals and clinics were better equipped than their predecessors, and were designed with greater sensitivity to their cultural environment. In the late twentieth century, the IHS made a concerted effort to involve tribal and local opinions in its design efforts and favored American Indian contractors. The IHS also took the opportunity to make the facilities more accessible to Navajo singers. With design help from the

MMA, and singers Frank Begay and Gerald Shirley, the Chinle hospital established this precedent in 1982 by offering a traditional healing center, complete with a ventilating system to handle ceremonial smoke and a long pipe to connect it with the earth below. Steering committees, NDOH employees, and traditional advisors all helped the NAIHS facilities appear more "Navajo." The government began to build new hospitals with their doors facing east toward the rising sun, as do the openings on Diné hogans. And Navajo artwork and signs utilizing both English and easily understood symbols made the interiors seem less foreboding. In an effort to help patients feel that the hospitals belonged to them, the Northern Navajo Medical Center in Shiprock included paintings of Navajos herding sheep and a ten-foot-high statue of a Navajo medicine man and his family by sculptor Tim Washburn.[37]

The NAIHS also placed a greater emphasis on improving patient-provider relations through total quality management efforts. It sought to make patients feel as though they were "guests" rather than hindrances. Some facilities added greeters and a few of the hospitals established special programs aimed at helping staff members to be more courteous,

The Native American Church of Navajoland headquarters in 2000.
Photograph by author.

helpful, and culturally sensitive to patients in hallways and waiting rooms. The NAIHS also worked to overcome problems with long waiting lines and provider continuity. Solutions to these problems were not easy. As Taylor McKenzie said in 1992, "I've been in this business almost thirty years and continuity of care is very hard to do. It's impossible almost. We talk about it and it sounds good, but when you really get down to the nuts and bolts, it's hard to do." Ironically, given that Navajos had once avoided the hospitals, the NAIHS began to encourage Navajos to rely more on home care and less on the hospitals for minor ailments in order to help alleviate overcrowding. Various hospitals also adopted triage and appointment systems to reduce waiting times and to enable patients to see the same physician over successive visits. By 1997, IHS surveys showed that patients were happier with the agency's services than in the past, largely because waiting times decreased.[38]

Perhaps optimal provider-patient relations were more easily pursued in clinics and health stations. Dr. Beulah Allen expressed pleasure that the IHS clinic in Tsaile, given its local focus and smaller size, allowed her and her patients to benefit from a greater continuity of care than in the large hospitals. She had a greater chance in Tsaile to develop long-term relationships with her patients. "I'm much closer to the people here," she said.[39]

Some of the small clinics also provided ample opportunities for community involvement in the 1980s and 1990s. The Dennehotso and Chilchinbeto communities followed in Rough Rock and Ganado's tradition of local medical control, by helping support and guide private clinics. While the IHS provided a large portion of the operating costs for these facilities, community members had a greater sense that these clinics "belonged" to them because they contributed their money and energy to them. When Chilchinbeto opened its clinic in the early 1980s, twelve master weavers from the community wove a 600-pound, 28-foot by 26-foot rug, intending to sell it and donate the proceeds to the facility. The community managed to get by and keep their rug until 1997 when funding shortages finally compelled them to sell it for $2 million to keep the clinic. "I'm glad to hear that it will be used for its intended purpose," said weaver Agnes Laughter.[40]

The IHS often found it easier to provide good facilities than the employees necessary to operate them. After 1973, the IHS faced a recruitment dilemma when the Doctor-Dentist Draft ended. The agency obtained limited relief during the early 1970s through the early 1980s by

seeking help from the National Health Service Corps, a scholarship program aimed at supplying physicians to underserved areas. But still unable
to adequately compete with private providers for new physicians, the IHS
tried to replace the defunct draft with loan repayment programs and, after
the Indian Health Care Improvement Act of 1976, with scholarship
obligation programs. Through these means, the NAIHS succeeded in expanding the number of physicians serving the Navajo Nation from 114 in
1976, to 154 in 1979, and 197 in 1991.[41]

While able to maintain its access to qualified young physicians, the
NAIHS found it more difficult to compete with the private sector for
certain specialists, such as orthopedic surgeons, anesthesiologists, and
psychiatrists. IHS pay scales were simply not competitive. In 1991, an IHS
specialist could make between $90,000 and $100,000 a year, plus bonuses,
compared to the $245,000 the average anesthesiologist and the $283,000
the average orthopedic surgeon made in the United States. The IHS also
had considerable trouble competing with health maintenance organizations for much-sought-after family physicians.[42]

Scholarship repayment programs also proved relatively ineffective in
preventing physician turnover. In 1991, NAIHS recruiter Ray Bayles
estimated that the average physician stayed only 3.3 years, although
fifteen of the Navajo Area doctors had been there for more than twelve.
Those who stayed were often attracted to the reservation because of the
recreational possibilities, fascination with Navajo culture, and community spirit. Many of the non-Navajo professionals also created links to
the Navajo Nation through marriage. Furthermore, as Dr. Don Lewis-
Kratsik at Fort Defiance pointed out, some medical doctors preferred
IHS employment because its comprehensive health care model and
paucity of specialists allowed physicians the opportunity to take part in
a wider variety of duties. Indeed, many NAIHS physicians in the 1980s
and 1990s were skilled and dedicated providers, but high turnover
among the ranks of younger physicians, who had joined the NAIHS to
fulfill obligations, tended to compromise larger efforts at health care
continuity.[43]

Although plagued by such personnel problems, the IHS benefited
from many dedicated and innovative employees. Whether clinical care
providers or public health workers, employees had to react daily to a wide
variety of medical dilemmas. "You might walk into the office one day and
get hit with a half dozen different things," said Patrick Bohan, Navajo

Area IHS chief of environmental health services during the 1990s. "There's a food outbreak over at this place. Someone is reporting cattle around a spring over here. Over here we have a case of plague. You may get hit with three or four things so you have to be able to change gears like that." While employees may have objected to some bureaucratic regulations, the IHS did allow them the freedom to use their own judgment and skills in responding to diverse situations. Some employees were able to accomplish a great deal with little money. When a team of IHS sanitarians connected a large incidence of broken hips among elderly Navajos to poorly constructed steps outside their homes, for example, they bought lumber and repaired the steps. Geri Bahe-Hernandez, director of community health services at Tuba City in the 1990s, also proved innovative, devising ways to combat teenage pregnancy during her school visits. She used a simulated pregnancy apron called a "sympathy belly" and tapes of crying babies to "simulate the costs of bringing a child into the world."[44]

Improvements in Western medical delivery also resulted from tribal government initiatives, including cooperative efforts with the IHS. The tribe's major role in health care in the 1980s and 1990s lay in the fields of environmental, preventive, and behavioral health. The Navajo Division of Health (NDOH, formerly the DHIS) directed most of these activities. In 1981, the agency also assumed the functions of the Navajo Health Authority, ending that group's term of service to the Navajo Nation.[45]

The NDOH functioned as a tribe-controlled agency independent of the IHS, but the two organizations attempted to coordinate their efforts. According to NDOH Project Coordinator Peggy Nakai, the NDOH acted in support of the larger reservation medical program by "filling in some of those gaps from our end, to help the IHS so that they can do more for the people." Navajo employees, working either in the NDOH, the Tribal Health and Social Services Committee, or the NAIHS's Office of Tribal Affairs, facilitated communication between the tribal and federal agencies. Navajos such as NAIHS Tribal Affairs Director Ellouise DeGroat were particularly skilled mediators because they could draw on wide administrative experience gained from employment in both IHS and tribal health offices.[46]

Public health activity after 1980 exemplified the cooperative relationship between the tribe and the federal government, but also the logistic difficulties they faced in making that relationship work. For example, the IHS and the Navajo Tribal Utility Authority (NTUA) had to closely coordinate their efforts in sanitation and water projects to achieve maximum results with minimal funds. The IHS had to choose carefully where it developed piped-water projects, because the NTUA had to be able to afford to operate those projects after their completion. This consideration forced IHS engineers to rely on cisterns to meet the needs of people in sparsely populated areas. But working together, the NAIHS and NTUA were able to provide running water to 24,500 out of 40,100 Navajo homes by 1998 and estimated that they would be able to reach a goal of 100-percent coverage by 2006. In addition to the joint sanitation efforts, IHS sanitarians and field medical officers operated in conjunction with the tribe-administered CHR program to staff field health stations, conduct school education and immunization services, and assist elderly and disabled people in their homes.[47]

The IHS and tribe also combined forces in health education efforts. Public health workers, community health nurses, CHRs, the tribal radio station (KTNN), and the *Navajo Times* all helped disseminate information about impending epidemics and self-care. Some health education efforts required a great deal of effort on the part of medical workers, but relatively inexpensive billboards across the reservation and adjacent to IHS facilities helped convey messages such as "Lifestyle of the Past: Beat Diabetes with Fitness and Nutrition," and "Keep the Tradition: Buckle Up."

The tribe played a particularly large role in health education efforts to fight the spread of HIV. During the late 1980s, the IHS responded relatively slowly to the small but steadily increasing number of AIDS cases on Indian reservations. By the early 1990s, Navajo leaders and community members viewed it as a high priority problem. Larry Curley, director of the NDOH, urged the tribe to take action in 1992, arguing that "[W]e have to come up with a policy that will treat the problem in an appropriate way to our culture." In the late 1980s and 1990s, a variety of tribe- and community-sponsored groups emerged to lead the awareness effort, including the Central Navajo AIDS Coalition, the Navajo Nation AIDS/HIV Network, and beginning in 1993, the NDOH-administered Navajo Nation AIDS Office.[48]

While the Navajo Nation focused on health education as a response to HIV, the IHS took advantage of drug therapy innovations to treat patients already infected by the disease. By 1998, the NAIHS could point to some encouraging results. Largely attributable to the combined effect of the drugs Crixivan, AZT, and 3TC, the number of AIDS deaths on the reservation fell from six out of twenty patients in 1996, to three out of twenty-seven in 1997.[49]

The Navajo Nation and IHS also worked to control diabetes, but with less encouraging results. Navajos living with diabetes had access to a fairly wide variety of clinical services, including dialysis treatments offered through the IHS, community-operated clinics such as one at Dennehotso, Arizona, and the nongovernment Total Renal Care network. However, the great distance between these facilities and Navajo homes, and poor roads in parts of the reservation, turned treatment into an ordeal. "There were some people that had to go for dialysis treatments three times per week, and it was an all-day affair," said Peggy Nakai. "They had to get up early in the morning and be transported to Tuba City where the nearest dialysis center is."[50]

In addition to direct medical services, the IHS and the NDOH addressed diabetes through health education and nutrition programs. For instance, the NDOH administered the Women, Infants and Children program, the Navajo Nation Food Distribution Program, and the New Dawn program, which encouraged Navajos to eat better and more traditional foods by learning horticulture and food storage methods. But in spite of these efforts, the disease grew more problematic.[51]

The IHS and tribe also worked to reduce auto-accident fatalities, even though traditionally conceived Western medicine seemed less capable of success in this regard. Medical providers attacked the problem by expanding their medical activities in creative ways. The NAIHS purchased video cameras for the Navajo Nation Police Department for taping suspected DWI offenders and supplied infant seats to Navajo drivers whenever possible. In a telling illustration of how far the IHS had come in expanding its scope and accommodating Navajo concepts, the Northern Navajo Medical Center asked singer Jones Benally to bless 260 car seats in July 1997. Benally walked among the seats, lined up on the Shiprock High School football field bleachers, blessing them with corn pollen. As a *Navajo Times* columnist pointed out, car seats were now protecting Navajo infants riding in the back of trucks, as cradle boards once protected them on the back of horse-drawn wagons.[52]

The Navajo Nation used multiple tactics to deal with auto accidents.

It became one of the first tribal governments to impose mandatory seat-belt laws, preceding the state of Arizona in its initiative. Assisted by NAIHS employees, the Navajo Nation also attempted to reduce fatalities with a DWI law that included mandatory sentences and punishments more severe than those found in New Mexico state laws. Navajo residents worked to make reservation highways safer by raising awareness of the dangers posed by drinking and driving. In 1996, community members from San Juan County, New Mexico, sponsored the "Sacred Journey to Save Lives," a marathon, health fair, and "sobriety powwow," staged along State Highway 44. In combination with better-constructed highways, all of these efforts contributed to declining numbers of auto-accident deaths.[53]

Alcoholism treatment efforts also contributed to safer roadways, and helped the Navajo Nation to deal with a wide variety of alcohol-related illnesses. IHS efforts to reduce alcoholism on Indian lands rose steadily after P.L. 94-437 transferred existing government programs to the agency. Between 1978 and 1987, nationwide IHS expenditures dealing with alcoholism increased from $3.8 million to $24.8 million. After 1990 the IHS devoted special attention to preventive programs for young people through its Teen Life Center and other programs. Other detoxification and counseling services were available to Navajos through a variety of private organizations, including the Southwest Indian Foundation, Friendship Services, Good Orderly Directions, the Path of Renewal, and, in Gallup, the Na'nizhoozhi Center, Inc.[54]

The tribe fought particularly hard against alcoholism, first through the Office of Navajo Economic Opportunity and later through the NDOH. The NDOH's Behavioral Health Division addressed alcohol and substance abuse through a combination of preventive and counseling efforts and incorporated the use of traditional healers and sweat baths in its procedures. In the 1990s, the NDOH also began planning a "Navajo Nation Mobile Treatment Unit" and a larger "Navajo Nation Recovery Center," both of which planned to combine the use of Western-style therapy with traditional healing.[55]

Many involved with Navajo health care believed that traditional ways offered the best solutions to the alcoholism crisis. Although both auto-accident fatality and cirrhosis rates declined, clinical care professionals had difficulty addressing alcoholism and drug abuse, because the underlying causes for these problems remained. Mary Roessel, a psychiatrist at the

Northern Navajo Medical Center during the 1990s, questioned the value of sending people with substance abuse problems away for treatment in medical centers, and she looked for ways to combine traditional methods with community- and family-based treatment. When patients go to clinical facilities, she pointed out, "[T]hey're away from their problems, their family, and all the different behaviors that kept their health problems going," Roessel explained. When they return, she said, "[T]hey might have changed but the family hasn't had any opportunity to change and the same group of people are there to drink with; the same problems of unemployment are there too."[56]

Neither the IHS, the tribe, nor any other supplier of Western medicine could offer miracle solutions to the health care dilemmas that continued to plague Navajos at the end of the century. Certainly, better funding would have helped them achieve higher levels of success, and perhaps bring Navajo health patterns to parity with national averages. Western medicine alone, however, could only do so much to deal with HIV, cancer, diabetes, accidents, alcoholism, and other medical threats that grew as the old killers gradually faded. But by working together, and by implementing an increasingly comprehensive medical strategy, the Navajo Area IHS and Navajo tribe had made great strides.

Toward Full Control

By the 1980s, and especially by the 1990s, the Navajo Nation did much more than to advise the IHS or provide supplementary medical services. In public and behavioral health, the Navajo government played a central role in delivering care to the Navajo people. Navajos were present not only in tribal programs, but throughout the IHS structure, from ancillary staff to physicians and administrators. Clearly the Navajo Nation had the desire, the personnel, and the experience necessary to take full advantage of the self-determination process.

So an obvious question remained: Why had the Navajo Nation not taken control over the hospitals and clinics upon which its people relied? It would seem that since the hospitals and clinics were at the heart of the Western medical system, and the most concrete symbols of its presence in Navajo country, that the tribe would make use of contracting programs to take over their administration. For decades, the Navajos had been as involved or more involved in Western medical delivery than any other tribe. Yet in 1992, only the Navajo Area and Billings Area had not taken over the administration of government hospitals. In contrast, tribes in the Alaska, Nashville, California, Bemidji and Portland Areas administered the majority of their health care facilities through P.L. 93-638. Nationwide, the IHS still operated forty-two hospitals while tribes administered only eight, but ninety-three of 158 health centers were tribe administered.[57]

Of course, the Navajos had shown that they could exercise control over Western medical delivery in other ways, that is, that 638 contracting was not the only way to obtain their health care goals. But the Navajo Nation's hesitancy to take the 638 option did not reflect a lack of desire to administer its own clinics and hospitals. Instead, tribal leaders recognized that, as the largest reservation population with the most expensive network of medical facilities, caution was paramount. A variety of factors slowed down the Navajo tribe's 638 contracting process, including shifting leadership in the tribal government. Some tribal leaders were enthusiastic about the process, while others were concerned that the Navajo Nation did not possess the expertise necessary to administer the IHS services efficiently. Certainly, the complexities of operating hospitals as large as the Gallup Indian Medical Center were great. But to meet this challenge, the Navajo Nation could draw from a large and growing pool of skilled Navajo administrators, physicians, and nurses. In addition, the NHA and NDOH had already taken many of the steps necessary to prepare the Navajo Nation for the task.[58]

Employee concerns also slowed the 638 process. Many Navajo and non-Navajo employees were somewhat hesitant about the prospect of contracting because they feared that their wages, benefits, and maybe even their positions could be at risk. When the Fort Defiance Indian Health Board expressed an interest in operating its newly planned hospital as a community venture, some employees expressed their doubts. "There's a lot of concern about how this will affect employees working here now as far as our federal benefits are concerned and the possibility that the running of the hospital will be affected by local or tribal politics," said one worker.[59]

Most of these concerns were secondary compared to the issue of funding. Past inadequacies in the 638 contracting procedure, both in the degree of continued federal influence and the lack of funds, caused the Navajo Nation to be very cautious in its approach. Historical experiences had taught the tribal leadership to be wary of any federal attempt to abrogate its responsibilities to Indian people. The Navajo leadership did not worry as much about the return of "termination" in its older form, than about "termination by non-appropriation" or underfunding. As NDOH official Peggy Nakai observed in 1993:

> [T]here is no money in 638 contracting. When you contract from the government, say $300,000 for this year—thereafter it's only $300,000. They don't add to it. That's basically one of the drawbacks of 638 contracting. There's no money in it. You may be doing it as a way to provide better services than the IHS did and as a result the demand for your services will increase, but you don't have enough money to pay for that increase.

Conversely, as NAIHS Chief Medical Officer Dr. Doug Peter pointed out, 638 contracting locked funds in, so funding levels were less susceptible to downward fluctuations in the federal budget. But the fear remained that the Navajo Nation would be left with greater responsibilities without the funds necessary to maintain current levels of care.[60]

In spite of such concerns, many Navajos saw real advantages to the contracting process as it would apply to IHS facilities. Pasquelita Waseta-Joe, a representative from Red Lake Chapter, contended that one of the greatest advantages would be the "flexibility" to "develop your program to have services according to the needs of the community." Others felt that the Navajos might be able to stretch their funds further than could the federal government, or pointed out that financial troubles would plague reservation medical care either way.[61]

In the mid-1990s, other options became available to the Navajo Nation. In contrast to 638 contracting, in which tribes would take fixed sums from the federal government on a program-by-program basis, and in which the IHS would maintain a degree of authority, newer "self-governance" compacts offered a means for tribes to take total control over the medical system in a single step. As IHS Director Dr. Michael Trujillo explained, through self-governance, tribes had the option to negotiate base budgets with the IHS that they would keep as a guaranteed sum, while other funds would be appropriated annually by Congress.[62]

In 1995, the Navajo Division of Health established a Navajo Nation Health Care Design Team to look into the possibility of administering the

NAIHS's network of facilities. At a meeting in Albuquerque, New Mexico, in early 1998, the team made public its plan to assume a $280 million-contract from the IHS, along with its six hospitals and dozens of clinics. The plan called for a complete transfer to the tribe and for fusing IHS services together with the NDOH. "The mission of the Navajo Nation Health Care System," as the design team referred to the proposed result of the tribal transfer, "is to elevate the health status and quality and quantity of life of Navajo people through the provision of culturally appropriate, responsive, cost effective, high quality health care services that are prevention oriented and reflect our respect for the teachings and gifts of both western medicine and traditional healing." The Tribal Council planned to meet in October 2000 to decide whether to approve the plan. Even if the Navajo Nation were to assume the NAIHS's role, the tribe would still be heavily reliant on outside funding sources, including the federal and state governments through contract arrangements, Medicare, and Medicaid. However, choosing to administer the IHS facilities would represent another landmark in the Navajo Nation's effort to incorporate Western medicine on Navajo terms.[63]

The Native American Church of Navajoland

Formalized as the Native American Church of Navajoland, peyotism continued to offer healing to thousands of Navajos. Previously, the Navajo leadership outlawed peyote and served as its primary opponent, but in the 1980s and 1990s, the tribal government acted as one of the NAC's greatest protectors. Along with many Navajos, the leadership had come to view the peyote religion as not only an "Indian," but also as a distinctly "Navajo" practice.

One of the NAC's greatest strengths on the Navajo Nation had been its ability over time to accommodate multiple identities. James Tomchee, president of the NAC of Navajoland in the 1980s, summed up its growing link to Diné ways and its multicultural nature:

By the way the peyote ceremony is practiced, I would say about 99 percent of whatever is taking place in there is basically Navajo. Prayers are all in Navajo; many Navajo traditional prayers have been integrated and incorporated into the ceremonies. . . . So right now, NAC consists of three belief doctrines: Plains Indian, the Judeo-Christian and the Navajo.

In fact, according to Tomchee, NAC members saw themselves as protectors of, rather than threats to, Navajo traditional ceremonialism. For instance, the presence of liquor had corrupted many of the ceremonies, so the NAC's role in controlling alcoholism made it an ally to the traditional ways. Tomchee thus saw positive links between the NAC and traditional healing. Some healers, of course, still saw any links between the NAC and traditional ways as corruptive. However, most healers and NAC members, including Tomchee, agreed that the two forms of spirituality remained distinct from one another.[64]

By the mid-1990s, official Navajo membership in the NAC had reached approximately 60,000. Many others had not become registered members but took advantage of the peyote religion as a supplemental form of spirituality and medicine. The NAC, of course, had not become universally accepted among the Diné, but many recognized its healing powers. The NAC provided special comfort to people suffering from chronic ailments that Western medicine seemed powerless to cure, including cancer.[65]

Even though Navajo and federal law protected the Native American Church, its members still found their religious rights challenged off the reservation. In 1990, a U.S. Supreme Court decision allowed states the right to prohibit peyote use as a drug. *Employment Division, Department of Human Resources of Oregon et al. v. Alfred Smith et al.* stemmed from an incident in Oregon, where two Indian men, Alfred Smith and Galen Black, had been fired from a drug rehabilitation group because they were NAC members. Twenty-two states, including California, had laws in the early 1990s that did not conform to the federal standards for peyote possession. In addition, while Navajo peyotists in Arizona did have legal protection, the state placed the burden of proof on NAC members, who had to document their affiliation with the organization to avoid prosecution.[66]

In response to these perceived threats, a group of American Indian leaders, including Peterson Zah, former NAC of Navajoland President David Clark, and its then-leader Robert Billie Whitehorse, petitioned the federal government to provide new protection for the peyote religion. In particular they sought amendments to the American Indian Religious Freedom Act (AIRFA) of 1978. Speaking in front of members of the Senate Select Committee on Indian Affairs in February 1993, Zah argued that "[O]ppression, persecution, and discrimination are consistently experienced by members of the Native American Church outside of the

Navajo Nation." Similarly, Whitehorse went before the U.S. House Subcommittee on Native American Affairs, explaining to the congressional delegates that "We are a spiritual people. We cannot be asked to leave our religion at home. Nor can we be asked to restrict our travel or our employment options based on a patchwork of dangerous state laws." As a sign of support, thousands of Navajos sent letters to senators and representatives in favor of the amendments, and the Navajo Tribal Council authorized funds to pay for one hundred NAC members to travel to Washington, D.C., as lobbyists.[67]

Navajo efforts paid off in 1994, when the House and Senate approved H.R. 4230, amending AIRFA. The new law placed the burden on states to prove "overriding interests" before violating the rights of NAC members. Further encouraging news for the NAC arrived in April of 1997, when the Department of Defense established a new policy allowing military personnel to attend peyote ceremonies while on leave.[68]

The Native American Church took other steps to ensure that peyote's healing power would pass on to future generations. In addition to protecting the rights of its members to use peyote, the NAC attempted to protect the increasingly scarce cactus itself. By 1996, the NAC had raised $127,000 from its members and helped establish security measures for licensed peyote growers in southern Texas, aimed at protecting peyote from thieves who sometimes climbed fences to steal the plant. The NAC also initiated a policy whereby only skilled collectors could harvest the cactus, because too many had been destroyed by improper gathering techniques. With a $25,000 grant from the Navajo Nation, Diné NAC members also began constructing their first official church on the reservation in 1996, a 1,300-square-foot structure including a large meeting room, offices, and a cultural museum, as well as a traditional hogan in the back and room for teepees. With this building, the Native American Church of Navajoland provided a concrete symbol of the religion's connection to the land surrounded by the four sacred mountains.[69]

Traditional Healing

During the century's last twenty years, traditional healing practices were threatened by the same forces that jeopardized their existence in the 1960s and 1970s. Traditional healers, most of whom were over fifty years old, looked upon changes in Navajo country with apprehension. Signs of accelerating cultural and language loss among the young people particularly worried them. As a *Navajo Times* editorial claimed in 1980, the elders

> see the Navajo youth torn between two cultures and many deciding that the Anglo culture is best. They see a breakdown with the clanship system and Navajo youths breaking clan laws by marrying within the clan. They say that these problems will continue through the 1980s and will probably get worse unless the Navajo people make a concerted effort to return to their traditions and language.

Alfred Yazzie, a former police officer and a singer, summed up modern trends and worries saying, "[T]oday we live in a world of politics, a fast-paced world, and we are forgetting ourselves." Harry Walters, a teacher of Navajo culture at Diné College, believed that the Navajos were suffering the consequences. "We are out of balance," he said. "Our people are disregarding our traditional laws and all of this affects the environment and it also affects our behavior."[70]

The loss of ceremonies and traditional practitioners seemed to accelerate in the 1980s and 1990s. Whereas the NHA had estimated that there were at least 1,029 healers on the reservation in 1979, healers in the 1990s estimated that there were only seven hundred ceremonial practitioners. No matter the estimates, Navajo elders did not doubt that their numbers were dwindling. "It's not a problem of the future," Earnest Becenti said in 1991 about the shortage of healers, "it's a problem we face right now." Taylor Dixon seconded Becenti's opinion. "Whatever we do, we had better start doing it soon, because we are coming to the point where it may be too late."[71]

In spite of these continuing concerns, there were signs that the Navajo Nation would retain its healing practices and traditional cultural beliefs well into the future. While increased gang activity and statistics showing that 60 percent of Navajo children did not speak their native language troubled many adults, evidence existed of enduring, if not growing interest, on the part of young people and adults alike, in traditional healing. As Jennie Joe has argued, there had been a "renaissance of indigenous medicine" among American Indians nationwide, in part because of a "re-awakening of cultural pride" and in part because, like other Americans, they were dissatisfied with Western medicine's ability to treat chronic ailments.[72]

Indeed, a casual observer could see that traditional beliefs still ran deep in Diné society. In the summer of 1994, some Navajo workers at the Navajo Nation Health, Social Services, and Community Development offices in Window Rock spotted snakes, traditionally considered a cause of disharmony and illness, inside their building. Many of them, who an intern in the office thought had "lost a little attentiveness to spirituality" before the incident, requested singers to cleanse them and the structure and showed a renewed interest in the traditional beliefs. Stories of miraculous cures achieved through traditional healing were not uncommon among people who spent time on the reservation. Many Navajos could tell stories such as Elton Naswood's, a college student who became afflicted with a serious rash that non-Indian physicians could not cure. He returned home to a healer who decided that Naswood had violated a taboo and brought sickness upon himself by playing with a cactus as a small boy. Naswood was amazed that the healer knew about the cactus without being told. The healer applied an herbal remedy to affected areas of his skin, and the rash disappeared the following day. Others, including non-Navajos and medical workers, told of sings curing life-threatening diseases, such as cancer.[73]

Many Navajo organizations and individuals took action to preserve the ceremonies to meet the continued demand for traditional healing. The Medicine Men's Association (MMA, known as the Diné Spiritual and Cultural Society from 1990 to 1999) continued to serve as the Navajo Nation's central body for protecting, promoting, and preserving traditional healing. Many traditional practitioners, however, remained outside the group, either because they had difficulty traveling to meetings or because they still opposed the organization.[74]

Among their many activities, the MMA helped the tribe petition the federal government to aid it in the quest to reclaim lost cultural paraphernalia. The Native American Graves Protection and Repatriation Act (NAGPRA), passed in 1990, assisted such efforts by giving Indian people legal recourse to claim skeletal remains and other items from museums, universities, and other public institutions. In 1996, implementing NAGPRA, the Navajo Nation regained possession of a Nightway jish (a bundle used in traditional ceremonies) that had once belonged to Hosteen Hataał ii Walker and had since fallen, illegally, into the hands of a private dealer. By agreement with the Navajo Nation, Wilbert Williams, the healer's grandson, took back the jish and promised to never let it leave Navajo country. A cause for celebration, the bundle's return set a precedent for the future repatriation of traditional items and symbolized the Diné effort to reclaim their ceremonies.[75]

The Navajo tribal leadership also took more direct action to preserve traditional healing. Recognizing the urgency posed by declining numbers of singers, the Tribal Council Education Committee began working with the MMA in 1997 on plans for a tribe-sponsored apprentice healer training program—the first such program since the Rough Rock Demonstration School's Navajo Mental Health Program ceased operating in 1983. With support from Navajo President Albert Hale and other tribal leaders, the apprentice program planned to train two groups of healers during a given year, divided into those training for summer ceremonies and those hoping to conduct winter ceremonies. The tribe planned to pay a $400-per-month stipend to students and $500 to teachers. The Navajo Medicineman Apprenticeship Program, as it was designated, began recruiting students in 1999.[76]

Many Navajos, and some students of Navajo traditional healing, remained confident that the old ways would endure because the Diné needed them and would find ways to keep them. As scholar Charlotte Frisbie wrote, "[T]here is no immediate reason to suspect that traditional [Navajo] religion, which has already withstood a variety of enormous internal and external pressures, will suddenly lose its resilience. Why should age-old flexibility, accommodation, tolerance, and inclusiveness cease? Why should traditional epistemology, which has long supported the continual process of adaptation, fail?"[77]

Irvin Tso served as a testament to their optimism. In 1984, at the age of fifteen, Tso became the youngest Navajo healer. "When I saw my first ceremony, with the chanting, prayers, and sand painting, it drew me in so much that I knew immediately that this is what I wanted to be," Tso later explained. His struggle to attain that goal exemplified the obstacles young Navajos faced in balancing their desire to become healers with modern demands, and the strong desire and discipline some of them demonstrated. "I would go to school, come back and do my homework until nine P.M. or ten P.M.," said Tso. "My uncle, Norris Nez, who was teaching me, would come over and we would go over the chants and prayers until one A.M. or three A.M. Then I would go to sleep and get up at seven A.M. to get ready for school."[78]

As the Diné focused more on preserving their traditional medical practices, IHS health care grew more receptive to the traditional concerns of its patients, adding more concrete support to their policy of cross-cultural cooperation. In addition to giving traditional hogans a place in the hospitals for healers and patients to use as they saw fit, the Navajo Area IHS hired Jones Benally as permanent staff at Winslow in 1996 to offer traditional services to patients in a hogan he erected on hospital grounds.[79]

In addition to overtures from the Indian Health Service, the federal government showed greater respect for the Navajo healers by allowing Diné patients to deduct traditional ceremonies from their income taxes. Also, in 1990, the Veterans Administration agreed to experiment with a plan to reimburse Navajo veterans for traditional healing services, and in 1996, the U.S. Department of Veterans Affairs (DVA) granted the Navajo Nation DVA funds for that purpose. The first ten Navajo veterans to benefit from the reimbursement program received grants averaging $250. Meanwhile, some private companies, including Broken Hills Property Minerals in Farmington, included traditional healing in their medical plans in the 1980s and 1990s.[80]

It is likely that Navajo insistence on the importance of their traditional ways combined with changing American attitudes about health care in general to encourage the continued growth of the cross-cultural process. Scholars have suggested that the rising popularity of "alternative" (or "new age") medicine among the general American population made non-Indians, including government medical providers, more receptive to traditional practices. As Americans became increasingly dissatisfied with Western medicine's weaknesses in treating chronic ailments and with the relative inattention they found from primary care providers, millions looked for other forms of healing. According to a 1993 study, one in three American adults were taking advantage of some form of alternative healing, including acupuncture, chiropractic, and herbal remedies. Native medicine, including Navajo healing, drew particular interest. The holistic approach, common to many Native cultures, appealed to non-Indians mentally and emotionally, and many others believed that Native American herbalists possessed secret medical knowledge that could cure seemingly incurable diseases. While "new-age" interest in Navajo healing could be viewed by some Diné as intrusive, it also may have encouraged medical providers to be more accepting of the traditional needs of their Navajo patients.[81]

More receptive IHS attitudes toward the healers also reflected respectful relations between individual medical employees and the Navajo community. Respect, however, did not always translate into understanding. Cross-cultural accommodation was not complete and perhaps never will be. Indeed, because so few non-Indian IHS employees served the Navajo Nation for more than two or three years, and because they were trained in Western medicine, they were more likely to view their relationship with Navajo healers as one of coexistence rather than cooperation. As Jennie Joe has argued, physicians and healers got along better than they used to, but they had not yet become "colleagues."[82]

But many non-Navajo medical providers moved beyond "coexistence" with traditional healing. Those non-Navajo medical providers who chose to stay in Navajo country long term often formed stronger cross-cultural bonds and were more likely to form cooperative relationships with the healers. According to Dr. Don Lewis-Kratsik at the Fort Defiance hospital, many physicians displayed a willingness to administer herbal remedies that traditional healers sent for their patients. Such accommodation required physicians to find a balance between their professional judgment and the healers' wishes. Lewis-Kratsik faced such a challenge when a patient experiencing a severe skin rash came to Fort Defiance covered in ashes from an earlier healing ceremony. The healer insisted that the ash could not be washed away for a specified period of time, which made it difficult for Lewis-Kratsik to attend to the patient as he normally would. In another instance, a healer sent an herbal concoction for a seriously ill patient who was receiving nourishment intravenously. In both cases, Lewis-Kratsik did all he could to heed the wishes of the healers without compromising his own treatments.[83]

Diné College offered even those non-Navajo medical workers who had not been in the area long a chance to learn about Navajo ways. In 1985, the Continuing Education Department at the college began its Navajo Cultural Orientation for Health and Social Services Providers program. This two-and-a-half-day immersion program helped orient health care providers to the IHS by asking them to participate in social games designed to give them a better understanding of common cross-cultural tensions. The program staff also used the opportunity to describe some of the Navajo outlooks on healing, and reinforced those lessons by taking students on tours of traditional hogans. Later in the course, the program staff discussed methods that could be used to integrate traditional and Western medicine.[84]

Although IHS nurses and other professionals were enthusiastic about the program, few physicians participated, and when the staff contracted with the Gallup Indian Medical Center to conduct the course for its medical doctors, they were somewhat disappointed with the results. According to Fran Kosik, the project's original coordinator and a one-time IHS nurse, some physicians interpreted the showing of a film about the importance of traditional healing as an attack on their beliefs. "There were a couple of surgeons in particular," she recalls, "who were turned off by the whole thing and ended up leaving the room. My impression was that these people were required to come, so they weren't really open to the whole thing." Consequently, Kosik and the new coordinator, Lena Fowler, decided against contracts with the IHS that required employees to attend, favoring strictly voluntary participation.[85]

Beginning in the mid-1990s, the K'e Project also facilitated better relations between IHS physicians and healers, and even involved NAC roadmen in this process. Funded through the U.S. Department of Health and Human Services, the K'e Project provided family counseling that took advantage of both "traditional and western modalities." In accordance with its cross-cultural philosophy, the project worked closely with IHS mental health workers, the BIA, and NDOH Behavioral Health Services personnel. It focused on bringing IHS officials, traditional healers, and roadmen together to try to establish written guidelines for traditional Navajo ceremonies and peyote rituals, hoping that this would make it easier for Navajo healers and NAC practitioners to obtain contract payments from the IHS. The project complemented ongoing efforts by the MMA to facilitate contracts with the IHS and private insurance companies by setting standards for its members.[86]

Of course, changing IHS attitudes about traditional healing also reflected the growing number of Navajo medical professionals employed by the agency. Many of the Navajo students who began attending medical school during the 1970s and 1980s, including Beulah Allen, M.D., Lori Arviso Alvord, M.D., and Mary Roessel, M.D., returned to serve the Navajo Nation. Like many Navajo adults, Allen and Alvord had come of age at a time when schools discouraged Diné children from speaking their language and practicing their cultural traditions. At the end of the century, however, Allen and Alvord were among many Navajos who felt strongly connected to their people and took a new interest in the old ways. "I began to honor and cherish my tribal membership," Alvord wrote, "and in the years that followed I came to understand that such membership is central to mental health, to spiritual health, to physical health." Both women made an effort to learn the language, and both came to know the power of the traditional ceremonies in their lives. As such, they formed cooperative relationships with traditional healers, and they could empathize with patients who utilized both Western medicine and Navajo healing.[87]

Lori Arviso Alvord, who served as a surgeon at GIMC (she was the first Navajo woman to become a surgeon) before leaving to accept a position on the faculty at Dartmouth in 1998, always looked for ways to shape her services to meet Navajo cultural standards. She found the task particularly rewarding because she could see a connection between the healing ways she learned in medical school, and those she learned from her people. The body's internal balance, as taught to her in medical school, conformed to the spiritual balance of hózhǫ. Because she experienced life as both a physician and as a patient, she came to understand that she could break down the cultural and spiritual barriers that sometimes existed between Western medicine and her patients. Realizing that patients regarded direct questions about their bodies as rude and embarrassing, she let patients communicate key medical information to her at their own pace through conversation; she used Navajo terms whenever possible and she showed proper respect by only revealing the necessary parts of their bodies during physical examinations.[88]

Although Alvord had a very difficult time deciding to leave the Navajo Nation for Dartmouth, she found that she could continue to serve her tribe by aiding young Indian medical students, and by using her new position to teach others of the importance of cross-cultural medical accommodation. In a book she wrote with Elizabeth Cohen Van Pelt, *The Scalpel and The Silver Bear,* Alvord encouraged non-Indians to learn more about Native medical ways, not only so they could be more sensitive providers to Indian people, but also because Navajo and other Native beliefs in holistic medicine offered solutions for the shortcomings of modern medicine. "It is my hope and vision that groups of people can learn from one another—that the culture of medicine can learn from the culture of Native Americans," she wrote, "and that both can be richer for the experience."[89]

Mary Roessel shared Allen's and Arviso's commitment to blending multiple forms of healing. She grew up with a strong understanding of and respect for traditional beliefs and practices. Her father Robert Roessel, although a non-Indian, had an abiding interest in Navajo culture, and her mother, Ruth Roessel, was a well-known Navajo educator. As a young person, Dr. Roessel recalled meetings between psychiatrist Karl Menninger and her grandfather, who practiced traditional medicine. Having observed Menninger's respect for "the Navajo way of healing," Roessel became interested in psychiatry. "Maybe that would be a profession that would really compliment my background as a Navajo," she thought. "I wouldn't have to compromise too much of myself to be able to practice as a doctor." She went on to advocate a cross-cultural approach to mental health, and as a psychiatrist at the IHS hospital in Shiprock, she devised numerous programs aimed at incorporating traditional healers and traditional concepts into the mental health process.[90]

Debra Watchman acted as a different kind of Navajo medical pioneer in 1996 when she became the first Navajo licensed chiropractor. Watchman became interested in "how the body works" while growing up on a ranch, and her experiences with physical therapists after a horseback riding accident fueled her desire to heal with her hands. As did other Navajo medical providers, she saw a strong connection between her form of healing and what Navajo singers and diagnosticians did. "I've experienced the traditional ways of healing," she explained. "I've watched medicine people use their hands as an x-ray, the power of the crystals and the coals. I believe very much in the Navajo way. But I would like to see what I can do as a healer too." At the same time, she believed that certain cases required the assistance of a medical doctor and tried to establish a rapport with local practitioners. Watchman's experience exemplified the complexity of the medical accommodation process for the Navajos and provided yet another option for Diné patients.[91]

No Navajo person's individual views on health and healing were or are representative of those of the rest of the Diné population, but Annie Kahn from Lukachukai, Arizona, may have summed up how many Navajos had come to view healing in the twentieth century. Kahn assisted cross-cultural medical accommodation by instructing non-Navajo medical providers about traditional Diné healing. She saw the power in non-Navajo forms of education, communication, and medicine, and incorporated them into her identity as a Diné. While working to establish relationships with IHS physicians, she devoted much of her time to teaching students at Diné College about the importance of tradition. "Because I want to be understood, I have to work twice as hard. This is ancient beauty itself." Kahn said:

I know the earth and the mountains. I'm also glad that your society put up some kind of school and gave me a piece of paper and a pencil to write. In the days of old, the medicine women also had to work twice as hard because they had to work without the help of science, without the help of hospitals, transportation, modern goods. . . . I have learned that white man's education, his medicine, and his science is learned by exploring—by trial and error. This later led me to believe that my children and their children's children would need both cultures—the western and the Native American medicine.[92]

· CONCLUSION ·

THE "MYSTERY ILLNESS"

In May 1993, young people were dying in the New Mexico portion of the Navajo reservation and no one knew why. The victims experienced flu-like symptoms for a few days before they began gasping for air as their lungs filled with fluid. Out of a group of four Navajo men and women who experienced this acute respiratory distress syndrome, three died, including a track star from the Santa Fe Indian School, his fiancée, and her brother's girlfriend. Bruce Tempest, a physician at the Gallup Indian Medical Center, was baffled by the young runner's death, and alarmed when he heard that this had not been an isolated case. Immediately after learning that the runner's fiancée had died with similar symptoms a few days earlier, Tempest began calling other IHS physicians across the reservation and alerted the New Mexico state medical examiner that they might have an epidemic on their hands.[1]

The "Mystery Illness," as some press releases termed it, terrorized Navajos and non-Navajos alike throughout the late spring and early summer of 1993. Before it ran its course, sixty-seven Americans had been infected, including twenty-two Navajos (of whom twelve died). Although the early cases tended to be young Navajos, the death toll included people ranging in age from twelve to sixty-nine and extended as far away as eastern Texas. By 3 June, epidemiologists at the Centers for Disease Control (CDC) in Atlanta, Georgia, had isolated its cause, and newspapers two days later relayed to the public that the killer was hantavirus, borne by the deer mouse and other rodents.[2]

A discussion of the hantavirus epidemic of 1993 has been saved for the conclusion because reactions to it, on the part of both Navajos and non-Indians, are illustrative of many of the major themes in twentieth-century Navajo health care. Because it happened so quickly, appeared to be so catastrophic, and gained so much attention on the reservation and nationwide, it spotlighted various long-term trends in Navajo medical care for two months. In the process, it became evident how extensively things had changed on the Navajo Nation during the century. It demonstrated that Western medicine and Diné healing had reached a point where they were able to work cooperatively to meet shared goals. It also showed how far Western medical science had come since its early days on the reservation. Yet at the same time, the epidemic showed that much had stayed the same. Evidence of the enduring influence of Navajo traditional beliefs and practices during the epidemic was unmistakable. Reactions to the epidemic revealed that many Navajos were still ambivalent toward the Indian Health Service and the federal government, more than half a century after Navajos had accepted Western medicine.

Between May and July, state and federal medical providers, tribal health workers, and traditional healers came together in a massive cooperative effort to track down and defeat the "mystery illness." While the CDC studied tissue samples on the other side of the country, New Mexico Department of Health workers, IHS employees, and tribal community health representatives scoured the reservation looking for clues. IHS clinics and hospitals treated those who were in need, and attempted to calm the fears of hundreds of people who invaded their lobbies asking to be tested. Meanwhile, political leaders did what they could to help. Tribal President Peterson Zah delivered public service announcements over the air waves, while senators from the Four-Corners states pushed through a $6-million emergency aid package for the reservation.[3]

Peterson Zah understood early on that practitioners of Western and Navajo medicine could be more effective working together than working alone, and he focused on the need to supplement the CDC, IHS, and Navajo Division of Health activity with help from traditional practitioners. Noting that "Western medicine has its limits," Zah dispatched tribal employees to seek information from the healers. The Navajo president admitted that the tribe required modern medical services and statistical studies to combat the epidemic, but "in certain situations," he said, "we have to rely on what we have lived with, traditionally, for all these years."[4]

Zah's approach proved highly effective, as the traditional healers played a vital role in aiding the epidemiological investigation. Throughout late May, IHS and CDC efforts to track down the cause behind the illness were inconclusive. Medical researchers considered and eliminated almost every factor they could think of, including plague, influenza, pneumonia, and a chemical known as phosphene (a sister compound to phosgene), sometimes used on the reservation to eradicate prairie dogs. Then Navajo elders and healers gave them some critical clues. They pointed out that the reservation had an unusually large harvest of piñon nuts that year and that rodents seemed to be more abundant. This information steered the investigation down the track that eventually led to the solution. Researchers found that an unusually wet winter had indeed led to flourishing piñons, which fed a larger number of rodents that invaded dwellings and spread hantavirus through their saliva and droppings.[5]

According to Ben Muneta, a Navajo physician working as an IHS epidemiologist, the healers had reasons for noting the connection between the piñons and the rodents. From discussions with older healers, Muneta learned that the Diné may have devised preventive measures against this particular disease centuries before. One woman in Monument Valley informed Muneta that the traditional ways told Navajos never to touch mice or allow them into their homes because the animals could cause disease. She also knew that this illness could spread through the air and that people must burn anything with which the mice had contact. Younger people considered those teachings embarrassing or illogical and had since ignored them, but the healers knew. Muneta realized that "The traditional healers are also scientists with centuries of experience."[6]

After discovering the possible connection between the epidemic and deer mice, employees from these organizations worked together to trap rodents for CDC researchers, laboring in 100-degree heat and risking exposure to the disease. At the same time, CHRs worked feverishly on Navajo language videotapes and brochures to educate people about possible dangers and, together with IHS environmental health employees, devised techniques for disinfecting homes. The IHS and NDOH also approved the emergency use of a drug known as ribavirin, which seemed to help impede the disease if administered to patients soon after symptomatic onset.[7]

Working alone, the CDC and IHS probably would have tracked down the hantavirus. In fact, although this particular epidemic resulted from a new mutation of the disease, the American medical community knew that hantaviruses had been present in North America for an indeterminate amount of time. Had it not been for budget cuts to the Army's hantavirus research, as scholar Laurie Garrett points out, the CDC and IHS may have been better prepared to respond than they were. Similarly, the healers may have brought the epidemic under control themselves, given enough time, based on their long experience with the ailment, or ones like it. However, it took cooperation between the Western medical practitioners and the healers to identify the disease as quickly as they did. Once the healers had helped the CDC identify the cause, the medical workers developed treatments and prevention measures that brought that particular outbreak under control (the disease has reemerged several times in the Four Corners area since that time, indicating that it is probably an endemic, if not necessarily an epidemic threat).[8]

The hantavirus example provides deeper insight into why Navajos have continued to value their traditional healing practices in the twentieth century. First and foremost, many Navajos follow the old teachings because they are handed down to them by the Holy People and are connected to their lives in every way; the traditional ceremonies are part of their cultural identity. Moreover, as many non-Indians have observed, the traditional practices have an enduring appeal because they provide emotional and mental support in times of great stress. As Muneta learned during the hantavirus epidemic, the traditional healers also understand a great deal about health care and offer those benefits to their patients. Whether passed down from the Holy People, learned over centuries of trial and error, or both, the traditional healing ways possess specific knowledge that has enabled the Navajos to thrive.

At the same time, the 1993 epidemic shed light on the forces that have threatened Diné healing. On one hand, signs of Navajo adherence to the traditional beliefs were overwhelming. By early June, it became difficult for Navajo patients to find traditional healers who did not already have long waiting lists of people seeking cleansing ceremonies. Yet the epidemic also prompted tribal elders to stress that far too many people had turned away from the traditional practices or treated them without proper respect.[9]

Many healers and elders believed that the Holy People were punishing the Navajos with this illness—that improper conduct had thrown the Diné out of harmony. "In the Navajo way, danger of this magnitude is not supposed to affect us because the Holy People protect us," said Lola Begay from Hardrock. "What have we done to deserve this?" Lori Belone of

Tolani Lake had an answer: "We have committed all the wrongs, sold, displayed, and lost our most religious possessions." In addition to a general loss of tradition, Belone had a long list of recent abuses of the old ways, including the playing of the Navajo shoe game after the winter and the disrespect shown by KTNN radio in broadcasting the traditional Monster Slayer story.[10]

Some healers, such as Earnest Becenti, believed that death had come to the Navajo Nation because too many young people failed to follow the traditions. As evidence of this, a few pointed to the high percentage of victims in the early days of the epidemic who were young and seemingly healthy. Other explanations included Mae Bekis's suggestion that the illness could be punishment for violating Diné Bikéyah with uranium mines. Becenti also wondered if the Navajos were paying for damage people had done to their world with "satellites, rockets, jet planes, pollution, and war." "There is a hole in the sky," he said, "and bad things are pouring through it." But Becenti also knew a solution: "We need to get back into harmony."[11]

Navajo interpretations of the illness reveal that Western medicine and traditional healing have never melded; they are still distinct from one another in the way they explain and treat illness. Western medical providers might explain that the healers helped them to track down the "cause" of the "mystery illness," but the healers did not see deer mice or even hantavirus as the "cause." As scholar Maureen Schwarz has argued, the healers might agree that the hantavirus existed and that the IHS could help them combat it, but nobody could "cure" it except the Navajos themselves. As in the beginning, Western medicine could coexist and even cooperate with Navajo traditional medicine, but never replace it.[12]

The hantavirus epidemic also illuminated the attitudes many Navajo people had toward the IHS, revealing both a continued reliance on its services and a mistrust of both the agency's intentions and those of the federal government. To a degree, criticisms leveled against the IHS during the outbreak were unfair, but they reflected a deep-seated ambivalence about government services based on decades of experience. In mid-June 1993, Tribal Council delegates began considering two resolutions, one asking for a multistate investigation of discrimination against Navajos because of the hantavirus, and the other asking for an independent investigation of the IHS and other federal agencies that responded to the epidemic. While the latter measure failed to pass, in part because Peterson

Zah opposed it, the actions reflected a mistrust of the IHS. Tribal Council Health and Social Services Committee Chairwoman Genevieve Jackson also criticized the IHS for being slow to report news of the epidemic. Rumors began to emerge by June that the federal government may have covered up the effects of biological warfare agents escaped from the Fort Wingate depot in New Mexico.[13]

Most tribal political leaders dismissed the alleged cover-up stories as unfounded rumors, but negative feelings directed toward the IHS were real, probably because people associated the agency with intrusive media coverage and a wave of discrimination Navajos faced from non-Indians. Critics believed they had found direct evidence of such dubious associations when the media began broadcasting information taken from a patient's file. People assumed that the IHS had released the information, but agency employees denied the charge. "Here we were trying desperately to protect patient confidentiality, and the public trust was eroding," said Bruce Tempest. "We were getting it from both sides, being accused of giving the press confidential information on the one hand, and charged with some conspiratorial cover-up on the other."[14]

Navajo families were particularly upset when local and national media reporters flocked to Navajo country, knocking on people's doors and asking questions about dead loved ones. One cartoon in the *Navajo Times* summed up how many people seemed to feel. A small girl stands at the door of a hogan, while outside awaits a herd of reporters, who strongly resemble rodents. "Grandma, Grandpa come quick! There's a whole bunch of rodents outside our house. What should we do?" the girl says. "Shut the door!" comes the reply from inside.[15]

In addition to the general disregard for Navajo residents shown by the media, Peterson Zah and others were upset by the tendency for some newspapers and television networks to refer to the mystery illness in its early days as "Navajo flu" or "Navajo disease." Navajos then had to deal with the discrimination that followed that stigma. Stories emerged of tourists driving across the reservation wearing surgical masks, and of waitresses and jewelry store merchants wearing protective gloves and masks when dealing with Navajo customers. Even worse, a school in the San Fernando Valley in California canceled a planned visit from Navajo school children, and the University of New Mexico required Navajo students enrolled for summer session and basketball camp to get clearance from the IHS.[16]

It would seem that the IHS had very little, if anything, to do with a variety of negative incidents on and off the reservation in those months, but a general sense that it was a non-Navajo institution, sponsored by a federal government that could not be trusted, continued to cast a shadow over the agency. Still, the agency proved more culturally sensitive than did one of its state counterparts. New Mexico Department of Health officials did not improve government relations with the tribe when they advised the Navajos not to hold healing ceremonies lest they stir up the disease from dirt floors.[17]

Despite criticisms of the IHS during the tense days of the hantavirus epidemic, the IHS had shown, both during the epidemic and in general, that working in conjunction with the tribe, it could accomplish a great deal. Overall, Western medical services, largely administered through the IHS, but coming from tribe, community, missionary, state, and private sources as well, improved significantly among Navajos in the last half of the twentieth century. In particular, the comprehensive model of care had been very effective in dealing with infectious diseases and infant mortality. Western medical providers also became increasingly respectful of Navajo ways and needs in the latter half of the twentieth century. To some extent, these changed cultural attitudes resulted from an influx of Navajo administrators, physicians, nurses, and other medical employees into the agency. On the other hand, underfunding and understaffing contributed to high rates of staff turnover that reduced Western medicine's effectiveness in Navajo country. Although many Navajos recognized the benefits of Western medicine, and the IHS in particular, many still believed that much needed to be improved, both in terms of the quantity and quality of services provided and the cultural sensitivity with which they were delivered.

Because the Navajo Nation's leaders recognized the desire on the part of its people to use multiple forms of medical care, the tribal government became increasingly involved in promoting Western medicine, traditional healing, and eventually the Native American Church as the century progressed. Throughout the twentieth century, the Navajo Nation played ever increasing roles in advising Western medical providers, lobbying for better services, and supplementing those services with their own. Since the 1970s, the tribe also considered the option of taking full control of Western medicine. Although budget worries caused the Navajo Nation to hesitate in this regard, there were signs that in the near future Navajos would have even greater influence over medical care on the reservation.

During the twentieth century, the Navajos, sometimes working against and sometimes with the U.S. government and other non-Navajo groups, overcame a great deal in their quest for medical self-determination. Among the obstacles standing in their way were government assimilationist and termination policies, poorly conceived and funded medical services, and internal disputes over the desirability and proper use of certain forms of healing. Navajos still faced similar challenges at the end of the century, and not all Navajos, of course, agreed about the course of action they should take to maintain their medical choices in the future. Nonetheless, tribal leaders, healers, roadmen, nurses, physicians, and patients had made a concerted effort to retain access to multiple forms of healing, not as "alternatives" to each other, but as combined forces leading toward health, harmony, and long life.[18]

· NOTES ·

List of Abbreviations

AIOHC   Navajo Transcripts, American Indian Oral History Collection, 1967–72, MSS 314 BC, Center for Southwest Research, University of New Mexico, Albuquerque, microfilm

AR   *The Arizona Republic* (Phoenix)

ASU   Arizona State University, Tempe

BBW   Virginia Brown, Ida Bahl and Lillian Watson Collection, MS 269, Special Collections, Cline Library, Northern Arizona University, Flagstaff

BGCP   Barry Goldwater Congressional Papers, Arizona Historical Foundation, Tempe

BGPIA   Barry Goldwater Papers, Indian Affairs Series, Arizona Historical Foundation, Tempe

CCF   Central Classified Files, Records of the Bureau of Indian Affairs, National Archives, Washington, D.C.

CCMO   Correspondences of Chief Medical Officers, Window Rock Agency, Records of the Bureau of Indian Affairs, National Archives, Pacific Southwest Region Branch, Laguna Niguel, Calif.

CHP   Carl Hayden Papers, C-MSS-1, Arizona Room, Hayden Library, Arizona State University, Tempe

CSR   Center for Southwest Research, Zimmerman Library, University of New Mexico, Albuquerque

DCP   Dennis Chávez Papers, CSR

DIHC   Division of Indian Health Correspondence, RG 513, National Archives II, College Park, Md.

GI   *Gallup (N.Mex.) Independent*

IHS   Indian Health Service

MKUP   Morris K. Udall Papers, MS 325, The University of Arizona Library, Special Collections, University of Arizona, Tucson

NAIHS   Navajo Area Indian Health Service

NAND   Native Americans and the New Deal: The Office Files of John Collier, 1933–45, University Publications of America, microfilm
NHA   Navajo Health Authority, Window Rock, Ariz.
NT   *Navajo Times* (Window Rock, Ariz.)
NTCM   *Navajo Tribal Council Minutes, Major Council Meetings of American Indian Tribes* (Frederick, Md.: University Publications of America, 1991), microfilm
NYT   *New York Times*
PFCP   Paul Fannin Congressional Papers, Arizona Historical Foundation, Tempe
PG   *The Phoenix Gazette*
RFN   Reports of Field Nurses, 1931–43, Records of the Health Division, Records of the Bureau of Indian Affairs, National Archives, Washington, D.C.
SANSR   Superintendents Annual Narrative and Statistical Reports, M1011, Records of the Bureau of Indian Affairs, National Archives, Washington, D.C.
SF   Subject Files, Records of the Indian Health Service, National Archives II, College Park, Md.
USDHEW   U.S. Department of Health, Education, and Welfare
USDHHS   U.S. Department of Health and Human Services
USPHS   U.S. Public Health Service

Preface

1. Sonlatsa Jim-James, "Diné Way," in *Reinventing the Enemy's Language: Contemporary Native Women's Writings of North America*, eds. Joy Harjo and Gloria Bird (New York: W. W. Norton and Company, 1997), 488–93.
2. *Navajo Times* (hereinafter cited as NT), 10 October 1996, 9; *Arizona Republic* (hereinafter cited as *AR*), 10 April 1997, HL1–HL2.
3. Robert Trennert has provided a strong overview of federal medical efforts among the Navajos, and Navajo reactions to those services, in the late nineteenth and early twentieth centuries. He describes early federal efforts to use Western medicine as a tool to assimilate the Navajo by compelling them to reject traditional practices. See Robert A. Trennert, *White Man's Medicine: Government Doctors and the Navajo, 1863–1955* (Albuquerque: University of New Mexico Press, 1998). Other books dealing with Navajo health care and traditional healing include, but are not limited to the following: by historians—Donald L. Parman, *The Navajos and the New Deal* (New Haven, Conn.: Yale University Press, 1976); and Peter Iverson, *The Navajo Nation* (Westport, Conn.: Greenwood Press, 1981; Albuquerque: University of New Mexico Press, 1983) (page citations are to the reprint edition); anthropological studies—Alexander H. Leighton and Dorothea C. Leighton, *The Navaho Door: An Introduction to Navaho Life* (Cambridge, Mass.: Harvard University Press, 1944; New York: Russell and Russell, 1967); Dorothea Leighton and Clyde Kluckhohn, *Children of the People* (Cambridge, Mass.: Harvard University Press, 1947); Charlotte J. Frisbie, *Navajo Medicine Bundles or Jish: Acquisition, Transmission, and Disposition in the Past and Present* (Albuquerque: University of New Mexico Press, 1987); Gary Witherspoon, *Language and Art in the Navajo Universe* (Ann Arbor: University of Michigan Press, 1977); John R. Farella, *The Main Stalk: A Synthesis of Navajo Philosophy* (Tucson: University of Arizona Press, 1984); Gladys A. Reichard, *Navaho Religion: A Study of Symbolism* (New York: Pantheon Books, 1950; Tucson: University of Arizona Press, 1983); by sociologists, demographers

and others—Cheryl Howard, *Navajo Tribal Demography, 1983–1986: A Comparative and Historical Perspective* (New York: Garland Publishing, 1993); Stephen J. Kunitz, *Disease Change and the Role of Medicine: The Navajo Experience* (Berkeley: University of California Press, 1983); John Adair, Kurt Deuschle, and Clifford R. Barnett, *The People's Health: Medicine and Anthropology in a Navajo Community* (New York: Appleton-Century-Crofts, 1970; rev. and exp. ed., Albuquerque: University of New Mexico Press, 1988); Robert L. Kane and Rosalie A. Kane, *Federal Health Care (With Reservations!)* (New York: Springer Publishing Company, 1972).

Chapter 1

1. Leland C. Wyman, "Navajo Ceremonial System," in *Southwest*, ed. Alfonso Ortiz, vol. 10 of *Handbook of North American Indians*, ed. William C. Sturtevant (Washington, D.C.: Smithsonian Institution, 1983), 536; Clyde Kluckhohn and Dorothea Leighton, *The Navaho*, rev. ed. (Garden City, N.Y.: The Natural History Library/Anchor Books/Doubleday, 1962).

2. Sam D. Gill, "Navajo Views of Their Origin," in *Southwest*, ed. Alfonso Ortiz, 502–5; Wyman, "Navajo Ceremonial System," 537–43; Frank Mitchell, *Navajo Blessingway Singer: The Autobiography of Frank Mitchell, 1881–1967*, ed. Charlotte J. Frisbie and David McAllester (Tucson: University of Arizona Press, 1978), 155; Alexander Leighton and Dorothea Leighton, "Therapeutic Values in Navajo Religion," in *Arizona Highways* 43, no. 8 (August 1967): 2–13.

3. Witherspoon, *Language and Art*, 19–25; Frisbie, *Navajo Medicine Bundles or Jish*, 1–5; Farella, *The Main Stalk*, 34.

4. Donald Sandner, *Navaho Symbols of Healing* (New York: Harcourt Brace Jovanovich, 1979), 23–30; Wyman, "Navajo Ceremonial System," 537–39.

5. Sandner, *Navaho Symbols*, 41–78; Wyman, "Navajo Ceremonial System," 543–48.

6. Wyman, "Navajo Ceremonial System," 536; Frisbie, *Navajo Medicine Bundles*, 1–5; Sandner, *Navaho Symbols*, 33–35.

7. Kluckhohn and Leighton, *The Navaho*, 201. See also Jerrold E. Levy, Raymond Neutra, and Dennis Parker, *Hand Trembling, Frenzy Witchcraft, and Moth Madness: A Study of Navajo Seizure Disorders* (Tucson: University of Arizona Press, 1987).

8. Howard Gorman, interview by Daniel Tyler, Ganado, Ariz., 25 October 1968, Tape 533, p. 15, Roll 3, Navajo Transcripts, American Indian Oral History Collection, 1967–72, MSS 314 BC, CSR (hereinafter cited as AIOHC); Wyman, "Navajo Ceremonial System," 536; Kluckhohn and Leighton, *The Navaho*, 201.

9. Witherspoon, *Language and Art*, 34; Frisbie, *Navajo Medicine Bundles*, 1–5.

10. Kluckhohn and Leighton, *The Navaho*, 184–87; James Kale McNeley, *Holy Wind in Navajo Philosophy* (Tucson: The University of Arizona Press, 1981).

11. Clyde Kluckhohn, *Navaho Witchcraft* (Cambridge, Mass.: The Museum, 1944; Boston: Beacon Press, 1967) (page citations are to reprint edition); Kluckhohn and Leighton, *The Navaho*, 187–92.

12. Wyman, "Navajo Ceremonial System," 536–38; Sandner, *Navaho Symbols*, 30–33 and 44–46; William Morgan, "Navaho Treatment of Sickness: Diagnosticians," *American Anthropologist* 33, no. 3 (July-September 1931): 390–402; Charlotte J. Frisbie, "An Approach to the Ethnography of Navajo Ceremonial Performance," in *Ethnography of Musical Performance*, comps. Norma McLeod and Marcia Herndon (Norwood, Pa.: Norwood Editions, 1980), 87.

13. Sandner, *Navaho Symbols*, 40–47; Wyman, "Navajo Ceremonial System," 536–57; Left Handed, *Left Handed, Son of Old Man Hat: A Navaho Autobiography*, recorded by Walter Dyk (1938; Lincoln: University of Nebraska Press, 1996), 251–52.

14. Clyde Kluckhohn and Dorothea Leighton estimated that in the 1930s, singers received between $5 and $500, depending on their reputation, the ceremony's complexity, and the cost of materials. Kluckhohn and Leighton, *The Navaho*, 226–27.

15. For more on the Yeibichai, see James C. Faris, *The Nightway: A History and a History of Documentation of a Navajo Ceremonial* (Albuquerque: University of New Mexico Press, 1990).

16. Mitchell, *Navajo Blessingway Singer*, 179.

17. Kluckhohn and Leighton, *The Navaho*, 194–96; Wyman, "Navajo Ceremonial System," 556; Leighton and Leighton, "Therapeutic Values," 3; Mitchell, *Navajo Blessingway Singer*, 227.

18. Leighton and Kluckhohn, *Children of the People*, 26.

19. Witherspoon, *Language and Art*, 29–30; Luci Tapahonso, *Sáanii Dahataal, The Women Are Singing: Poems and Stories* (Tucson: University of Arizona Press, 1993), 33; McNeley, *Holy Wind*.

20. Leighton and Kluckhohn, *Children of the People*, 1–26.

21. Ibid., 1–26, 31–39. In fact, the Navajos had established practices that were very effective in combating waterborne diseases. Concerns about witchcraft compelled Navajos to carefully dispose of bodily waste, which limited the risk of contaminating their water. Harry S. Wise, "The Ecology of Disease in the Navajo Camp," 1965, Box 3, Folder 197, Virginia Brown, Ida Bahl, and Lillian Watson Collection, MS 269, Special Collections, Northern Arizona University, Flagstaff (hereinafter cited as BBW).

22. Trennert, *White Man's Medicine*, 4–5; Howard, *Navajo Tribal Demography*, 4–5; Kluckhohn and Leighton, *The Navaho*, 33.

23. Left Handed, *Left Handed*, 68–69.

24. Leighton and Leighton, *The Navaho Door*, 62–63.

25. Trennert, *White Man's Medicine*, 3; Virgil J. Vogel, *American Indian Medicine* (Norman: University of Oklahoma Press, 1970), 148–61.

26. Franc Johnson Newcomb, *Hosteen Klah: Navaho Medicine Man and Sand Painter* (Norman: University of Oklahoma Press, 1964), 117. Singers also allow for variation in other ways such as providing for two-, five-, and nine-night versions of some of the chantways. Wyman, "Navajo Ceremonial System," 543; Charlotte Frisbie, "Temporal Change in Navajo Religion: 1868–1990," *Journal of the Southwest* 34, no. 4 (winter 1992): 457–514.

27. Jerrold E. Levy, "Navajo Health Concepts and Behavior: The Role of the Anglo Medical Man in the Navajo Healing Process," 1 August 1963, p. 8, Museum of Northern Arizona, Flagstaff; Leighton and Leighton, "Therapeutic Values"; Evon C. Vogt, "Navaho," in *Perspectives in American Indian Culture Change*, ed. Edward H. Spicer (Chicago: University of Chicago Press, 1956; Chicago: University of Chicago Press, 1961), 301–7 (page citations are to the reprint edition).

28. Erwin H. Ackerknecht, *A Short History of Medicine*, rev. ed. (Baltimore: Johns Hopkins University Press, 1982); Lynn Payer, *Medicine and Culture: Varieties of Treatment in the United States, England, West Germany, and France* (New York: Penguin Books, 1988).

29. Ackerknecht, *A Short History of Medicine*, 64–68, 218–26; Paul Starr, *The Social Transformation of American Medicine* (New York: Basic Books, 1982), 35–37.

Chapter 2

1. Robert Roessel, "Navajo History, 1850–1923," in *Southwest,* ed. Alfonso Ortiz, 510–11, 517; William Haas Moore, *Chiefs, Agents, and Soldiers: Conflict on the Navajo Frontier, 1868–1882* (Albuquerque: University of New Mexico Press, 1994), 1–20; Trennert, *White Man's Medicine,* 22–25.

2. Trennert, *White Man's Medicine,* 26–33.

3. Trennert, "White Doctors Among the Navajos, 1868–1928" (paper presented at Western History Association Annual Meeting, Tulsa, Okla., October 1993), 15; Garrick Bailey and Roberta Glenn Bailey, *A History of the Navajos: The Reservation Years* (Santa Fe, N.Mex.: School of American Research Press, 1986), 166–67.

4. Trennert, *White Man's Medicine,* ix; Ruth M. Raup, for U.S. Public Health Service (hereinafter cited as USPHS), U.S. Division of Public Health Methods, *The Indian Health Program from 1800 to 1955* (Washington, D.C.: GPO, 1959), 1–2; U.S. Department of Health, Education, and Welfare (hereinafter cited as USDHEW), USPHS, *The Indian Health Program: The U.S. Public Health Service* (Washington, D.C.: GPO, 1963), 14.

5. Trennert, *White Man's Medicine,* 40–43; Raup, *Indian Health Program,* 2–3; H. J. Hagerman, Commissioner to the Navajo Tribe, 28 July 1924, p. 22, Roll 90, Superintendents Annual Narrative and Statistical Reports, M1011, Records of the Bureau of Indian Affairs, National Archives, Washington, D.C. (hereinafter cited as SANSR); Mitchell, *Navajo Blessingway Singer,* 113; Albert M. Wigglesworth, "Albert M. Wigglesworth, Frontier Doctor (1872–1964): A Memoir," Arizona Historical Society, Tucson, 1986.

6. Iverson, *The Navajo Nation,* 12; Moore, *Chiefs, Agents, and Soldiers,* 113; Bailey and Bailey, *A History of the Navajos,* 60–61, 143; Trennert, *White Man's Medicine,* 79.

7. During the administration of President Ulysses S. Grant, different Christian denominations were given responsibility for different agencies. In the Navajos' case, Presbyterians had formal control. However, other Protestant denominations and Catholics were allowed to establish their own missions. Francis Paul Prucha, *The Great Father: The United States Government and the American Indians,* abridged ed. (Lincoln: University of Nebraska Press, 1986), 152–66; Betty Stirling, *Mission to the Navajo* (Mountain View, Calif.: Pacific Press Publications Association, 1961), 12, 36–39, 47; Trennert, *White Man's Medicine,* 44–52; J. Rockwood Jenkins, *The Good Shepherd Mission to the Navajo* (Phoenix, Ariz.: Author, 1955), 11; Bailey and Bailey, *A History of the Navajos,* 171; Rev. John Dolfin, *Bringing the Gospel in Hogan and Pueblo* (Grand Rapids, Mich.: Van Noord, 1921), 211, 218–19.

8. Dolfin, *Bringing the Gospel,* 209.

9. Ibid., 214–19.

10. Prucha, *The Great Father,* 288–91; Trennert, *White Man's Medicine,* 95–96.

11. USDHEW, USPHS, *The Indian Health Program: The U.S. Public Health Service* (Washington, D.C.: GPO, 1972), 18–19; Raup, *Indian Health Program,* 4–7.

12. Trennert, *White Man's Medicine,* 109–12; Kunitz, *Disease Change,* 147–50; Sandra K. Schackel, "'The Tales Those Nurses Told!': Public Health Nurses Among the Pueblo and Navajo Indians," *New Mexico Historical Review* 65 (April 1990): 225–49.

13. Annual Report, 16 June 1915, p. 8, Roll 89, SANSR; Annual Report, 5 August 1916, Roll 89, SANSR; Annual Report, 5 November 1920, pp. 5–6, Roll 89, SANSR; August F. Duclos, Annual Statistical Report, 31 August 1925, pp. 768–69, Roll 90, SANSR; Robert W. Young, ed. and comp., *The Navajo Yearbook, 1951–1961,* vol. 8

(Window Rock, Ariz.: U.S. Department of Interior, Bureau of Indian Affairs, Navajo Agency, 1961), 316.

14. Tom Allen, interview by Daniel Tyler, Fort Defiance, Ariz., 1 October 1968, Tape 534, Roll 3, AIOHC.

15. Schackel, "'The Tales Those Nurses Told!,'" 229–30; Annual Report, 1 March 1919, p. 5, Roll 89, SANSR.

16. Annual Report, 8 October 1912, p. 1, Roll 89, SANSR; Howard Gorman, interview, AIOHC; Wigglesworth, "A Memoir," 88.

17. William H. McNeill, *Plagues and Peoples* (New York: Anchor Books/Doubleday, 1989; New York: Anchor Books/Doubleday, 1989), 255 (page citation is to the reprint edition); Trennert, *White Man's Medicine*, 122–27; Alexander H. Leighton and Dorothea C. Leighton, recorders, *Lucky: The Navajo Singer*, ed. and annot. Joyce J. Griffen (Albuquerque: University of New Mexico Press, 1992), 134–37.

18. H. J. Hagerman, Report, 28 July 1924, p. 26, Roll 90, SANSR.

19. "Authorization of Appropriations and Expenditures for Indian Affairs (Snyder Act) November 2, 1921," in *Documents of United States Indian Policy*, 2d ed., ed. Francis Paul Prucha (Lincoln: University of Nebraska Press, 1996), 320–21; Robert Trennert, "Indian Sore Eyes: The Federal Campaign to Control Trachoma in the Southwest, 1910–1940," *Journal of the Southwest* 32 (summer 1990): 121–49; Trennert, *White Man's Medicine*, 130.

20. Prucha, *The Great Father*, 293; "Meriam Report, 1928," in *Documents of United States Indian Policy*, ed. Francis Paul Prucha, 219–21; Trennert, *White Man's Medicine*, 136–38.

21. Jennie Joe, "Navajo Singers and Western Medical Doctors" (paper presented at the American Historical Association Annual Meeting, Chicago, 27–30 December 1991), 8; Newcomb, *Hosteen Klah*, 106; Trennert, *White Man's Medicine*, 32–34.

22. Sandner, *Navaho Symbols*, 46; Trennert, *White Man's Medicine*, 32–34.

23. Jack Johnson, interview by Tom Ration, October 1968, p. 199, Tape 181, Roll 3, AIOHC; Moore, *Chiefs, Agents, and Soldiers*, 187–98; Bailey and Bailey, *A History of the Navajos*, 33; Mitchell, *Navajo Blessingway Singer*, 132; Trennert, *White Man's Medicine*, 41, 107–8. Lansing quote in *Stories of Traditional Navajo Life and Culture*, ed. Broderick H. Johnson (Tsaile, Ariz.: Navajo Community College Press, 1977), 108.

24. Trennert, *White Man's Medicine*, 107–08; Annual Report, 4 December 1923, p. 6, Roll 89, SANSR; Eastern Navajo Agency, Annual Report, August 1927, Roll 90, SANSR.

25. Adair et al., *The People's Health*, 1970, 27–28.

26. Ibid.

27. Kunitz, *Disease Change*, 147; Young, *The Navajo Yearbook, 1951–1961*, vol. 8, 89–90; Parman, *The Navajos and the New Deal*, 219. By 1930, Navajos could seek hospital care at Kayenta, Arizona (47 beds, opened in 1929); Leupp, Arizona (29 beds, 1929); Toadlena, Arizona (12 beds, 1927); Crownpoint, Arizona (32 beds, 1914); Fort Defiance, Arizona (28 beds, 1912); Tuba City, Arizona (6 beds, 1911); Tohatchi, New Mexico (12 beds, 1927); Shiprock, New Mexico (41 beds, built in 1908 and replaced in 1915); and Fort Wingate, New Mexico (35 beds, 1889, off the reservation). From Norman K. Eck, *Contemporary Navajo Affairs: Navajo History*, vol. 3, part B (Rough Rock, Ariz.: Navajo Curriculum Center, Rough Rock Demonstration School, 1982), 45–47.

28. Parman, *The Navajos and the New Deal*, 223; Trennert, *White Man's Medicine*, 178–81; W. W. Peter, Navajo Health Policy, 13 April 1935, p. 12, Roll 8, Native Americans and the New Deal: The Office Files of John Collier, 1933–45, University Publications

of America, microfilm (hereinafter cited as NAND); Annual Report, 15 August 1910, p. 12, Roll 89, SANSR; W. W. Peter, Navajo Health Policy, 13 April 1935, p. 12, NAND; Annual Report, 15 August 1910, p. 12, Roll 89, SANSR.

29. The BIA constructed a new sanatorium off the southern end of the reservation at Winslow, Arizona, in 1933, and replaced an older hospital with a sixty-five–bed facility at Crownpoint, New Mexico, in 1939. Another new hospital was located at Chinle, Arizona (1932), with twelve beds. In Eck, *Contemporary Navajo Affairs,* 167; W. W. Peter, Navajo Health Policy, 13 April 1935, p. 2, Roll 8, NAND; Address by Edgar B. Meritt, 12 November 1928, p. 3, Roll 1, *Navajo Tribal Council Minutes, Major Council Meetings of American Indian Tribes* (Frederick, Md.: University Publications of America, 1991), microfilm (hereinafter cited as NTCM); Parman, *The Navajos and the New Deal,* 225; Annual Report, 15 August 1910, p. 12, Roll 89, SANSR; Statement by W. W. Peter, Navajo Executive Committee Meeting, minutes, 5 February 1935, p. 2, Box 5, Folder 3, Thomas Dodge Papers, MSS033, Arizona Room, Arizona State University (hereinafter cited as TDP); Sallie Jeffries, "Relationships of Hospital Personnel," *Navajo Medical News* 7, no. 4 (25 November 1940): 1.

30. Civil Service regulations required all physicians to have graduated from a "Class A medical school" within four years prior to their application. In L. W. White to W. W. Peter, March 12, 1935, p. 2, Central Navajo Box, Navajos, 1907–1939, Central Classified Files, Records of the Bureau of Indian Affairs, National Archives, Washington, D.C. (hereinafter cited as CCF); Medical News, 29 July 1937, Box 5, Folder 25, TDP; W. W. Peter, Annual Report, 5 August 1936, p. 1, Roll 90, SANSR; Parman, *The Navajos and the New Deal,* 224; Raup, *Indian Health Program,* 11; Sallie Jeffries, "Relationships of Hospital Personnel," 1.

31. W. W. Peter to L. W. White, 11 February 1935, Central Navajo Box, Navajos, 1907–1939, CCF.

32. Schackel, "'The Tales Those Nurses Told!,'" 226–49.

33. Ibid., 243–46; Elizabeth Forster to Mrs. Burge, 7 November 1932, Box 3, Records of Field Nurses, 1931–43, Records of the Health Division, Records of the Bureau of Indian Affairs, National Archives, Washington, D.C. (hereinafter cited as RFN).

34. Raup, *Indian Health Program,* 12; Schackel, "'The Tales Those Nurses Told!,'" 248–49; Seba Ates, Field Nurse Monthly Reports, June-October 1933, Box 3, RFN. See also Field Nurse Monthly Reports, 1931–1943, Boxes 3, 23, 33, RFN; Bertha Lips, Field Nurse Monthly Report, July 1932, Box 3, RFN; Domitilla Showalter, Field Nurse Monthly Reports, 5 March and 30 April 1943, Box 33, RFN.

35. Parman, *The Navajos and the New Deal,* 195; Seba Ates, Narrative Report, December 1933, Box 3, RFN.

36. Edna Gerken, "How the Navajos Improve Their Health," *Childhood Education* 18 (March 1942): 315–18; Medical News, 26 October 1937, p. 4, Box 5, Folder 25, TDP; Parman, *The Navajos and the New Deal,* 195–206, 226.

37. U.S. Department of the Interior Memorandum for the Press, 22 May 1939, Box 8, TDP; Annual Report, 1931, Roll 90, SANSR; Hospital Reports, 1 July–31 December 1932, 1 July 1932–30 June 1933, 10 July 1933, 21 October 1937, 16 September 1938, Box 42, 1932 and 1937–1938, Navajo Agency, Hospital Reports, 1923–38, Records of the Health Division, Records of the Bureau of Indian Affairs, National Archives, Washington, D.C.; Circular Letter to Physicians and Nurses Navajo-Hopi Area, 25 June 1937, p. 2, Box 1, Folder 17, TDP; Raup, *Indian Health Program,* 15; Trennert, *White Man's Medicine,* 191–95; U.S. Department of the Interior Memorandum for the Press, 22 May 1939, Box 8, TDP.

38. Annual Report, 5 November 1920, Roll 89, SANSR; Statement by W. W. Peter, Navajo Executive Committee Meeting, minutes, 5 February 1935, p. 4, Box 5, Folder 3, TDP; Parman, *The Navajos and the New Deal*, 227–30; Leighton and Leighton, *The Navaho Door*, 38; *Navajo Medical News* 7, no. 4 (25 November 1940): 20–23.

39. Medical News, 26 October 1937, p. 1–2, Box 5, Folder 25, TDP; Annual Report, 1931, Roll 90, SANSR.

40. Gertrude Hosmer to Commissioner, 2 May 1940 and 19 December 1941, E. R. Fryer to Commissioner, 3 March 1942, W. W. Peter to Kenneth Setzler, 7 February 1942, Gertrude Hosmer to Commissioner, 6 January 1942, Box 104, Navajos, 1940–45, CCF; Hospital Reports, 10 July 1933, 21 October 1937, Box 42, Navajo Agency, Hospital Reports, 1923–1938, Records of the Health Division, Records of the Bureau of Indian Affairs, National Archives, Washington, D.C.; Elizabeth V. Duggan to Commissioner, 22 April 1935, and L. L. Elliott to W. W. Peter, 27 December 1934, Box 13, Reports of Medical Directors: Northern Navajo Agency, 1930–35, Records of the Health Division, Records of the Bureau of Indian Affairs, National Archives, Washington, D.C.

41. W. W. Peter, Navajo Health Work, July 1936, Roll 10, NAND; Statement by Toadechenie Chischille, Minutes of the Eleventh Annual Session of the Navajo Tribal Council, 7–8 July 1933, p. 49, Roll 1, NTCM.

42. Stephen C. Jett, "Pete Price, Navajo Medicineman (1868–1951): A Brief Biography," *American Indian Quarterly* 15 (winter 1991): 91–101; David M. Brugge, "Henry Chee Dodge: From the Long Walk to Self-Determination," in *Indian Lives: Essays on Nineteenth- and Twentieth-Century Native American Leaders*, eds. L. G. Moses and Raymond Wilson (Albuquerque: University of New Mexico Press, 1993), 91–107.

43. Dr. C. H. Koentz speech, 10 December 1928, pp. 1–12, Roll 1, NTCM; H. J. Hagerman, J. C. Morgan, et al., Minutes of the Fifth Annual Session of the Navajo Tribal Council, 7–8 July 1927, pp. 3–8, 68–72, 76–83, Roll 1, NTCM.

44. Statements by W. W. Peter and Pete Price, Proceedings of the Meetings of the Navajo Tribal Council and the Executive Committee, 17–20 January 1938, p. 76, Roll 1, NTCM.

45. Ibid., 76–77.

46. Annual Report, 5 August 1936, Roll 90, SANSR; Statement by W. W. Peter, Navajo Executive Committee Meeting, minutes, 5 February 1935, TDP; J. G. Townsend to Haven Emerson, 17 January 1935, W. W. Peter to Commissioner, 22 December 1934, Haven Emerson to J. G. Townsend, 26 December 1934, Central Navajo Box, CCF; Navajo Tribal Council, "Health—Establishment of Committee on," 18 January 1938, in *Navajo Tribal Council Resolutions, 1922–1951* (Window Rock, Ariz., 1952), 133; Statement by W. W. Peter, et al., Proceedings of the Meetings of the Navajo Tribal Council and the Executive Committee, 17–20 January 1938, p. 160, Roll 1, NTCM.

47. Statements by W. W. Peter, J. C. Morgan, et al. Proceedings of the Meeting of the Navajo Tribal Council, 15–19 May 1939, pp. 34–35, Roll 1, NTCM; Navajo Tribal Council, "Dental Revolving Fund," 23 July 1937, 4 June 1940, and "Health—Dental Program," 19 May 1939, in *Navajo Tribal Council Resolutions*.

48. W. W. Hill to John Collier, 28 December 1934, Central Navajo Box, Navajos, 1907–1939, CCF; Kenneth R. Philp, *John Collier's Crusade for Indian Reform, 1920–1954* (Tucson: University of Arizona Press, 1977).

49. W. W. Peter to G. W. Helms, 2 June 1938, Box 1, Folder 20, TDP; Annual Report, 5 August 1936, Roll 90, SANSR.

50. Navajo Service Physician to W. W. Peter, 26 June 1940, Box 104, Navajos, 1907–1939, CCF.

51. J. C. Morgan, "A Voice from an Indian," 1932, The Navajo Nation Museum, Window Rock.

52. Clarence G. Salsbury with Paul Hughes, *The Salsbury Story: A Medical Missionary's Lifetime of Public Service* (Tucson: University of Arizona Press, 1969), 119.

53. Florence Crannell Means, *Sagebrush Surgeon* (New York: Friendship Press, 1955), 3–12, 50; Salsbury, *The Salsbury Story*, 119–23; Red Point was also an informant for Gladys Reichard, indicating that he was willing to cooperate with non-Navajos interested in Navajo healing. See Reichard, *Navaho Religion*.

54. Salsbury, *The Salsbury Story*, 119–23.

55. Means, *Sagebrush Surgeon*, 83; Frank Walker of St. Michael's Mission to Richard Van Valkenburg in Tucson, 3 and 16 February 1944, and Father Anselm at St. Michaels Mission to Van Valkenburg, 8 January 1945, Richard Van Valkenburg Papers, MS 831, Box 2, Folder 6, Arizona Historical Society.

56. Means, *Sagebrush Surgeon*, 97; Salsbury, *The Salsbury Story*, 154.

57. Iverson, *The Navajo Nation*, 44; Cora Salsbury, *Forty Years in the Desert: A History of Ganado Mission, 1901–1941* (Chicago: Press of Physicians' Record Co., n.d.), 30.

58. There is at least one report sent to Collier in 1934 saying that missionaries in the Eastern Navajo jurisdiction disrupted a healing ceremony. W. W. Hill to Collier, 28 December 1934, Central Navajo Box, Navajos, 1907–1939, CCF,; Annual Report, 4 December 1923, Roll 89, SANSR; Iverson, *The Navajo Nation*, 44.

59. Father Berard Haile, O.F.M., report to Rev. Bernard Espelage, O.F.M.D.D., Bishop of the Diocese of Gallup, New Mexico, 20 May 1941, Box 3, Folder 10, and Haile to Espelage, 20 May 1941, Box 3, Folder 10, Berard Haile Papers, Southwest Collections, University of Arizona, Tucson; Iverson, *The Navajo Nation*, 36; Fr. Murray Bodo, O.F.M., ed., *Tales of an Endishodi: Father Berard Haile and the Navajos, 1900–1961* (Albuquerque: University of New Mexico Press, 1998).

60. Parman, *The Navajos and the New Deal*, 221–24.

61. W. W. Peter to G. W. Helms, 2 June 1938, Box 1, Folder 20, TDP.

62. David F. Aberle, *The Peyote Religion Among the Navaho* (Chicago: Aldine Publishing Co., 1966; Norman: University of Oklahoma Press, 1982), 17 (page citations are to the reprint edition).

63. Aberle, "The Peyote Religion Among the Navajo," in *Southwest*, ed. Alfonso Ortiz, 558–69.

64. Ibid.; Omer C. Stewart, *Peyote Religion: A History* (Norman: University of Oklahoma Press, 1987), 293–317.

65. Aberle, *The Peyote Religion*, 109–10.

66. Ibid., 182; Thomas J. Csordas, "The Sore That Does Not Heal: Cause and Concept in the Navajo Experience of Cancer," *Journal of Anthropological Research* 45 (1989): 457–77.

67. Aberle, *The Peyote Religion*, 109–14.

68. Ibid., 110–11; Howard Gorman, "The Growing Peyote Cult and the Use of Peyote on the Navajo Indian Reservation," 18 May 1940, Roll 12, NAND.

69. Aberle, *The Peyote Religion*, xxv; Aberle, "The Peyote Religion," 558–69.

70. Statements by Roy Kinsel, Sam Gorman, Hola Tso, et al., Proceedings of the Meeting of the Navajo Tribal Council, 3–6 June 1940, Roll 1, NTCM; Aberle, *The Peyote Religion*, 113; Navajo Tribal Council, "Peyote—Prevent Use of," 3 June 1940, in *Navajo Tribal Council Resolutions*, 107–8.

71. John Collier to Secretary Ickes, 6 December 1940, Roll 13, NAND.

Chapter 3

1. Population estimate for 1950 from Young, *The Navajo Yearbook, 1951–1961*, 328; Kunitz, *Disease Change*, 150.
2. Alison R. Bernstein, *American Indians and World War II: Toward a New Era in Indian Affairs* (Norman: University of Oklahoma Press, 1991), 70; Iverson, *The Navajo Nation*, 49.
3. Statements by J. C. Morgan, Scott Preston, et al., 22–24 June 1942, p. 87, Roll 1, NTCM; Ruth M. Raup, *Indian Health Program*, 29.
4. Young, *The Navajo Yearbook, 1951–1961*, 90; Dr. Herbert Knudtson to Mrs. Bayles Ricketson, 29 July 1947, Box 190, Folder N, Correspondences of Chief Medical Officers, Window Rock Agency, Records of the Bureau of Indian Affairs, National Archives, Pacific Southwest Region Branch, Laguna Niguel, Calif. (hereinafter cited as CCMO).
5. W. W. Peter to H. K. Mangum, 23 May 1942, Box 104, Navajos 1940–1943, CCF; Kunitz, *Disease Change*, 150; W. W. Peter to L. T. Hoffman et al., Memorandum, 6 June 1942, Box 104, Navajos 1940–1943, CCF.
6. Esther F. Bacon, Field Nurse Monthly Reports, 2 October 1943–4 January 1944, Box 33, Reports of Field Nurses, 1931–1943, Records of the Health Division, Records of the Bureau of Indian Affairs, National Archives, Washington, D.C.; Knudtson to Ricketson, 29 July 1947, Box 190, Folder N, CCMO.
7. Statement by Allan Harper, Proceedings of the Meeting of the Advisory Committee, Navajo Tribal Council, 29 August–5 September 1949, NTCM; Dr. Raymond Mundt to Dr. Henry Kassel, 6 April 1948, Box 190, Folder M, CCMO.
8. Donald J. Hunt to Dr. R. B. Snavely, 25 October 1946, Box 190, Folder N, CCMO.
9. Mundt to Kassel, 6 April 1948, Box 190, Folder M, CCMO.
10. Iverson, *The Navajo Nation*, 50–56; Editorial, *Indian Truth* 23, no. 3 (September-December 1946): n.p.; Ruth Falkenburg Kirk, "Indian Welfare: The Navaho," *Public Welfare* (April 1946): n.p.
11. *New York Times* (hereinafter cited as *NYT*), 12 March 1949, 10, 14 March 1949, 25, 7 July 1949, 27, 23 July 1949, 8, 9 October 1949, 38, 15 October 1949, 16, 18 October 1949, 29, 19 October 1949, 11, 21 October 1949, 24. Also Young, *The Navajo Yearbook, 1951–1961*, 1–5; Bureau of Indian Affairs, Summary of Navajo Developments, February 1949, Box 82, Folder 32, Dennis Chávez Papers, CSR.
12. Young, *The Navajo Yearbook, 1951–1961*, 67, 71–78; Orme Lewis to Senator Saltonstall, July 7, 1954, Box 159, Navajos 1953–54, CCF.
13. J. A. Krug to Sam Rayburn, n.d., Box 82, Folder 32, DCP.
14. Kenneth D. Claw to "Doctor," 1 December 1947, Box 190, Folder N, CCMO; Dr. Ralph B. Snavely to John H. Provinse, 10 December 1946, Box 4, Navajos 1942–47, CCF.
15. Nell Murbarger, "White Man's Medicine in Monument Valley," *Desert Magazine* 21 (July 1958): 5–10.
16. Salsbury, *The Salsbury Story*, 196; Means, *Sagebrush Surgeon*, 126.
17. Salsbury, *The Salsbury Story*, 198–99, 220–21.
18. Statements by Allan Harper, Roger Davis, et al., Proceedings of the Meeting of the Advisory Committee, Navajo Tribal Council, 24 January–2 February 1950, NTCM; Burnet M. Davis, Memorandum, 12 June 1953, Box 159, Navajos 1952–1953, CCF.
19. Dorothea Leighton, "As I Knew Them: Navajo Women in 1940," *American Indian Quarterly* 6, nos. 1–2 (spring/summer 1982): 34–51; Talcott Parsons and Evon Z. Vogt, "A Biographical Introduction," in Clyde Kluckhohn, ed., *Navaho Witchcraft*, ix–xxii;

Dorothy Ragon Parker, "Choosing an Indian Identity: A Biography of D'Arcy McNickle" (Ph.D. diss., University of New Mexico, 1988), 129–45; John Collier, unpublished draft of Foreword to Leighton and Leighton, *The Navaho Door*, Roll 7, NAND.

20. Leighton and Leighton, *The Navaho Door*; Leighton and Leighton, "Therapeutic Values in Navajo Religion," p. 13, Roll 7, NAND.

21. Leighton and Leighton, *The Navaho Door*, 58–77; Leighton and Leighton, "Therapeutic Values."

22. John Collier to L. K. Frank, 30 December 1941, Box 104, Navajos 1940–1943, CCF; Leighton and Leighton, "Therapeutic Values."

23. Kluckhohn and Leighton, *The Navaho*; Leighton and Kluckhohn, *Children of the People*; John Collier to Dr. Laura Thompson, 10 March 1942, Roll 12, NAND.

24. Adair et al., *The People's Health*, 1988, 23; "Medical Dictionary: English to Navajo," Medical Division, Navajo Service, Window Rock, Ariz., 1941, Museum of Northern Arizona, Flagstaff; William H. Kelly, "Applied Anthropology in the Southwest," *American Anthropologist* 56 (1954): 708–16.

25. Robert W. Young, foreword to Adair et al., *The People's Health*, 1988, xi–xv; Young, ed. and comp., *The Navajo Yearbook, 1958*, vol. 7 (Window Rock, Ariz.: U.S. Department of Interior, Bureau of Indian Affairs, Navajo Agency, 1958), 48.

26. Adair et al., *The People's Health*, 1970, 32.

27. Statements by Kurt Deuschle, Annie Wauneka, et al., 12 February 1954, Roll 9, NTCM.

28. Adair et al., *The People's Health*, 1988, 12, 41.

29. Ibid., 26.

30. Statements by J. M. Stewart, Thomas Dodge, et al., 9–11 July 1943, p. 17, Roll 1, NTCM; Statements by Scott Preston, Thomas Dodge, et al., Proceedings of the Delegation of the Navajo Tribal Council in Washington, D.C., 13–25 May 1946, p. 13, Roll 3, NTCM; U.S. House Committee on Indian Affairs, *Statements on Conditions among the Navajo Tribe: Hearings before the Committee on Indian Affairs, House of Representatives*, 79th Cong., 2d sess. (Washington, D.C.: GPO, 1946).

31. Statement by Roger Davis, 17–19 July 1944, Roll 1, NTCM; D'Arcy McNickle to Ralph B. Snavely, 18 June 1946, McNickle to John Cooper, 17 June 1946, J. M. Stewart to Snavely, 25 March 1946, Fred Loe to Col. J. C. Harding, 27 February 1946, Stewart to Ernest W. McFarland, 22 March 1946, Box 4, Navajos 1942–1947, CCF.

32. Statements by Norman Littell, Howard Gorman, et al., 3–5 November 1947, Roll 4, NTCM; Statements by Allan Harper, Roger Davis, et al., Proceedings of the Meeting of the Advisory Committee, Navajo Tribal Council, 27–29 July 1949, Roll 4, 24 January–2 February 1950, Roll 5, NTCM.

33. Statements by J. C. Morgan, Scott Preston, Paul Begay, et al., 22–24 June 1942, 44–45, Roll 1, NTCM.

34. Ibid., 49.

35. Statements by Berard Haile, Bizahalani Bekis et al., 2 March 1954, pp. 41–75, Roll 9, NTCM.

36. Ibid.; Bodo, *Tales of an Endishodi*, xxi–xxii.

37. Aberle, *The Peyote Religion*, 110–19.

38. Statements of David Clark, Sam Ahkeah, Scott Preston, et al., Proceedings of the Delegation of the Navajo Tribal Council in Washington, D.C., 13–25 May 1946, Roll 3, NTCM.

39. Aberle, *The Peyote Religion*, 113–19.

40. "Annie Dodge Wauneka: Tsennjikini Clan—House Beneath Cliff People," in Virginia Hoffman and Broderick H. Johnson, *Navajo Biographies* (Rough Rock, Ariz.: Diné Inc. and Board of Education, Rough Rock Demonstration School, The Navajo Curriculum Center, 1970), 292–307; Mary C. Nelson, *Annie Wauneka: The Story of an American Indian* (Minneapolis, Minn.: Dillon Press, 1972).

41. Steven Spencer, "They're Saving Lives in Navaho Land," *Saturday Evening Post* 227 (April 1955): 96.

42. Ibid.; Journal of the Navajo Tribal Council, 13 May 1954, p. 2, 12 February 1954, 1–4, Box 82, Folder 36, DCP; Statements by Kurt Deuschle, Annie Wauneka, et al., 12 February 1954, Roll 9, NTCM.

43. Journal of the Navajo Tribal Council, 9 February 1954, pp. 5–6, 12 February 1954, pp. 1–4, Box 82, Folder 36, DCP; Statements by Allan Harper, Roger Davis, et al., Proceedings of the Meeting of the Advisory Committee, Navajo Tribal Council, 24 January–2 February 1950, Roll 5, NTCM; Statements by Kurt Deuschle, Annie Wauneka, et al., 12 February 1954, Roll 9, NTCM.

44. John R. Wunder, *"Retained by The People": A History of American Indians and the Bill of Rights* (New York: Oxford University Press, 1994), 97–123; Prucha, *The Great Father*, 340–56.

45. Prucha, *The Great Father*, 343–44; Kunitz, *Disease Change*, 152; "Comments of the Department of the Interior on the Recommendations of the Commission on Organization of the Executive Branch of the Government Concerning the Department of the Interior," 26 May 1949, Box 6, Folder 18, William J. Zimmerman Jr. Papers, 1933–65, MSS 517 BC, CSR.

46. Fitzhugh Mullan, M.D., *Plagues and Politics: The Story of the United States Public Health Service* (New York: Basic Books, 1989); Odin W. Anderson, *Health Services in the United States: A Growth Enterprise Since 1875* (Ann Arbor, Mich.: Health Administration Press, 1985), 42–43; USDHEW, USPHS, *History, Mission, and Organization of the Public Health Service* (Washington, D.C.: GPO, 1976).

47. Marcia Wilson, "The Federal Trust Responsibility and the Obligation to Provide Health Care to Indian People," 10 March 1980, Law Library, Arizona State University (hereinafter cited as ASU).

48. U.S. House, "Debate on Transferring Maintenance and Operation of Hospital Facilities for Indians to Public Health Service, H.R. 303," *Congressional Record*, 83d Cong., 2d sess., 1954, 100:5507.

49. Statement by Sen. Arthur Watkins of Utah, in U.S. House, "Debate on Transferring," 8945, 8959–67.

50. Statement by Sen. Barry Goldwater of Arizona, in U.S. House, "Debate on Transferring," 8969, 8970–73; Peter Iverson, *Barry Goldwater: Native Arizonan* (Norman: University of Oklahoma Press, 1997), 151–88.

51. Statements by Roger Davis, Warren Spaulding, Frank Bradley, Sam Ahkeah, et al., 1 June 1954, Roll 10, NTCM.

52. Ibid., 290–91.

53. Ibid., 277–92.

54. Ibid., 281–82.

55. Annual Report to Governor of Arizona, n.d., Box 3, Folder 8, pp. 20–25, Orme Lewis Collection, Arizona Historical Foundation, Tempe.

56. Raup, *Indian Health Program*, 22–24; NYT, 29 May 1954, 10; Young, *The Navajo Yearbook, 1951–1961*, 69; "Transfer of Indian Health Services, August 5, 1954," in *Documents of United States Indian Policy*, ed. Prucha, 236–37.

Chapter 4

1. Prucha, *The Great Father*, 359.
2. Other tribes in the Albuquerque Area were the United Pueblo Council, the Mountain Utes, the Southern Utes, the Jicarilla Apaches, and the Mescalero Apaches. Young, *The Navajo Yearbook, 1951–1961*, 69; *NYT*, 18 December 1955, 76; Raup, *Indian Health Program*, 23–24; George Bock, "Window Rock Sub-Area Comments on the Review of the Organization of the Albuquerque Area," p. 9, 1 March 1967, Box 2, Administrative Management Folder, Subject Files, Records of the Indian Health Service, National Archives II, College Park, Md. (hereinafter cited as SF), 1965–1972; USDHEW, USPHS, *The Indian Health Program* (Washington, D.C.: GPO, 1963), 26; Surgeon General to Arthur Watkins, 29 August 1957, letter and attached report, Box 4, Folder 4, Division of Indian Health Correspondence, Records of the Indian Health Service, National Archives II, College Park, Md. (hereinafter cited as DIHC); USDHEW, USPHS, *Health Services for American Indians* (Washington, D.C.: GPO, 1957), 6.
3. Young, *The Navajo Yearbook, 1951–1961*, 89–90.
4. Address by James R. Shaw before Governors' Interstate Indian Council at Sheridan, Wyoming, 6 August 1956, p. 3, Box 7, Folder 7, William J. Zimmerman Jr. Papers, 1933–65, MSS 517 BC, CSR; U.S. House and Senate Joint Committee on Navajo-Hopi Indian Administration, *Legislation Concerning the Navajo Tribe: Hearings before the Joint Committee on Navajo-Hopi Administration on General Legislative Matters Concerning the Navajo Tribe of Indians*, 86th Cong., 2d sess., 29 January 1960 (Washington, D.C.: GPO, 1960), 33–34.
5. Statement by James Shaw, Navajo Tribal Council Minutes, 7 April 1955, p. 210, A-290, Arizona State Museum Archives, Tucson; "Report of U.S. Public Service to Navajo Chapter Presidents," 31 August 1956, p. 3, Box 4, Folder 4, DIHC; Young, *The Navajo Yearbook, 1951–1961*, 89–90; Young, *The Navajo Yearbook, 1958*, 34.
6. Young, *The Navajo Yearbook, 1951–1961*, 71; Statement by Charles McCammon, 30 January 1961, Roll 5, pp. 8–10, NTCM; Kunitz, *Disease Change*, 159; Young, *The Navajo Yearbook, 1958*, 80–89; "Information to Be Used in the Preparation of the Statement to the Surgeon General's Advisory Committee: Nutrition," n.d., Box 4, Folder 4, DIHC; James Shaw to Area and/or Sub-Area Nutritionists, memorandum, 22 July 1957, Box 4, Albuquerque Personnel, 1955–1957 Folder, DIHC.
7. Statement by Manuel Begay, 29 June 1961, p. 968, Roll 6, NTCM; Albert Stevenson to Ralph Holtje, 3 January 1958, Box 5, Water, 1955–1957 Folder, DIHC; Young, *The Navajo Yearbook, 1951–1961*, 78; Young, *The Navajo Yearbook, 1951–1961*, 78–79.
8. Statement by Charles McCammon, Record of the Navajo Tribal Council, Budget Session, 3 April 1962, p. 16, Roll 7, NTCM.
9. Adair et al., *The People's Health*, 1988, 140–44.
10. Young, foreword to Adair et al., *The People's Health*, 1988, xii.
11. Adair et al., *The People's Health*, 1988, 47–62; Statement by Annie Wauneka, 12 February 1954, pp. 131–32, Roll 9, NTCM.
12. Adair et al., *The People's Health*, 1988, 47–62; Tom T. Sasaki, "Socioeconomic Survey of the Many Farms and Rough Rock Navajos," in Robert W. Young, ed. and comp., *The Navajo Yearbook, 1951–1961*, Vol. 8 (Window Rock, Ariz.: Navajo Agency, 1961), 103–13.
13. Young, foreword to Adair et al., *The People's Health*, 1988.

14. Adair et al., *The People's Health*, 1988, 85–108; Kurt Deuschle and John Adair, "An Interdisciplinary Approach to Public Health on the Navajo Indian Reservation: Medical and Anthropological Aspects," *Annals of New York Academy of Sciences* 84 (1960): 887–905.

15. Adair et al., *The People's Health*, 1970, 67–92.

16. Adair et al., *The People's Health*, 1988, 184–200.

17. Ibid., 143–59; Young, *The Navajo Yearbook*, 1958, 45; Henry Kassel and Annie Wauneka to Paul Jones, 15 March 1957, Box 4, Folder 4, DIHC; Annie Wauneka, "Welcome to the Third Working Conference of the Navajo Health Association, May 12, 1956," p. 7, *Navajo Health Association: Third Working Conference on Services for Hospitalized Navajo Tuberculosis Patients, Action on Health through Interpretation, May 11–13, 1956, Gallup, New Mexico*, Arizona State Museum Library, Tucson; Statement by Teddy McCurtain, 12 February 1962, Roll 7, NTCM.

18. Paul Jones to L. E. Burney, 27 August 1956, Box 480, Folder 11, Carl Hayden Papers, C-MSS-1, Arizona Room, Arizona State University, Tempe (hereinafter cited as CHP).

19. Walsh McDermott, Kurt Deuschle, John Adair, Hugh Fulmer, and Bernice Loughlin, "Introducing Modern Medicine in a Navajo Community," *Science* 131 (22 and 29 January 1960): 197–205, 280–87; Henry Kassel to Chief, Division of Indian Health, memorandum, 21 March 1957, Box 4, Folder 4, DIHC; Adair et al., *The People's Health*, 1970, 60, 140–49. The Indian Health Service (hereinafter cited as IHS) did not fund the clinic after the Cornell team departed because its administrators perceived a greater need in other portions of the reservation. Statement by Charles McCammon, 13 February 1962, Roll 7, pp. 16, 30, NTCM.

20. Paul Jones to Carl Hayden, 7 March 1960, Box 279, Folder 32, CHP; Statement by Annie Wauneka, U.S. House and Senate Joint Committee on Navajo-Hopi Indian Administration, *Legislation Concerning the Navajo Tribe*, 14–15.

21. Iverson, *The Navajo Nation*, 71; Paul Jones, "Address to the Navajo Health Association," 12 May 1956, pp. 4–6, Box 5, Navajo Agency, 1955–1957 Folder, DIHC.

22. Paul Jones to L. E. Burney, 27 August 1956, Box 480, Folder 11, CHP.

23. Dr. L. E. Burney, U.S. Surgeon General, to Paul Jones, Navajo Tribal Chairman, 1956, Box 480, Folder 11, CHP.

24. David R. L. Duncan, "Welcome to the Third Working Conference of the Navajo Health Association, May 12, 1956," p. 9, *Navajo Health Association: Third Working Conference*.

25. Annie Wauneka to James Shaw, 5 April 1960, Annie Wauneka et al. to Paul Jones, 11 March 1960, James Shaw to Annie Wauneka, 22 April 1960, 91st Cong., Box 13, Folder 5, Barry Goldwater Congressional Papers, Arizona Historical Foundation, Tempe (hereinafter cited as BGCP); Paul Jones and Annie Wauneka to Dennis Chávez, telegram, 18 February 1958, Dennis Chávez to Paul Jones, 19 February 1958, Box 83, Folder 21, DCP.

26. NT, 7 July 1966, 1–2, 4–5, 6 July 1967, 1, 10, 20 July 1967, 4, 13.

27. Iverson, *The Navajo Nation*, 57, 104; Edward T. Hall, *West of the Thirties: Discoveries Among the Navajo and Hopi* (New York: Doubleday, 1994), 53.

28. Bailey and Bailey, *A History of the Navajos*, 268, 282–85.

29. David W. Broudy and Philip A. May, "Demographic and Epidemiologic Transition Among the Navajo Indians," *Social Biology* 30 (spring 1983): 1–16; Howard, *Navajo Tribal Demography*, 45–60.

30. Figures in the first three rows are taken from USDHEW, USPHS, Health Services and Mental Health Administration, IHS, *Indian Health Trends and Services, 1970 Edition*, PHS Pub. No. 2092 (Washington, D.C.: Office of Program Planning and Evaluation,

Program Analysis and Statistics Branch, January 1971), 14. The last two rows are from Sixten S. R. Haraldson, "Health and Health Services Among the Navajo Indians," *Journal of Community Health* 13 (fall 1988): 130. The "all Indian" statistic is from U.S. Department of Health and Human Services, (hereinafter cited as USDHHS), USPHS, IHS, Office of Planning, Evaluation, and Legislation, Division of Program Statistics, *Indian Health Service: Trends in Indian Health, 1992* (Washington, D.C.: GPO, 1992), 30. No "all Indian" data are listed for 1970.

31. USDHEW, USPHS, IHS, *Indian Health Trends and Services, 1970*, 7–10; John Cobb to Charles Mallary, "Maternal and Child Health Annual Report," 27 July 1959, Box 3, Folder 142, BBW.

32. Howard, *Navajo Tribal Demography*, 140–41; Adair et al., *The People's Health, 1988*, 156–57; Edison E. Newman, Sanitarian Director, "Planning the Navajo Family," 23 December 1966, Box 18, Training Programs, Planning the Navajo Family Folder, SF, 1965–1972.

33. Sen. Paul Fannin, "Indian Health Service," speech, 24 April 1970, p. 2, Tucson, Arizona, 91st Cong., Box 57, Folder 24, Paul Fannin Congressional Papers, Arizona Historical Foundation, Tempe (hereinafter cited as PFCP).

34. Young, *The Navajo Yearbook, 1951–1961*, 100; Howard, *Navajo Tribal Demography*, 206.

35. James Bondurant, "Typhoid Fever in the Shiprock Area," 17 January 1958, Box 6, Shiprock Hospital, 1956–1957 Folder, DIHC; Henry Kassel, "Maternal and Child Health Monthly Activity Report, December 1957, Highlight: Epidemic of Infectious Hepatitis," 3 January 1958, Box 4, Folder 1, DIHC; E. F. McIntyre, Assistant Area Medical Officer, Albuquerque Sub-Area, "Preliminary Report: Infectious Hepatitis Epidemic, Navajo Reservation, Indian Boarding School and Community Townspeople, Chinle, Arizona, December 1957," 5 January 1958, Box 4, Folder 1, DIHC; Van H. Dyer to Kassel and Bondurant, telegram, 13 February 1958, Bondurant to Assistant Area Medical Officer in Charge, Window Rock Sub-Area Office, memorandum, 12 February 1958, Kassel to Huston K. Spangler, Assistant Chief, Field Health, 17 February 1958, Box 4, Albuquerque Personnel, 1955–1957 Folder, DIHC.

36. USDHEW, USPHS, IHS, *Indian Health Trends and Services, 1970*, 28.

37. Ibid., 56; Cobb to Mallary, "Maternal and Child Health Annual Report," 27 July 1959, Box 3, Folder 142, BBW.

38. Wise, "The Ecology of Disease"; Bailey and Bailey, *A History of the Navajos*, 281.

39. Public Health Service, "Trachoma," 24 April 1964, pamphlet, Box 2, Folder 85, BBW; "Special Report on Plague Epidemic," n.d., Box 3, Folder 249, BBW; Margaret M. Turnbull and Bernice W. Loughlin, "Nursing Service at the Intertribal Ceremonial at Gallup, New Mexico," 1964, Box 4, Folder 242, BBW.

40. McIntyre, "Preliminary Report," January 5, 1958, pp. 3–4, Box 4, Folder 1, DIHC; Turnbull and Loughlin, "Nursing Service at the Intertribal Ceremonial at Gallup, New Mexico," 1964, Box 4, Folder 242, BBW; George Bock, "Report to the Navajo Tribal Council," 10 April 1967, pp. 7–8, Box 4, Window Rock Folder, SF, 1965–1972; *NT*, 1 September 1966, 10, 15, 11 August 1966, 7.

41. Howard, *Navajo Tribal Demography*, 198–202.

42. Ibid., 196–97; Tom Joe, interview by Tom Ration, Smith Lake, New Mexico, January 1969, Tape 53, Billy Short and Tom Ralton, interview by Austin Leiby, n.p., 11 August 1968, Tape 136, Roll 1, AIOHC; Mr. Roanhorse, Community Action Committee, recorded by Tom Ration, n.p., February 1969, Tape 311, Roll 2, Ned Yazzie, interview by Tom Ration, n.p., February 1969, Tape 315, Roll 2, Rex Becenti,

Jr., interview by Tom Ration, Tohatchi, New Mexico, n.p., December 1969, Tape 367, Roll 3, AIOHC; Buck Chamber, "The Drinking Problem of the Navajos," *NT*, 18 March 1965, 14, 1 February 1968, 11, 21 March 1968, 12; Statement by Paul Jones, 8 December 1958, pp. 30–31, Part 2, Roll 2, NTCM; Statement by Charles McCammon and Scott Preston, Navajo Tribal Council Minutes, Budget Session, 23 April 1962, Roll 7, NTCM; Statement by Carl Beyal, Statement McCammon, 8 December 1964, pp. 54, 57–58, Part 2, Roll 11, NTCM.

43. Stephen J. Kunitz and Jerrold E. Levy, *Drinking Careers: A Twenty-Five-Year Study of Three Navajo Populations* (New Haven, Conn.: Yale University Press, 1994), 1–28, 181–90.

44. Indian Health Service Task Force on Alcoholism, "Alcoholism: A High Priority Health Problem, Document 1, Draft 2," 2 June 1969, and Robert J. Savard, "The Navajo Alcoholic: A Man Yearning for Social Competence," n.d., Box 7, SF, 1965–1968; "Summary of Activities Related to Alcoholism—Albuquerque Area," n.d., Box 7, Activities Related to Alcoholism Summary Folder, DIHC; *NT*, 24 February 1966, 9, 25 May 1967, 5, 28 November 1968, 12.

45. Kunitz, *Disease Change*, 65; Kunitz and Levy, *Drinking Careers*, 55–57.

46. Kunitz and Levy, *Drinking Careers*, 181–85.

47. Ibid., 185–86; Howard, *Navajo Tribal Demography*, 171–85.

48. Bureau of Ethnic Research, Department of Anthropology, University of Arizona, "Social and Economic Resources Available for Indian Health Purposes in Five Southwestern States" (report prepared for the USPHS, Tucson, Ariz., 15 June 1956), vol. 2, "Arizona," p. 6, vol. 3, "New Mexico," p. 2, vol. 4, "Nevada, Utah, and Colorado," p. 16, Arizona State Museum Library, Tucson.

49. McIntyre, "Preliminary Report," 5 January 1958, Box 4, Folder 1, DIHC.

50. Bureau of Ethnic Research, "Social and Economic Resources Available for Indian Health Purposes in Five Southwestern States," vols. 2–4; Stanley Leland to Henry Kassel, 14 June 1956, Kassel to Leland, 28 June 1956, J. O. Dean to Kassel, 3 August 1956, Box 4, Equipment and Supplies, 1953–1957 Folder, DIHC; Statements by Charles McCammon, Annie Wauneka, et al., 8 December 1964, pp. 57–60, Part 2, Roll 11, NTCM; Surgeon General to Arthur Watkins, 29 August 1957, Box 4, Folder 4, DIHC; Statement by Annie Wauneka, U.S. House and Senate Joint Committee on Navajo-Hopi Indian Administration, *Legislation Concerning the Navajo Tribe*, 15.

51. Kassel to Leland, 28 June 1956, 3 August 1956, Box 4, Equipment and Supplies, 1953–1957 Folder, DIHC; Statement by Annie Wauneka, Navajo Tribal Council Minutes, Budget Session, 25 April 1963, p. 238, Part 2, Roll 9, NTCM.

52. States were allowed a great deal of flexibility under the Medicaid program, but they were not allowed to exclude eligible people by race. Alexander to Goldwater, 3 March 1969, Alexander to John Rhodes, 3 March 1969, Rhodes to Alexander, 10 March 1969, Goldwater to Alexander, 14 March 1969, 91st Cong., Box 6, Folder 3, BGCP; *NT*, 7 July 1966, 18; Arizona Commission of Indian Affairs, "1968 Survey Follow-Ups," Phoenix, Arizona, 1968, Box 1, Folder 2, Charles F. Gritzner Collection, MSS 044, Arizona Room, ASU; Starr, *The Social Transformation*, 369–70.

53. "Report of U.S. Public Service to Navajo Chapter Presidents," 31 August 1956, p. 4, Box 4, Folder 4, DIHC.

54. Donald L. Fixico, *Termination and Relocation: Federal Indian Policy, 1945–1960* (Albuquerque: University of New Mexico Press, 1986), 151–56; Billy Tochin, interview by Michael Husband, Torreon, New Mexico, 26 February 1970, AIOHC; Tom

Joe, interview, AIOHC; Ray Yazzie, interview by Michael Husband, n.p., 19 February 1970, Tape 471, Roll 3, AIOHC.

55. George Bertino to Carl Hayden, 8 August 1967, E. S. Rabeau to Hayden, 3 May 1967, Minnie Moore to Hayden, 12 May 1965, Grace Rowley to Hayden, 10 May 1968, Box 315, Folder 46, CHP; F. W. Parker, Secretary of the McKinley County Medical Society, to Dennis Chávez, 25 February 1958, Paul Jones and Annie Wauneka to Joseph Montoya, telegram, 18 February 1958, O. G. O'Connor, Board of Directors, Gallup-McKinley Chamber of Commerce, to Chávez, 18 February 1958, A. L. Maisel, Bernalillo County Indian Hospital, to Chávez, 3 January 1958, Chávez to Maisel, 21 January 1958, Box 158, Folder 4, DCP; "Supplementary Notes—Background Statement on Gallup Hospital," n.d., Box 58, DCP; Clinton Anderson to William Stewart, Surgeon General, 22 June 1967, Mrs. James West to Anderson, 20 June 1967, Box 2, Medical Care, 1967, Albuquerque Folder, SF, 1965–1972; Carol Atwood to E. S. Rabeau, 4 March 1967, Rabeau to Atwood, 23 March 1967, Box 2, Medicare, 1967, Albuquerque Folder, Records of the Indian Health Service, National Archives II, College Park, Md.; Mrs. Bill Van Huss, Jr. to Marion Folsom, Secretary DHEW, 14 November 1957, I. W. Steele to Area Medical Officer in Charge, Albuquerque Area Office, memorandum, 12 December 1957, James Shaw to Van Huss, 26 December 1957, Box 5, Crownpoint, 1955–1957 Folder, DIHC.

56. F. W. Parker, Secretary of the McKinley County Medical Society, to Dennis Chávez, 25 February 1958, Paul Jones and Annie Wauneka to Joseph Montoya, telegram, 18 February 1958, O. G. O'Connor, Board of Directors, Gallup-McKinley Chamber of Commerce, to Chávez, 18 February 1958, A. L. Maisel, Bernalillo County Indian Hospital, to Chávez, 3 January 1958, Chávez to Maisel, 21 January 1958, Box 158, Folder 4, DCP; *Gallup Independent* (hereinafter cited as *GI*), 22 March 1961, 1, 26 May 1961, 1–2, 6, and 28 May 1961, 1.

57. GI, 22 March 1961, 1, 26 May 1961, 1–2, 6, 28 May 1961, 1; *NT*, 3 May 1961, 1; "United States Public Health Service Installations: Arizona and New Mexico, October 30-November 17, 1960," pp. 10–12, Box 7, Folder 3, DCP.

Chapter 5

1. James Shaw, "Indian Health Progress," Address at the Annual Indian Achievement Awards ceremony of the Indian Council Fire, 25 September 1959, Chicago, Ill., pp. 1–2, 9–11, Box 7, Folder 7, William J. Zimmerman Jr. Papers, 1933–65, MSS 517 BC, CSR.

2. "Report of U.S. Public Health Service to Navajo Chapter Presidents," 31 August 1956, pp. 4–5, Box 4, Folder 4, DIHC; Statements by Joseph McPherson, Annie Wauneka, et al., pp. 189–204, 15 January 1959, Part 2, Roll 2, NTCM.

3. Statements by Joseph McPherson, Annie Wauneka, et al., 15 January 1959, pp. 189–227, Part 2, Roll 2, NTCM.

4. Ibid., 207–11, 225–27.

5. Ibid., 225; Statements by Clifford Beck, Annie Wauneka, et al., 4 November 1961, pp. 155–65, Part 2, Roll 7, NTCM.

6. Kane and Kane, *Federal Health Care*, 38–43.

7. Ibid.; USDHHW, USPHS, Health Services and Mental Health Administration, "Evaluation of Community Health Representative Program," 13 February 1970, p. 1, Box 3, Folder 209, BBW.

8. Kane and Kane, *Federal Health Care,* 39–41; USDHHW, USPHS, "Evaluation of Community Health Representative Program," 13 February 1970, Box 3, Folder 209, BBW.

9. Iverson, *The Navajo Nation,* 89–91.

10. *NT,* 29 August 1963, 7, 18 March 1965, 14, 17 March 1966, 19, 11 April 1968, 1, 4, 28 November 1968, 12, 14 August 1969, 14.

11. Jerry S. Bathke, Diné Bitsiis Baa Aha Yaa, Inc., September Newsletter, 7 October 1970, 92d. Cong., Box 155, Folder 11, BGCP; Statement by James Bondurant, 11 July 1960, pp. 6–7, Part 2 Roll 4, NTCM; George Bock, "Report to the Navajo Tribal Council," 10 April 1967, pp. 13–14, Box 4, Window Rock Folder, SF, 1965–1972; *NT,* 28 November 1968, 1, 6 February 1969, 1, 14 August 1969, 1, 28 August 1969, 2; Stephen J. Kunitz and Jerrold Levy, *Navajo Aging: The Transition from Family to Institutional Support* (Tucson: University of Arizona Press, 1991), 123; Statement by Carl Beyal, Record of the Navajo Tribal Council, Budget Session, 15 May 1963, p. 673, Part 2, Roll 9, NTCM; Statements by Frankie Howard, Sevier Vaughn, John Begaye, et al., Record of the Navajo Tribal Council, Budget Session, 9 July 1964, pp. 547–50, Part 2, Roll 10, NTCM.

12. Paul Jones, Chairman of the Navajo Tribal Council, Address to the College of Medical Evangelists, 8 March 1957, in Stirling, *Mission to the Navajo,* 143–47; Statements by Charles McCammon and Samuel Billison, 12 February 1962, p. 54, Part 2, Roll 7, NTCM.

13. Murbarger, "White Man's Medicine," 5–10; *NT,* 20 February 1964, 11.

14. Statements by Manuel Begay, Howard Gorman, et al., Record of the Navajo Tribal Council, Budget Session, 26 June 1962, pp. 1064–1067, Part 2, Roll 8, NTCM.

15. Arthur Watkins to James Shaw, 13 December 1956, Box 4, Cooperation, 1955–1957 Folder, DIHC; Alexander Leighton, "Some Impressions of the U.S. Public Health Service with Regard to the Navaho Indians," 11 October 1957, Box 4, Albuquerque, Organization 1957 Folder, DIHC.

16. *NT,* 1 December 1966, 20, 30 March 1967, 4, 21 September 1967, 1. St. Mary's Hospital had also served the area since the early decades of the twentieth century, but the nuns did not focus their efforts on the Navajo reservation. The facility had also served as a tuberculosis sanatorium. Raymond Estrada, discharge planner, Rehoboth-McKinley Hospital, interview by author, Gallup, N.Mex., 3 December 1993.

17. Estrada, interview; *NT,* 21 September 1967, 1.

18. Project HOPE, "Proposal for Development of the Navajo Indian Program at Ganado," n.d., 91st. Cong., Box 58, Folder 9, PFCP; William Walsh to Fannin, 26 June 1969, Fannin to Walsh, 10 July 1969, 91st. Cong., Box 58, Folder 13, PFCP.

19. John King, director of development, Sage Memorial Hospital, interview by author, Ganado, Ariz., 2 October 1992; *NT,* 24 July 1969, 15, 11 September 1969, 15–16. A few churches, including the Catholic Church, Lutheran Church, and the Church of Latter Day Saints, continued to provide limited clinical services to Navajos in the 1960s and 1970s. Will Stapleton and Patricia Heredia, "A History: Churches Contribute to Navajo Nation Health Care," *NT,* 8 April 1976, B-10, B-13.

20. Rough Rock News, "Navajo Mental Health," *The Rough Rock News,* 18 March 1970.

21. Adair et al., *The People's Health,* 1988, 161–78; *NT,* 27 April 1978, 19.

22. Impressions taken from AIOHC and Johnson, *Stories of Traditional Navajo Life and Culture.*

23. Aberle, *The Peyote Religion*, 1982, xliii–xlvi; Bailey and Bailey, *A History of the Navajos*, 280.

24. Aberle, *The Peyote Religion*, xliii–xlvi; Deescheeny Nez Tracy, interview in *Stories of Traditional*, ed. Johnson, 158–59; Charlie Brown, interview in *Stories of Traditional*, 147; John Dick, interview in *Stories of Traditional*, 200; Frisbie, "Temporal Change," 492.

25. Tracy, interview, *Stories of Traditional*, 164.

26. Thomas Clani, interview in *Stories of Traditional*, ed. Johnson, 248; Howard Gorman, interview, AIOHC; Tom Ration, interview in *Stories of Traditional*, ed. Johnson, 324.

27. Mitchell, *Navajo Blessingway Singer*, 292.

28. Adair et al., *The People's Health*, 1988, 161–79; Tracy, interview, *Stories of Traditional*, 165.

29. Tracy, interview, *Stories of Traditional*, 164.

30. Dick, interview, *Stories of Traditional*, 200.

31. Tom Joe, interview, AIOHC; Jack Johnson, interview by Tom Ration, Black Mountain, Arizona, October 1968, p. 5, Tape 181, Roll 1, AIOHC.

32. George Bock, "The Medicine Men," *PHS World* 2, no. 4 (April 1967): 33.

33. Adair et al., *The People's Health*, 1988, 162–68.

34. Ibid., 161–76; Frisbie, "Temporal Change," 477–78.

35. Hosteen Klah shared ceremonies with Franc Newcomb. Newcomb, *Hosteen Klah*; Howard Gorman, interview, AIOHC; Tracy, interview, 160.

36. Iverson, *The Navajo Nation*, 114–23.

37. Dr. Robert L. Bergman, interview by Brad Steiger, in *Indian Medicine Power*, by Brad Steiger (Atglen, Pa.: Whitford Press, 1984), 51; Rough Rock News, "Navajo Mental Health," *The Rough Rock News*, 18 November 1970; Robert A. Roessel, *Navajo Education in Action: The Rough Rock Demonstration School* (Chinle, Ariz.: Navajo Curriculum Center, Rough Rock Demonstration School, 1977), 83–85; Frisbie, "Temporal Change," 495; Robert Roessel, former director of Rough Rock Demonstration School and president of Navajo Community College, interview by author, Round Rock, Ariz., 29 July 1997.

38. Rough Rock News, "Navajo Mental Health." In reports to the Tribal Council and official publications, Bock frequently borrowed from some of the Leightons' original reports to explain how physicians and healers could work cooperatively. The IHS also became more open to traditional healing officially by advertising examples of cooperation between physician and healers in its publications, such as in Bock, "The Medicine Men," and USDHEW, USPHS, "After Antibiotics: The Fire Dance," *Medical News* (10 June 1959), n.p.

39. Rough Rock News, "Navajo Mental Health"; Bergman, interview, *Indian Medicine Power*, 47–51.

40. Hoke Denetsosie, interview in *Stories of Traditional*, ed. Johnson, 100–102.

41. Aberle, *The Peyote Religion*, xxxvii–xlviii.

42. Ibid., xi; NYT, 14 November 1962, 52, 15 November 1962, 41, 7 May 1963, 47, and 25 August 1964, 35.

43. Dr. Robert L. Bergman, interview by Joel Bernstein, Window Rock, Ariz., 1 July 1970, Tape 643, Roll 3, AIOHC.

44. Aberle, *The Peyote Religion*, xxxviii; Mitchell, *Navajo Blessingway Singer*, 1978, 316; Iverson, *The Navajo Nation*, 86–87.

Chapter 6

1. Bock, "Report to the Navajo Tribal Council," 10 April 1967, pp. 5–6, Box 4, Window Rock Folder, Subject Files, 1965–1972, Records of the Indian Health Service, National Archives II, College Park, Md.; USDHEW, USPHS, Division of Indian Health, Navajo Area Office, *Health Highlights: Trends in DIH Facility Workloads, Navajo Area* (Albuquerque, N.Mex.: Albuquerque Area, Program Analysis Branch, 1968), 2, 23.

2. Navajo Health Authority (hereinafter cited as NHA), "The American Indian School of Medicine, Briefing Paper on AISOM," October 1975, unpublished report, p. 1, Box 1, Folder 9, Manuel Lujan Papers, 1971–81, MSS 142 BC, CSR; Robert Roessel, interview.

3. Ida Bahl, *Nurse Among the Navajos* (Northvale, N.J.: Shepherd Publishing, 1984), 135–41.

4. Kane and Kane, *Federal Health Care*, 47–59; Richard Bozof, "Some Navaho Attitudes Toward Available Medical Care," *American Journal of Public Health* 62 (December 1972): 1620–24.

5. Statement by Charles McCammon, 27 November 1961, p. 16, Part II, Roll 6, NTCM; Geri Bahe-Hernandez, director of community health services at Tuba City Hospital, interview by author, Tuba City, Ariz., 4 February 1993; Kane and Kane, *Federal Health Care*, 47–52.

6. Lena Fowler, coordinator of Navajo Community College Cross-Cultural Training Project, interview by author, Tuba City, Ariz., 4 February 1993; Fran Kosik, director of development, Sage Memorial Hospital, interview by author, Tuba City, Ariz., 4 February 1993; Frisbie, *Navajo Medicine Bundles*, 258.

7. Alexander H. Leighton and Donald A. Kennedy for the USPHS, "Pilot Study of Cultural Items in Medical Diagnosis: A Field Report," 1 July 1957, pp. 11–12, Box 4, Folder 248, BBW.

8. Bock, "The Medicine Men"; Robert Young, Ph.D., professor emeritus, University of New Mexico, interviews with author, 5 April 1992, 8 February 1993.

9. Nealtha J. Stone response to "History of Indian Service Nursing Questionnaire," 6 August 1974, Box 1, Folder 7, BBW; Bock, "The Medicine Men," 34; Bernice W. Loughlin, "Aide Training Reaches the Navajo Reservation," *American Journal of Nursing* 63 (July 1963): 106–9; Leighton and Kennedy, "Pilot Study of Cultural Items," 11–12, BBW; Kane and Kane, *Federal Health Care*, 83; Henry W. Winship, III, "Pharmacy Goes West: Cultivating the Navajo Indians," *Journal of the American Pharmaceutical Association*, n.s., 4 (December 1964): 594–99.

10. Kane and Kane, *Federal Health Care*, 50. Non-Indian nurses frequently commented that their Navajo colleagues were often more opposed to traditional healing beliefs than they were. One nurse who worked at Crownpoint in the 1940s could not remember her Navajo coworker acting "any different" from the Anglo nurses and argued that it really did not matter how they approached Navajo culture because "we couldn't do anything until the doctors told us anyway." Mrs. Joseph Kraft, interview by Daniel Tyler, Fort Defiance, Ariz., 21 November 1969, p. 20, Tape 529, Roll 3, AIOHC.

11. Robert Kane and Douglas McConatha, "The Men in the Middle: A Dilemma of Minority Health Workers," *Medical Care* 13, no. 9 (September 1975): 736–43; Jennie Joe, former member of NHA and current faculty member of University of Arizona, interview by author, Tucson, Ariz., 22 January 1993.

12. Kane and Kane, *Federal Health Care*, 47–9; Bozof, "Some Navaho Attitudes," 1620–24.

13. Jennie Joe, interview; *NT*, 18 July 1963, 3, 24 October 1963, 8; Robert Roessel, interview; Kane and Kane, *Federal Health Care*, 50.

14. Kane and Kane, *Federal Health Care*, 57; Statement by Charles McCammon, 12 February 1962, p. 51, Roll 7, NTCM.

15. Statement by Annie Wauneka, 25 April 1963, p. 238, Part, Roll 9, NTCM; *NT*, 18 July 1963, 3, 5 March 1964, 2; Iverson, *The Navajo Nation*, 154; Kane and Kane, *Federal Health Care*, 44.

16. When Wauneka complained about poor conditions affecting other patients in the Gallup Indian Medical Center while hospitalized in 1971, the secretary of the Department of Health, Education, and Welfare, Congressman Morris Udall from Arizona, and IHS officials paid attention—they investigated the complaint on a point-by-point basis. Annie Wauneka, interview by S. I. Myers of the History Department of St. Louis College, Klagetoh, Ariz., no. 74, *New York Times* Oral History Program, Listening to Indians, 19 October 1975, Labriola Center, Arizona State University, Tempe; Elliott Richardson, Secretary of Health, Education, and Welfare to Morris K. Udall, House of Representatives, n.d., Richardson to Wauneka, n.d., Emery Johnson, Director of Indian Health Service, "Report on Conditions in the Gallup Indian Medical Center," n.d., Udall to Richardson, 11 January 1972, Wauneka to Richardson, n.d., Box 561, Folder 3, Morris K. Udall Papers, MS 325, Special Collections, The University of Arizona Library, University of Arizona, Tucson (hereinafter cited as MKUP).

17. R. L. Gorrell, "Clinic Cares at Lukachukai," *Arizona* (19 November 1978): 11; "History of Indian Service Nursing Questionnaire," Box 1, Folders 7–14, BBW.

18. "History of Indian Service Nursing Questionnaire," Box 1, Folders 7–14, BBW.

19. Barbara Munn, Navajo Area Indian Health Service (hereinafter cited as NAIHS) employee, interview by author, Window Rock, Ariz., 4 March 1993; Statement by McCammon, 12 February 1962, p. 51, Roll 7, NTCM.

20. Kane and Kane, *Federal Health Care*, 22–33; Steven Borowsky, M.D., former IHS physician on Cheyenne River Reservation, interview by author, Phoenix, Ariz., 18 August 1997.

21. *NT*, 18 January 1973, A7.

22. University of New Mexico, "Indian Health Care, Turnover Rate of Registered Nurses," unpublished report, Box 3, Folder 9, Barry Goldwater Papers, Indian Affairs Series, Arizona Historical Foundation, Tempe (hereinafter cited as BGPIA); Lillian Watson, "A Report on Hospital Nursing Services Status in the IHS Hospital at Shiprock, July 31, 1979," unpublished report, Box 7, Folder 467, BBW.

23. *NT*, 18 September 1975, A3, 25 September 1975, 1, A8.

24. Letter to Jackson, 2 October 1974, 93d Cong., Box 4, Folder 23, PFCP.

25. Borowsky, interview; Memorandum by Benjamin M. Bravence, Division of Indian Health, "Health Communication Program Procedures Document," Box 18, Bravamara Health Communications Training Folder, SF, 1965–1972; Staff of the Navajo Health Education Project, University of California School of Public Health, for USDHHW, USPHS, Division of Indian Health, *Orientation to Health on the Navajo Indian Reservation: A Guide for Hospital and Public Health Workers*, (Washington, D.C.: GPO, 1961); Kane and Kane, *Federal Health Care*, 78–102.

Chapter 7

1. "Dr. Taylor McKenzie: Kinlichii'nii Clan—Red House People," in Hoffman and Johnson, *Navajo Biographies*, 308–21; *NT*, 25 September 1975, A10.

2. Paul Chaat Smith and Robert Allen Warrior, *Like a Hurricane: The Indian Movement from Alcatraz to Wounded Knee* (New York: The New Press, 1996), 28–29; Vine Deloria, Jr., *Custer Died for Your Sins: An Indian Manifesto* (1970; reprint, New York: Avon Books, 1972), 140–41.

3. Borowsky, interview; *GI*, 29 January 1973, 1, 6; 30 January 1973, 1, 6, 1 February 1973, 2, 3 February 1973, 1, 2, 23 March 1973, 1, 6, 23 May 1973, 1, 6, 26 May 1973, 1, 6; *NT*, 1 February 1973, 1, A4. Mrs. Cutnose's first name is not listed in articles related to the incident.

4. *GI*, 29 January 1973, 1, 6, 30 January 1973, 1, 6, 1 February 1973, 2, 3 February 1973, 1, 3 February, 1973, 2, 23 March 1973, 1, 6, 23 May 1973, 1, 6, 26 May 1973, 1, 6; *NT*, 1 February 1973, 1, A4.

5. Ellouise DeGroat, NAIHS tribal relations director, interview by author, Window Rock, Ariz., 5 March 1993.

6. *NT*, 3 July 1975, 1, A7, 21 August 1975, 1, A6, 9 October 1975, 1, A3, 8 January 1976, A2.

7. *NT*, 8 January 1976, A2.

8. Ibid. Emery Johnson later apologized to the nurses, admitting that their complaints were valid, but that they had to be terminated for their failure to report for reassignment.

9. Ibid.; Iverson, *The Navajo Nation*, 204.

10. Patricia White, "Forced Sterilization Amongst American Indian Women," *Journal of Indigenous Studies* 1, no. 2 (1989): 91–96; Charles R. England, "A Look at the Indian Health Service Policy of Sterilization, 1972–76," *Red Ink* 3 (spring 1994): 17–21; Janet Karsten Larson, "And Then There Were None: Is Federal Policy Endangering the American Indian 'Species'?" *The Christian Century* (26 January 1977): 61–63.

11. England, "A Look," 18; Larson, "And Then There Were None," 61; Helen Temkin-Greener, "Surgical Fertility Regulation Among Women on the Navajo Indian Reservation," *American Journal of Public Health* (August 1969): 405–6, cited in England, "A Look," 18; Stephen Kunitz, *A Survey of Fertility Histories and Contraceptive Use Among a Group of Navajo Women*, Lake Powell Research Project Bulletin, ed. Priscilla C. Grew (Los Angeles: University of California, Collaborative Research on Assessment of Man's Activities in the Lake Powell Region, Research Applied to National Needs, National Science Foundation, 1976).

12. England, "A Look," 17–21; U.S. Comptroller General, General Accounting Office, *Activities of the Indian Health Service*, special report prepared at the request of the U.S. Congress, 1978, Box 601, MKUP.

13. Cate Gilles, Marti Reed, and Jacques Seronde, "Our Uranium Legacy," *Northern Arizona Environmental Newsletter* (summer 1990): 1–11; NHA, *Pictures of the Navajo: Their Health and Environment in 1980*, ed. Barbara Bayless Lacy (Window Rock, Ariz., 1980); Rita Goodman, "Secondary Sex Ratio and Birth Weights of Navajo Indians in an Area of Uranium Mining and Milling" (Master's thesis, Arizona State University, 1984); "Navajos Who Mined Uranium Dying from Lung Cancer," *The Albuquerque Tribune*, 17 August 1973.

14. In the 1950s, the PHS had obtained permission from the mining companies to conduct a health study in the mines in exchange for promising not to reveal the results to the laborers. Sandy Tolan, "Uranium Plagues the Navajos," *Sierra* 68 (November/

December 1983): 55–60; Susan E. Dawson, "Navajo Uranium Workers and the Effects of Occupational Illnesses: A Case Study," *Human Organization* 51 (winter 1992): 389–97; High Country News, "Experts Knew Miners Were at Risk," *High Country News*, vol. 22 (18 June 1990): 11–12.

15. Dawson, "Navajo Uranium Workers," 393; Tolan, "Uranium Plagues the Navajos," 56–57.

16. Dawson, "Navajo Uranium Workers," 392; Tony Davis, "Uranium Has Decimated Navajo Miners," *High Country News*, 18 June 1990, 1, 10; Sam Negri, "When Things Go Awry, Relax, Here Comes Muttonman," *Arizona Highways* 73 (July 1997): 32–35.

17. Francis Paul Prucha, *The Indians in American Society: From the Revolutionary War to the Present* (Berkeley: University of California Press, 1985), 80–103; Prucha, *The Great Father*, 364–65.

18. Senate Subcommittee on Indian Affairs of the Committee on Interior and Insular Affairs, *Indian Self-Determination and Education Program: Hearings before the Subcommittee on Indian Affairs on S. 1017 and Related Bills*, 93d Cong., 1st sess., 1 and 4 June 1973 (Washington, D.C.: GPO, 1973), 259–70.

19. Ibid.; Prucha, *The Great Father*, 378–80; USDHHS, USPHS, IHS, prepared by the National Indian Health Board and American Indian Technical Services, *The Indian Health Service's Implementation of the Indian Self-Determination Process* (Washington, D.C.: GPO, 1984); Kunitz, *Disease Change*, 47–48.

20. Prucha, *The Great Father*, 377; Emery Johnson, "Statement on Indian Health Programs, March 2, 1981," in *Documents of United States Indian Policy*, ed. Prucha, 298–300.

21. Kunitz, *Disease Change*, 65.

22. U.S. Comptroller General, General Accounting Office, *Progress and Problems in Providing Health Services to Indians*, a special report prepared at the request of the U.S. Congress, 11 March 1973, 1–4, MKUP; NT, 18 September 1975, A3, 25 September 1975, 1, A8.

23. Paul Fannin, "Indian Health Care: A Real Health Care Crisis," *Arizona Medicine* 32 (September 1975): 741–47.

24. Ibid., 741; Starr, *The Social Transformation*, 381.

25. NT, 14 March 1974, 1, 21 March 1974, A4, 4 April 1974, A12, 25 September 1975, A10, 12 February 1976, A11, 15 April 1976, A3, 12 August 1976, A8; "News from U.S. Senator Paul Fannin of Arizona," 25 September 1975, 94th Cong., Box 58, Folder 38, PFCP; Fannin to Peter MacDonald, 28 January 1976, 95th Cong., Box 26, Folder 11, BGCP; Navajo Comprehensive Health Planning Agency, "NCHPA Newsletter," September 1975, George James, Councilman, Tsaile-Wheatfields Chapter to Fannin, 94th Cong., Box 9, Folder 4, PFCP; NHA, "Statement of Testimony of the Navajo Health Authority Regarding Senate Bill 2938," n.d., 95th Cong., Box 26, Folder 9, BGCP; Public Law 94-437, 94th Cong., 2d. sess., 30 September 1976, i.e., *Indian Health Care Improvement Act of 1976*, U.S. *Statutes at Large* 90 (1976): 1400–14.

26. *Indian Health Care Improvement Act of 1976*, 1400–14.

27. NT, 21 March 1974, 1, 4, 29 May 1975, A2, 19 October 1975, A9, 7 October 1976, A3, 9 December 1976, A3, A11, 23 July 1981, 1, 3, 3 September 1981, 18, 25 August 1982, 14, 1 September 1982, 1, 4; Eck, *Contemporary Navajo Affairs*, 165, 185.

28. Iverson, *The Navajo Nation*, 125–26, 175.

29. Ibid., 156; Navajo Tribal Council, CMY-57–70, *Resolution of the Navajo Tribal Council: Establishing a Navajo Area Indian Health Advisory Board, 12 May 1970* (Window Rock, Ariz.: 1970); MacDonald to Fannin, August 10, 1971, 92d Cong., Box 46, Folder 11,

PFCP; Navajo Tribal Council, *CJN-62–72, Resolution of the Navajo Tribal Council: Rescinding Navajo Tribal Council Resolution CMY-57–70, and Creating a Navajo Area Indian Health Board and Eight Navajo Indian Health Service Unit Boards in Lieu Thereof, 15 June 1972* (Window Rock, Ariz., 1972); Crownpoint Service Unit Health Board, "Resolution, Supporting the Jackson-Fannin Bill," 2 April 1974, and Health Board, "New Liquor Outlet at Smith Lake," 2 April 1974, Box 46, Folder 7, Pete Domenici Papers, MSS 403 BC, CSR; Taylor McKenzie, M.D., Navajo Nation vice president, interview by author, Gallup, N.Mex., 5 February 1993.

30. Resolution of the Navajo Tribal Council, CJN-44-72, Establishing the Navajo Health Authority, 2 June 1972, NNM; NHA, *Annual Report, 1973* (Window Rock, Ariz., 1973); NHA, *Resolution 4R-1, Navajo Health Authority, Statement of Goals, Functions and Philosophy* (Window Rock, Ariz., 1973). The NHA conducted numerous studies on traditional healing and collected ceremonial and herbal knowledge through its ethno-medical encyclopedia and ethnobotany projects. "Navajo Beliefs Collected for Ethno-Medical Encyclopedia," *Navajo Area Health Education Center Newsletter* 1 (September 1976), 2, in *NT,* 30 September 1976.

31. Jennie Joe, interview; NHA, *Annual Report, 1973,* 3–10.

32. Frisbie, "Temporal Change," 496; Iverson, *The Navajo Nation,* 159; *NT,* 12 July 1973, B5, 25 April 1974, B1–B2, 1 August 1974, B16, 2 June 1977, B11, 27 December 1979, 4; "Dial 911 for All Emergencies," *Navajo Area Health Education Center Newsletter* 1 (December 1976), 3, in *NT,* 3 December 1976.

33. Starr, *The Social Transformation,* 402; *NT,* 18 July 1974, A10, 31 July 1975, A2, 23 March 1978, B8; 6 April 1978, 13; 27 April 1978, 17–18; 10 August 1978, B6, B12; 22 February 1979, A9, A17, A18.

34. *NT,* 17 February, 1977, A8, 5 March 1981, 19, 3 September 1981, 10–12, 28 April 1982, 17; Thomas Todacheeny, Gallup Indian Medical Center chief administrator, interview by author, Gallup, N.Mex., 4 February 1993.

35. George Bock, "Report to the Navajo Tribal Council," 3; "More Indian Nurses Needed to Staff Reservation Facilities," *Navajo Area Health Education Center Newsletter* 1 (December 1976), 2, in *NT,* 3 December 1976; NHA, "Petition to the Veterans Administration," August 1973, p. 3, Box 46, Folder 6, Domenici Papers, CSR.

36. Jennie Joe, interview; "Barriers to Medical Careers Discussed by Indian Med Students," *Navajo Area Health Education Center Newsletter* 1 (December 1976), 1, in *NT,* 3 December 1976.

37. *Indian Health Care Improvement Act of 1976; NT,* 12 April 1973, A8, 3 May 1973, 1, A4, 14 June 1973, A16, 18 April 1974, A-3, 21 April 1977, 3, 21 July 1977, A10, 10 August 1978, B9; "Kellogg Fellowship Graduates Work in Variety of Health Fields," *Navajo Area Health Education Center Newsletter* 2 (December 1977), 2, in *NT,* 22 December 1977; Kane and Kane, *Federal Health Care,* 31–32.

38. NHA, *Pictures of the Navajo,* 42; "Kellogg Fellowship Graduates," 2; "Aggressive Nurse Advisory Committee Works to Recruit, Retain Indian Nurses," *Navajo Area Health Education Center Newsletter* 1 (March 1977), 2, in *NT,* 31 March 1977; "Redesigned Nursing Program Emphasizes RN Degree," *Navajo Area Health Education Center Newsletter* 1 (September 1976), 2, in *NT,* 30 September 1976; Navajo Community College Newsletter, "Four Graduate from Nursing Program," *Navajo Community College Newsletter* 1 (January 1973): 1.

39. NHA, "American Indian School of Medicine," 1976, unpublished report, 95th Cong., Box 26, Folder 12, BGCP.

40. McKenzie's lobbying convinced Congress to include a Title VI in The Indian Health Care Improvement Act authorizing the Secretary of the DHEW to conduct a study "to determine the need for, and feasibility of" establishing the school. NHA, *Annual Report,* 1973, 13; NHA, *Annual Report, 1975* (Window Rock, Ariz., 1975), 8; *Indian Health Care Improvement Act of 1976*; Jasper L. McPhail, "American Indian School of Medicine," *Arizona Medicine* 34 (April 1977): 270–72; NHA, "American Indian School of Medicine," 2–9; McKenzie to Lujan, November 3, 1975, McKenzie to Meeds, 8 October 1975, Box 1, Folder 9, Manuel Lujan Papers, 1971–81, MSS 142 BC, CSR; McKenzie to Fannin, 11 February 1976, 94th Cong., Box 8, Folder 18, PFCP.

41. AISOM devised a plan of operation in which thirty-two to forty students would be selected. Students were to begin their pre-medical studies at Northern Arizona University and then move on to a clinical campus in Phoenix before being sent out to various IHS facilities. "Media Center Serves Area Health Personnel," *Navajo Area Health Education Center Newsletter* 2 (December 1977), 4, in *NT,* 22 December 1977; NHA, "AISOM Update #1," October 1975, Box 1, Folder 9, Manuel Lujan Papers, 1971–81, MSS 142 BC, CSR; McPhail, "American Indian School of Medicine," 272; McKenzie to Fannin, 11 February 1976, 94th Cong., Box 8, Folder 18, PFCP; Taylor McKenzie, interview.

42. Association of American Indian Physicians, "A Look Back," *Association of American Indian Physicians Newsletter* 25, no. 6 (July 1996): 1, 3; Indians Into Medicine, "Indians Into Medicine" report, Labriola Center, Arizona State University, Tempe.

43. Iverson, *The Navajo Nation,* 204; *NT,* 1 September 1977, B19.

44. "Barriers to Medical Careers," in *NT,* 3 December 1976, 1.

45. Emery Johnson to Goldwater, 10 May 1971, 91st Cong., Box 154, Folder 8, BGCP; Kayenta Chapter, "Resolution, Requesting the Navajo Tribal Council to Appropriate Funds for the Purchase of an Ambulance," 91st Cong., Box 92, Folder 2, BGCP; Randolph Begay, Councilman, Rock Point Chapter, to Goldwater, 95th Cong., Box 111, BGCP.

46. Roessel, *Navajo Education,* 122; "Written Report Following Oral Report to Task Force on Indian Health," p. 7, 95th Cong., Box 2, Folder 12, BGCP.

47. Iverson, *The Navajo Nation,* 157; Robert Roessel, interview; *NYT,* 5 May 1972, L13, 7 July 1972, 33.

48. Kitsilee Chapter to Haffner, on Kitsilee, n.d., 95th Cong., Box 2, Folder 12, BGCP; Roessel, *Navajo Education,* 122.

49. Roessel, *Navajo Education,* 122; Johnson to Rhodes, 21 May 1976, 94th Cong., Box 37, John J. Rhodes Papers, 1953–1983, MSS 002, Arizona Room, ASU.

50. Roberts to Scranton, 29 February 1976, 94th Cong., Box 37, Folder 1, Rhodes Papers, Arizona Room, ASU; Kitsilee Chapter to Haffner, on Kitsilee, n.d., Rough Rock Demonstration School, petition, 3 March 1976, 95th Cong., Box 2, Folder 12, BGCP; Yazzie to Haffner, 24 September 1976, Box 601, MKUP.

51. *Qua' Tqti,* 15 December 1977, 1; *NT,* 8 December 1977, A20.

52. Wallace Mulligan, "The Navajo Nation Health Foundation: The Sequel to Salsbury," *Arizona Medicine* 33 (January 1976): 52–54; *NT,* 15 August 1974, 1, 12 October 1977, A6.

53. Mulligan, "Navajo Nation," 52–54; *NT,* 28 April 1977, C9; 4 March 1976, B10.

54. Mulligan, "Navajo Nation," 52; *NT,* 9 September 1976, B2.

55. Mulligan, "Navajo Nation," 52; *NT,* 9 September 1978, B2; 28 April 1977, C9; 2 October 1975, A12; Lincoln to Udall, 11 March 1975, Udall to Morris Thompson,

BIA Commissioner, 21 March 1975, John Marshall, Acting Administrator of PHS, to Udall, 17 April 1975, Box 585, MKUP.

56. Navajo Nation Health Foundation, "Navajo Nation Health Foundation, 1990 Annual Progress Report" (Ganado, Ariz., 1991); King, interview.

57. *NT*, 14 March 1974, A10, 6 May 1976, A15; *GI*, 1 June 1973, 6; Jerome du Bois, "Medicine Men Organize to Protect Old Ways," *NT*, 27 April 1978, 19.

58. Frisbie, "Temporal Change," 492; Frisbie, *Navajo Medicine Bundles*, 263–64, 271.

59. *NT*, 10 November 1977, A4, 27 April 1978, 19; Robert Roessel, interview; *NYT*, 3 April 1977, 4, 7; Frisbie, "Temporal Change," 496–97.

60. *NT*, 10 November 1977, A4, 27 April 1978, 19; *NYT*, 3 April 1977, 4, 7; Frisbie, "Temporal Change," 496–97.

61. Frisbie, *Navajo Medicine Bundles*, 284–95.

62. Ibid.

63. Aberle, *The Peyote Religion*, xliv; du Bois, "Medicine Men," 19.

Chapter 8

1. Howard, *Navajo Tribal Demography*, 23–44, 122–23; Kunitz, *Navajo Aging*, 93; Kunitz, *Disease Change*, 62–86; Gregory Campbell, "The Changing Dimension of Native American Health: A Critical Understanding of Contemporary Native American Health Issues," *American Indian Culture and Research Journal* 13, nos. 3 and 4 (1989): 1–20; Broudy and May, "Demographic and Epidemiologic Transition," 1–16.

2. Entries marked with asterisks reflect statistics that are not provided by this source, but they demonstrate an accurate position of these causes by ranking as shown in USD-HHS, USPHS, NAIHS, Office of Program Planning and Development, *Navajo Area Indian Health Service, Area Profile, 1992* (Washington, D.C.: GPO, 1992). The all IHS clients statistics shown for the influenza and pneumonia and chronic liver disease and cirrhosis rates derive from USDHHS, USPHS, IHS, *Indian Health Service: Trends in Indian Health, 1992*, 43.

3. USDHHS, USPHS, IHS, *Regional Differences in Indian Health, 1992* (Washington, D.C., 1992), 55–56.

4. Howard, *Navajo Tribal Demography*, 86, 137–70.

5. Wilbert Gesler and Thomas C. Ricketts, *Health in Rural North America: The Geography of Health Care Services and Delivery* (New Brunswick, N.J.: Rutgers University Press, 1992), 16–46. I selected fifteen counties in a systematic random sample according to their scores for the availability of flush toilets, family income, unemployment rate, and mean daily average temperature in January. These variables were selected based on Stephen Kunitz's assessment that such variables would affect infant mortality (*Disease Change and the Role of Medicine*) and on derived statistical measures of association. Because the point of the study was to see how Navajo infant mortality rates compared over time to counties with similar economic and environmental conditions, ranges were first set for these variables according to the values given for counties overlapping with the Navajo reservation. States were selected subjectively to represent different regions of the United States with similar environmental conditions. The first county in each state and every fifth county thereafter was filtered through these variables to create the test group. Because areas defined as "rural" by the U.S. Census, based on the average size of population areas, were more likely to parallel the Navajo Nation in the abovemen-tioned ways than were metropolitan areas, only they were included in the sample. Counties were rejected if the *U.S. Decennial Population and Housing Census* of 1970

failed to designate them as "rural" or showed that a large proportion of the residents were American Indian. Of course, some American Indians were represented in the comparison counties, but relatively few would have been served by the Indian Health Service. Large non-Indian populations were accepted. Selected counties were drawn from Arkansas, Indiana, Kansas, Louisiana, Missouri, Montana, New Mexico, Nevada, Texas, West Virginia, and Wyoming.

6. *NT*, 15 June 1983, 1, 3, 26 May 1994, 1, A5, 28 July 1994, 1, A2, 16 March 1995, 1.

7. *NT*, 17 August 1989, 1–2, 16 April 1992, 9, 30 April 1992, 5, 8 October 1992, 9, 30 November 1995, A1-A2; Betty J. Claymore and Marian A. Taylor, "AIDS—Tribal Nations Face the Newest Communicable Disease: An Aberdeen Area Perspective," *American Indian Culture and Research Journal* 13, nos. 3 and 4 (1989): 21–31; Campbell, "The Changing Dimension of Native American Health," 4–8.

8. Howard, *Navajo Tribal Demography*, 198–200, 122–23.

9. *NT*, 27 February 1997, A5; USDHHS, USPHS, NAIHS, *Navajo Area Indian Health Service, Area Profile*, 1992, 7–9.

10. J. V. Neel, "Diabetes Mellitus: A 'Thrifty' Genotype Rendered Detrimental by 'Progress,'" *American Journal of Human Genetics* 14 [1984?]: 353–62, cited in Howard, *Navajo Tribal Demography*, 203–5; Sonya Yazzie, "Lifestyle Changes among the Navajo: Cause for Diabetes?" (paper presented at the 9th Annual Navajo Studies Conference, Fort Lewis College, Durango Colo., 1996); Elizabeth Cohen, "Good Medicine: First Navajo Woman Surgeon Operates Between Two Worlds," *New Mexico* 72 (August 1994): 26–31; Tracy, *Stories of Traditional Navajo Life and Culture*, 164.

11. Sonya Yazzie, "Lifestyle Changes Among the Navajo," 5.

12. *NT*, 14 October 1981, 18, 26 April 1985, 1, 2, 23 April 1992, 1, 2, 28 September 1995, A-3; *Phoenix Gazette* (hereinafter cited as *PG*), 22 February 1991, B11; Statement by Exendine in U.S. Senate Committee on Indian Affairs, *Issues of Indian Health and Health Care Reform: Hearing before the Committee on Indian Affairs on the National Health Care Reform and Its Implications for New Mexico Indian Health Programs at the Reservation and Urban Level*, 103d Cong., 2d sess., 8 April 1994, Shiprock, N.Mex. (Washington, D.C.: GPO, 1994), 293; USDHEW, USPHS, IHS, *Indian Health Trends and Services, 1970*.

13. Peter Iverson, *We Are Still Here: American Indians in the Twentieth Century* (Wheeling, Ill.: Harlan Davidson, 1998), 177; Haraldson, "Health and Health Services," 136; USDHHS, USPHS, IHS, *Indian Health Service: Trends in Indian Health, 1992*, 20.

14. Starr, *The Social Transformation*, 405–6; Theda Skocpol, *Boomerang: Clinton's Health Security Effort and the Turn Against Government in U.S. Politics* (New York: W. W. Norton & Company, 1996), 21–22.

15. "Indian Policy: Statement of Ronald Reagan, January 24, 1983," in *Documents of United States Indian Policy*, ed. Prucha, 301–2; *NT*, 26 March 1981, 1.

16. Statement by Exendine, Wood, et al., in U.S. Senate Committee on Indian Affairs, *Issues of Indian Health*, 293–405.

17. *NT*, 26 March 1981, 1, 9–10, 16 April 1981, 1, 18, 11 June 1981, 17, 16 July 1981, 20, 23 July 1981, 1, 3, 2 May 1982, 1, 5; Eldon Rudd to Bill Walker, Executive Director of Arizona Nursing Home Association, 14 March 1983, Box 156, Folder 3, Eldon Rudd Papers, 1962–87, MSS 119, Arizona Room, ASU.

18. *NT*, 12 January, 1984, 14, 2 February 1984, 3, 23 March 1984, 1, 2, Lois M. Fallis, Director of South Dakota Urban Indian Health, Inc., Pierre, S.D., to Goldwater, 9 March 1984, Ivan Sidney, Chairman of the Hopi Tribe, Kykotsmovi, to Goldwater, 9 May 1984, Elsie Ricklefs, Chairman, Hoopa Valley Business Council, Hoopa, Calif., to Goldwater, 27 August 1984, Members of the Senate Select Committee on Indian

Affairs to Goldwater, 10 October 1984, Box 1, Folder 20, BGPIA; National Congress of American Indians, "Position Statement on the Delivery of Health Services by the Indian Health Service," 21 February 1986, p. 7, Box 13, Folder 12, BGPIA.

19. U.S. Senate Select Committee on Indian Affairs to Robert Dole and Robert C. Byrd, 15 October 1986, Box 13, Folder 12, BGPIA; *AR*, 11 August 1989, C1; *PG*, 22 February 1991, B11; *NT*, 23 January 1985, 1.

20. Starr, *The Social Transformation*, 384–85; *NT*, 14 October, 1981, 16, 23 January 1985, 1, 28 September, 1995, A3; Jim Lang, third parties coordinator, NAIHS, interview by author, Window Rock, Ariz., 13 November 1992; Edward Hardiman, M.D., chief of internal medicine, Phoenix Area IHS, interview by author, Phoenix, Ariz., 27 August 1997.

21. Arizona Commission of Indian Affairs, *State-Tribal Relationships: A Report on the 8th Indian Town Hall, November 12–14, 1980, Held on the White Mountain Apache Reservation* (Phoenix, 1980), 26–31; Arizona Legislature, *Annual Report: Arizona Health Care Cost Containment System, July 1988-June 1989* (Phoenix, February 1990), 1; *The State of Arizona vs. The United States of America and Dr. Otis Bowen*, 10 July 1986, Box 13, Folder 12, BGPIA.

22. *Arizona vs. U.S. and Bowen*, Rhodes to Anderson, 16 May 1986, Box 13, Folder 12, BGPIA; *PG*, 29 September 1988, B1, 19 December 1988, B8; *AR*, 10 July 1991, A12.

23. Arizona Commission of Indian Affairs, *A Report of the Proceedings of the 16th Annual Indian Town Hall on the Theme: "Indian Land and Medicine," October 20 & 21, 1994, Arizona State University, West* (Phoenix, 1994), 22, 24–25; Statement by Genevieve Jackson, in U.S. Senate Committee on Indian Affairs, *Issues of Indian Health, Hearing*, 7.

24. U.S. Senate Select Committee on Indian Affairs, *Hearings before the Select Committee on Indian Affairs on S. 2482, to Amend the Indian Health Care Improvement Act and to Authorize Appropriations for Indian Health Programs*, 102d Cong., 2d sess., 1 April 1992 (Washington, D.C., GPO, 1992); USDHHS, USPHS, NAIHS, Area Director, Memorandum to CEOs, CDs, HPDP Coordinators, and Branch Chiefs, "FY 1992 HPDP Objectives," 8 October 1991, unpublished report, NAIHS Area Office, Window Rock, Ariz.

25. White House Domestic Policy Council, *The President's Health Security Plan* (New York: Random House, 1993), 26, 240–42; Philip R. Lee, "Reinventing Public Health," in *Health Care Reform in the Nineties*, ed. Pauline Vaillancourt Rosenau (Thousand Oaks, Calif.: Sage Publications, 1994), 74–82.

26. *NT*, 6 May 1993, 2.

27. Skocpol, *Boomerang*; Statement by McCain, in U.S. Senate Committee on Indian Affairs, *Issues of Indian Health*, 1–2; *GI*, 18 June 1993, 1–2.

28. Statements by Zah, Jackson, and Marshall, in U.S. Senate Committee on Indian Affairs, *Issues of Indian Health*, 4–10.

29. *NT*, 6 January 1994, 1–2, 31 March 1994, A10, 14 April 1994, A3; *PG*, 10 February 1994, B1; *AR*, 5 February 1994, B4.

30. *AR*, 5 February 1994, B4, 4 March 1994, A19, 24 April 1994, CL18; *PG*, 10 February 1994, B1; *NT*, 28 April 1994, A8, 7 July 1994, B4, 4 August 1994, A8.

31. U.S. Department of Justice, Civil Division, "Proposed Rules, Radiation Exposure Compensation Act," *Federal Register* 62 (23 May 1997): 28393–96; *NT*, 13 May 1993, 2, 21 November 1996, 1.

32. *AR*, 1 June 1993, B1; *NT*, 6 June 1996, A9, 21 November 1996, 1; Anna Aloysious, cited in Navajo Uranium Miner Oral History and Photography Project, *Memories Come to Us in the Rain And the Wind: Oral Histories and Photographs of Navajo Uranium Miners & Their Families* (Boston, Mass.: Author, 1997).

33. NT, 6 June 1996, A9, 17 April 1997, 1–2, 17 July 1997, A7, 26 March 1998, A8, 16 April 1998, 1, 23 April 1998, A10, 22 April 1999, A-1.

34. DHHS, PHS, NAIHS, *Navajo Area Indian Health Service, Area Profile*, 1992, 12–13; NT, 12 May 1981, 1–2, 25 August 1982, 14, 26 August 1993, 9, 28 October 1993, 1, 11 July 1996, B5, 10 July 1997, A2, 17 July 1997, A1, 19 February 1998, A10, 18 April 1998, A2, 21 January 1999, A-2.

35. Statement by Jackson, U.S. Senate Committee on Indian Affairs, *Issues of Indian Health*, 7.

36. NT, 21 December 1995, A11.

37. NT, 18 May 1995, 1; Jennie Joe, interview; USDHHS, USPHS, NAIHS, Chinle Hospital Steering Committee, *Dedication: Chinle Comprehensive Health Care Facility, August 28, 1982, Chinle, Navajo Nation* (Washington, D.C.: GPO, 1982); NT, 25 August 1982, 1, 4; AR, 23 December 1995, B-5; Frisbie, *Navajo Medicine Bundles*, 302–4.

38. Peggy Nakai, special projects coordinator for Navajo Division of Health, Department of Operations, interview by author, Window Rock, Ariz., 5 March 1993; NT, 13 October 1994, 1, A8, 20 November 1997, 1–2, A2; Taylor McKenzie, interview.

39. Beulah Allen, M.D., physician at NAIHS, Tsaile clinic, interview by author, Tsaile, Ariz., 31 July 1997; Navajo Nation, "A (Local) Doctor in the House," *Navajo Nation*, n.d., 31.

40. NT, 8 May 1997, A1, 2 October 1997, A1.

41. Gesler and Ricketts, *Health in Rural North America*, 5; Robert Graham, Assistant Surgeon General to Eldon Rudd, 12 December 1983, Rudd to Zah, 18 November 1983, Zah to Margaret Heckler, Secretary of DHHS, 21 November 1983, Box 153, Folder 2, Eldon Rudd Papers, Arizona Room, ASU; Doug Peter, M.D., chief medical officer and assistant area director for NAIHS, interview by author, Window Rock, Ariz., 5 March 1993; Todacheeny, interview; USDHHS, USPHS, IHS, *Comprehensive Health Care Program for American Indians and Alaska Natives* (Washington, D.C.: GPO, 1992), 24–25.

42. Doug Peter, interview; Todacheeny, interview; American Hospital Association, *Hospitals* (Chicago: Author, 20 January 1993), 12; NT, 26 October 1978, A26, 6 December 1979, 14, 19 May 1982, 12, 18 April 1991, 12.

43. NT, 18 April 1991, 1–2; Rodney Brod, Philip May, and Thomas Stewart, "Recruitment and Retention of Federal Physicians on the Navajo Reservation," *The Social Science Journal* 19 (October 1982): 53–66; Don Lewis-Kratsik, M.D., family physician at Fort Defiance NAIHS Hospital, interview by author, Fort Defiance, Ariz., 5 March 1993.

44. Pat Bohan, chief officer of environmental health services for NAIHS Office of Environmental Health and Engineering, interview by author, Window Rock, Ariz., 4 March 1993; Bahe-Hernandez, interview.

45. NT, 3 September, 1981, 10, 12; Nakai, interview.

46. NT, 3 September, 1981, 10, 12; Nakai, interview; DeGroat, interview.

47. NT, 6 July 1983, 1, 2; Lou Fox, chief officer of sanitation facilities construction branch office, NAIHS, Office of Environmental Health and Engineering, interview by author, Window Rock, Ariz., 5 March 1993; Bohan, interview; NT, 5 February 1998, A6.

48. NT, 20 August 1992, 1, 8 October 1992, 9, 30 November 1995, 1–2, 3 October 1996, 9; Statements by Roselyn Chapela and Navajo Nation AIDS Office, in U.S. Senate Committee on Indian Affairs, *Issues of Indian Health*, 29–30, 247–49.

49. NT, 12 December 1996, A5, 8 January 1998, A5.

50. Nakai, interview; *NT*, 17 October 1996, 9, 8 May 1997, A1, 15 January 1998, A3.

51. *NT*, 15 January 1998, A3.

52. Doug Peter, *NT*, 24 July 1997, A3.

53. Peter, interview; *NT*, 4 February 1993, 1–2, 25 May 1995, A3, 1 August 1996, A2, A8.

54. Kunitz and Levy, *Drinking Careers*, 193–95; Mary Roessel, M.D., psychiatrist with Northern Navajo Medical Center, interview by author, Shiprock, N.Mex., 6 August 1997; *NT*, 14 August 1980, 8, 16 April 1981, 1, 9, 28 April 1982, 17, 12 October 1995, A11.

55. Mary Roessel, interview; Nakai, interview.

56. Mary Roessel, interview; Robert Roessel, interview; *NT*, 5 September 1996, A6.

57. USDHHS, USPHS, IHS, *Regional Differences in Indian Health*, 1992, 13–19.

58. DeGroat, interview; Robert Roessel, interview.

59. *NT*, 14 April 1996, A2, A5.

60. Nakai, interview; Doug Peter, interview.

61. *NT*, 30 May 1996, A6.

62. Michael H. Trujillo, "An Indian Health Service Perspective on Self-Governance," p. 2, Labriola Center, Arizona State University, Tempe.

63. *NT*, 19 April 1996, A2, A5, 19 February 1998, A10, 13 August 1998, A2, 21 January 1999, A1.

64. James Tomchee, "President James Tomchee, Native American Church of Navajoland" (interview), *The Maazo Magazine: Navajo Life Stories* 1 (spring 1986): 30–35, 45; Robert Roessel, interview; Aberle, "The Peyote Religion," 558–69.

65. *NT*, 29 September 1996, 1, A2; Kunitz and Levy, *Drinking Careers*, 110–16; Tomchee, *Maazo Magazine*, 34. On the use of peyote to deal with cancer, see Csordas, "The Sore That Does Not Heal."

66. *NT*, 11 February 1993, 1–2, 8 April 1993, 8; Iverson, *We Are Still Here*, 181–82.

67. *NT*, 11 February 1993, 1–2, 8 April 1993, 8, 29 September 1994, 1, A2; Iverson, *We Are Still Here*, 181–82.

68. *NT*, 30 December 1993, 1, 2, 29 September, 1994, 1, A2, 17 April 1997, A1.

69. *NT*, 30 December 1993, 1, 2, 29 September, 1994, 1, A2, 17 April 1997, A1, 25 April 1996, A1, A3.

70. *NT*, 13 January 1980, 6, 2 January 1985, 1–2, *AR*, 16 December 1996, B1.

71. *NT*, 15 August 1991, 1, 5, 7 November 1991, 1–2, Robert Roessel, interview; Elton Naswood, student at Arizona State University, interview by author, Tempe, Ariz., 21 July 1997.

72. *NT*, 17 March 1994, 1, 6, 19 October 1995, B16; Jennie Joe, "Navajo Singers," 16.

73. *AR*, 16 December 1996, B1; *NT*, 18 August 1994, 1, A5; Naswood, interview; Robert Young, letter to author, 4 September 1992.

74. Arizona Indian: NOW, "Healing Without Hospitals," *Arizona Indian: NOW* 3, no. 2 (June 1980): 21.

75. Iverson, *We Are Still Here*, 188–89; *NT*, 19 September 1996, 5.

76. *NT*, 19 October 1995, B16, 31 December 1996, A7, 20 March 1997, A1, A3, 2 April 1998, A1.

77. *NT*, 7 November 1991, 1, A2; Robert Roessel, interview; Naswood, interview; Frisbie, "Temporal Change," 501.

78. *AR*, 4 November 1991, A1.

79. Kunitz and Levy, *Drinking Careers*, 217–21; *NT*, 10 October 1996, 9; *AR*, 10 April 1997, HL1-HL2.

80. Jennie Joe, "Navajo Singers," 16; *NT*, 28 July 1994, 1, A2, 27 November 1996, A10; *AR*, 10 April 1997, HL1-HL2.

81. Kunitz and Levy suggest that some Native Americans may be influenced by "new age" philosophies as well, demonstrating a two-way cultural interchange regarding medical beliefs and practices; Kunitz and Levy, *Drinking Careers*, 206–21; Jennie Joe, "Navajo Singers," 4–5; Melvin Konner, *Medicine at the Crossroads: The Crisis in Health Care* (New York: Pantheon Books, 1993), 16–18; Carol Wekesser, ed., *Health Care in America: Opposing Viewpoints* (San Diego, Calif.: Greenhaven Press, 1994), 95; James S. Gordon, "Alternative Medicine Should Be Considered Standard Medical Practice," in *Health Care in America: Opposing Viewpoints*, ed. Wekesser, 106–11.

82. Jennie Joe, interview; *AR*, 10 April 1997, HL2.

83. Lewis-Kratsik, interview.

84. *NT*, 11 July 1991, A6; Kosik, interview; Fowler, interview.

85. Kosik, interview; Fowler, interview.

86. *NT*, 4 April 1996, A7; Anonymous, "Healing without Hospitals," 21.

87. Beulah Allen, interview; Lori Arviso Alvord, M.D., surgeon at IHS Gallup Indian Medical Center, interview by author, Gallup, N.Mex., 5 August 1997; The Navajo Nation, "A (Local) Doctor in the House," 31; Lori Arviso Alvord, and Elizabeth Cohen Van Pelt, *The Scalpel and the Silver Bear* (New York: Bantam Books, 1999) 32.

88. Alvord, interview; Alvord and Van Pelt, *The Scalpel*.

89. Alvord and Van Pelt, *The Scalpel*, 3.

90. Mary Roessel, interview.

91. *NT*, 31 October 1996, A1 and A5, 16 October 1997, 1.

92. Perrone et al., "Annie Kahn: The Flower That Speaks in a Pollen Way," in Bobette Perrone, H. Henrietta Stockel, and Victoria Krueger, *Medicine Women, Curanderas, and Women Doctors* (Norman: University of Oklahoma Press, 1989), 29–44; *NT*, 11 July 1991, A6.

Conclusion

1. Laurie Garrett, *The Coming Plague: Newly Emerging Diseases in a World Out of Balance* (New York: Farrar, Straus and Giroux, 1994), 526–29; Denise Grady, "Death at the Corners," *Discover* 14, no. 12 (December 1993): 82–91.

2. Garrett, *The Coming Plague*, 537–46; *GI*, 5 June 1993, 1–2.

3. Garrett, *The Coming Plague*, 536–37; Grady, "Death," 88–89; *GI*, 1 June 1993, 1–2, 3 June 1993, 1; *NT*, 24 June 1993, 1–2.

4. *NT*, 3 June 1993, 1–2; *GI*, 3 June 1993, 1–2.

5. Garrett, *The Coming Plague*, 529–31, 536; Grady, "Death," 90.

6. Grady, "Death," 90.

7. Garrett, *The Coming Plague*, 536–37, 546; Grady, "Death," 88–89; "Navajo Nation Testimony on the Outbreak of Hantavirus," in U.S. Senate Committee on Indian Affairs, *Issues of Indian Health*, 220–21.

8. Hantavirus had originally been discovered by scientists during the Korean War in the 1950s. Garret, *The Coming Plague*, 535.

9. *NT*, 3 June 1993, 1–2; *GI*, 2 June 1993, 1.

10. *NT*, 3 June 1993, 1–2.

11. *NT*, 3 June 1993, 1–2, 10 June 1993, 1–2; *GI*, 3 June 1; Maureen Trudelle Schwarz, "The Explanatory and Predictive Power of History: Coping with the 'Mystery Illness,' 1993," *Ethnohistory* 42, no. 3 (summer 1995): 393.

12. For a more in-depth look at Navajo interpretations of the illness, see Schwarz, "Explanatory and Predictive Power."

13. *NT,* 9 June 1993, 1–2, 17 June 1993, 1–7, 1 July 1993, 1–2; *GI,* 1 July 1993, 1.

14. Garrett, *The Coming Plague,* 535.

15. Ibid., 536; *NT,* 10 June 1993, 4; *GI,* 4 June 1993, 1.

16. Garrett, *The Coming Plague,* 536; *GI,* 3 June 1993, 2, 15 June 1993, 1–2, 1 July 1993, 1.

17. *NT,* 10 June 1993, 1, 5; *GI,* 5 June 1993, 1–2.

18. Hopefully, future scholarship will illuminate the medical self-determination process further for the Navajo Nation, other American Indian groups, and non-Indian communities as well. It would be interesting to study further the reaction Navajos had to the tribal government's health care actions and attitudes. More detailed overviews of U.S. Indian health care policy would also be useful, as would studies of IHS relations with other tribes, and more historical studies of evolving state and missionary relations with American Indians. Multistate comparisons should yield particularly interesting insights into twentieth-century American Indian history. Much has already been done in the fields of anthropology, sociology, demography, and psychology on the topics of traditional healing and American Indian relations with Western medicine, but few historians have attempted overviews of those topics. As more historians turn to the twentieth century and the post–World War II era, health care issues should make up a greater portion of tribal histories.

▾ REFERENCES ▴

ARCHIVAL SOURCES

National Archives

Collections at the Main Branch, Washington, D.C.
Record Group 75. Records of the Bureau of Indian Affairs
Central Classified Files, 1907–53
Records of the Health Division
Reports of Field Nurses, 1931–43
Hospital Reports, 1923–38
Reports of Medical Directors: Northern Navajo Agency, 1930–35
Superintendents Annual Narrative and Statistical Reports from Field Jurisdictions
    of the BIA, 1907–38, microfilm
Collections at the Pacific Southwest Regional Branch, Laguna Niguel, Calif.
Record Group 75. Records of the Bureau of Indian Affairs
Window Rock Agency Files, Correspondence of Chief Medical Officers
Collections at College Park, Md.
Record Group 513. Records of the Indian Health Service
Division of Indian Health, Correspondence, 1955–58
Subject Files, 1965–72

Other Manuscript Collections

Arizona Historical Foundation, Tempe
Paul Fannin Congressional Papers
Barry Goldwater Congressional Papers
Barry Goldwater Indian Affairs Series
Orme Lewis Collection
Arizona State Museum Archives, Tucson
Navajo Tribal Council Minutes, 1970–78
Arizona State Historical Society, Tucson
Richard Van Valkenburg Papers
Arizona State University, Hayden Library, Arizona Room, Tempe
Thomas Dodge Papers MSS 033

Charles F. Gritzner Collection MSS 044
Carl Hayden Papers C-MSS 001
John J. Rhodes Papers MSS 002
Eldon Rudd Papers MSS 119
Native Americans and the New Deal: The Office Files of John Collier, 1933–1945, University Publications of America, Microfiche
Northern Arizona University, Special Collections, Cline Library, Flagstaff
Virginia Brown, Ida Bahl, and Lillian Watson Collection MS 269
Harold Osborne Papers MS 006
University of Arizona, The University of Arizona Library, Special Collections, Tucson
Berard Haile Papers
Morris K. Udall Papers MS 325
University of New Mexico, Zimmerman Library, Center for Southwest Research, Albuquerque
American Indian Oral History Collection, microfilm, MSS 314 BC
Dennis Chávez Papers MSS 394 BC
Pete Domenici Papers MSS 403 BC
Manuel Lujan Papers MSS 142 BC
William J. Zimmerman Jr. Papers MSS 517 BC

Dissertations, Theses, Author Interviews, and Published Sources

Aberle, David F. *The Peyote Religion Among the Navaho.* Chicago: Aldine Publishing Co., 1966; Norman: University of Oklahoma Press, 1982.
———. "The Peyote Religion Among the Navajo." In *Southwest,* edited by Alfonso Ortiz. Vol. 10, *Handbook of North American* Indians, 558–69.
Ackerknecht, Erwin H. *A Short History of Medicine.* Rev. ed. Baltimore: Johns Hopkins University Press, 1982.
Adair, John, Kurt W. Deuschle, and Clifford R. Barnett. *The People's Health: Medicine and Anthropology in a Navajo Community.* New York: Appleton-Century-Crofts, 1970.
———. *The People's Health: Medicine and Anthropology in a Navajo Community.* Rev. and exp. ed. Albuquerque: University of New Mexico Press, 1988.
Allen, Beulah. Interview by author. Tsaile, Ariz., 31 July 1997.
Alvord, Lori Arviso. Interview by author. Gallup, N.Mex., 5 August 1997.
Alvord, Lori Arviso, and Elizabeth Cohen Van Pelt. *The Scalpel and the Silver Bear.* New York: Bantam Books, 1999.
American Hospital Association. *Hospitals.* Chicago: Author, 20 January 1993.
Anderson, Odin W. *Health Services in the United States: A Growth Enterprise Since 1875.* Ann Arbor, Mich.: Health Administration Press, 1985.
Arizona Commission of Indian Affairs. *State-Tribal Relationships: A Report on the 8th Indian Town Hall, November 12–14, 1980, Held on the White Mountain Apache Reservation.* Phoenix, 1980.
———. *A Report of the Proceedings of the 16th Annual Indian Town Hall on the Theme: "Indian Land and Medicine," October 20 & 21, 1994, Arizona State University, West.* Phoenix, 1994.
Arizona Indian: NOW. "Healing Without Hospitals." *Arizona Indian: NOW* 3, no. 2 (June 1980): 21.
Arizona Legislature. *Annual Report: Arizona Health Care Cost Containment System, July 1988–June 1989.* Phoenix, February 1990.
The Arizona Republic (Phoenix), 8 November 1989–10 April 1997.

Association of American Indian Physicians. "A Look Back." *Association of American Indian Physicians Newsletter* 25, no. 6 (July 1996): 1, 3.

Bahe-Hernandez, Geri. Interview by author. Tuba City, Ariz., 4 February 1993.

Bahl, Ida. *Nurse Among the Navajos*. Northvale, N.J.: Shepherd Publishing, 1984.

Bailey, Garrick, and Roberta Glenn Bailey. *A History of the Navajos: The Reservation Years*. Santa Fe, N.Mex.: School of American Research Press, 1986.

Bergman, Robert L. Interview by Brad Steiger. In *Indian Medicine Power* by Brad Steiger. Gloucester, Mass.: Para Research, and Atglen, Pa.: Whitford Press, 1984, 48–53.

Bernstein, Alison R. *American Indians and World War II: Toward a New Era in Indian Affairs*. Norman: University of Oklahoma Press, 1991.

Bock, George. "The Medicine Men." *PHS World* 2, no. 4 (April 1967): 32–34.

Bodo, Fr. Murray, O.F.M. *Tales of an Endishodi: Father Berard Haile and the Navajos, 1900–1961*. Albuquerque: University of New Mexico Press, 1998.

Bohan, Pat. Interview by author. Window Rock, Ariz., 4 March 1993.

Borowsky, Steven. Interview by author. Phoenix, Ariz., 18 August 1997.

Bozof, Richard. "Some Navaho Attitudes toward Available Medical Care." *American Journal of Public Health* 62 (December 1972): 1620–24.

Brod, Rodney L., and Ronald Ladue. "Political Mobilization and Conflict among Western Urban and Reservation Indian Health Service Programs." *American Indian Culture and Research Journal* 13, nos. 3 and 4 (1989): 171–241.

Brod, Rodney, Philip May, and Thomas Stewart. "Recruitment and Retention of Federal Physicians on the Navajo Reservation." *The Social Science Journal* 19 (October 1982): 53–66.

Broudy, David W., and Philip A. May. "Demographic and Epidemiologic Transition Among the Navajo Indians." *Social Biology* 30 (spring 1983): 1–16.

Brugge, David M. "Henry Chee Dodge: From the Long Walk to Self-Determination." In *Indian Lives: Essays on Nineteenth- and Twentieth-Century Native American Leaders*, edited by L. G. Moses and Raymond Wilson, 91–107.

Campbell, Gregory R. "The Changing Dimension of Native American Health: A Critical Understanding of Contemporary Native American Health Issues." *American Indian Culture and Research Journal* 13, nos. 3 and 4 (1989): 1–20.

Claymore, Betty J., and Marian A. Taylor. "AIDS—Tribal Nations Face the Newest Communicable Disease: An Aberdeen Area Perspective." *American Indian Culture and Research Journal* 13, nos. 3 and 4 (1989): 21–31.

Cohen, Elizabeth. "Good Medicine: First Navajo Woman Surgeon Operates between Two Worlds." *New Mexico* 72 (August 1994): 26–28.

Csordas, Thomas J. "The Sore That Does Not Heal: Cause and Concept in the Navajo Experience of Cancer." *Journal of Anthropological Research* 45 (1989): 457–77.

Dawson, Susan E. "Navajo Uranium Workers and the Effects of Occupational Illnesses: A Case Study." *Human Organization* 51 (winter 1992): 389–97.

DeGroat, Ellouise. Interview by author. Window Rock, Ariz., 5 March 1993.

Deloria, Vine, Jr. *Custer Died for Your Sins: An Indian Manifesto*. New York: Avon Books, 1972.

Deuschle, Kurt, and John Adair. "An Interdisciplinary Approach to Public Health on the Navajo Indian Reservation: Medical and Anthropological Aspects." *Annals of New York Academy of Sciences* 84 (1960): 887–905.

Dolfin, Rev. John. *Bringing the Gospel in Hogan and Pueblo*. Grand Rapids, Mich.: Van Noord, 1921.

du Bois, Jerome. "Medicine Men Organize to Protect Old Ways," *Navajo Times* (27 April 1978): 19.

Eck, Norman K. *Contemporary Navajo Affairs: Navajo History*. Vol. 3, part B. Rough Rock, Ariz.: Navajo Curriculum Center, Rough Rock Demonstration School, 1982.

England, Charles R. "A Look at the Indian Health Service Policy of Sterilization, 1972–76."
    Red Ink 3 (spring 1994): 17–21.
Estrada, Raymond. Interview by author. Gallup, N.M., 3 December 1993.
Fannin, Paul. "Indian Health Care: A Real Health Care Crisis." Arizona Medicine 32
    (September 1975): 741–47.
Farella, John R. The Main Stalk: A Synthesis of Navajo Philosophy. Tucson: University of
    Arizona Press, 1984.
Faris, James C. The Nightway: A History and a History of Documentation of a Navajo
    Ceremonial. Albuquerque: University of New Mexico Press, 1990.
Fixico, Donald L. Termination and Relocation: Federal Indian Policy, 1945–1960. Albuquerque:
    University of New Mexico Press, 1986.
Fowler, Lena. Interview by author. Tuba City, Ariz., 4 February 1993.
Fox, Lou. Interview by author. Window Rock, Ariz., 5 March 1993.
Frisbie, Charlotte J. "An Approach to the Ethnography of Navajo Ceremonial Performance."
    In Ethnography of Musical Performance, compiled by Norma McLeod and Marcia Herndon.
    Norwood, Pa.: Norwood Editions, 1980, 75–104.
———. "Temporal Change in Navajo Religion: 1868–1990." Journal of the Southwest 34, no. 4
    (winter 1992): 457–514.
———. Navajo Medicine Bundles or Jish: Acquisition, Transmission, and Disposition in the Past
    and Present. Albuquerque: University of New Mexico Press, 1987.
Gallup (N.M.) Independent, 22 March 1961–1 July 1993.
Garrett, Laurie. The Coming Plague: Newly Emerging Diseases in a World Out of Balance. New
    York: Farrar, Straus, and Giroux, 1994.
Gerken, Edna. "How the Navajos Improve Their Health." Childhood Education 18 (March
    1942): 315–18.
Gesler, Wilbert, and Thomas C. Ricketts, eds. Health in Rural North America: The Geography
    of Health Care Services and Delivery. New Brunswick, N.J.: Rutgers University Press, 1992.
Gill, Sam D. "Navajo Views of Their Origin." In Southwest, edited by Alfonso Ortiz. Vol. 10,
    Handbook of North American Indians, 502–5.
Gilles, Cate, Marti Reed, and Jacques Seronde. "Our Uranium Legacy." Northern Arizona
    Environmental Newsletter (summer 1990): 1–11.
Goodman, Rita. "Secondary Sex Ratio and Birth Weights of Navajo Indians in an Area of
    Uranium Mining and Milling." Master's thesis, Arizona State University, 1984.
Gordon, James S. "Alternative Medicine Should Be Considered Standard Medical Practice."
    In Health Care in America: Opposing Viewpoints, edited by Carol Wekesser, 106–11.
Gorrell, R. L. "Clinic Cares at Lukachukai." Arizona (19 November 1978): 8–15.
Grady, Denise. "Death at the Corners." Discover 14, no. 12 (December 1993): 82–91.
Hall, Edward T. West of the Thirties: Discoveries Among the Navajo and Hopi. New York:
    Doubleday, 1994.
Haraldson, Sixten S. R. "Health and Health Services among the Navajo Indians." Journal of
    Community Health 13 (fall 1988): 129–42.
Hardiman, Edward. Interview by author. Phoenix, Ariz., 27 August 1997.
Harjo, Joy, and Gloria Bird, eds. Reinventing the Enemy's Language: Contemporary Native
    Women's Writings of North America. New York: W. W. Norton and Company, 1997.
High Country News. "Experts Knew Miners Were at Risk." High Country News 22 (18 June
    1990): 11–12.
Hoffman, Virginia, and Broderick H. Johnson. Navajo Biographies. Rough Rock, Ariz.: Diné
    Inc. and Board of Education, Rough Rock Demonstration School, The Navajo Curriculum
    Center, 1970.
Howard, Cheryl. Navajo Tribal Demography, 1983–1986: A Comparative and Historical
    Perspective. New York: Garland Publishing, 1993.

Indian Health Care Improvement Act of 1976. U.S. Statutes at Large 90 (1976): 1400–14.

Iverson, Peter. *Barry Goldwater: Native Arizonan.* Norman: University of Oklahoma Press, 1997.

———. *The Navajo Nation.* Westport, Conn.: Greenwood Press, 1981; 3d pbk. printing, Albuquerque: University of New Mexico Press, 1989.

———. *We Are Still Here: American Indians in the Twentieth Century.* Wheeling, Ill.: Harlan Davidson, 1998.

Jeffries, Sallie. "Relationships of Hospital Personnel." *Navajo Medical News* 7, no. 4 (25 November 1940): 1–7.

Jenkins, J. Rockwood. *The Good Shepherd Mission to the Navajo.* Phoenix: Author, 1955.

Jett, Stephen C. "Pete Price, Navajo Medicineman (1868–1951): A Brief Biography." *American Indian Quarterly* 15 (winter 1991): 91–101.

Jim-James, Sonlatsa. "Diné Way." In *Reinventing the Enemy's Language: Contemporary Native Women's Writings of North America,* edited by Joy Harjo and Gloria Bird, 488–93.

Joe, Jennie. Interview by author. Tucson, Ariz., 22 January 1993.

———. "Navajo Singers and Western Medical Doctors." Paper presented at the American Historical Association Annual Meeting, Chicago, Ill., 27–30 December 1991.

Johnson, Broderick H., ed. *Stories of Traditional Navajo Life and Culture.* Tsaile, Ariz.: Navajo Community College Press, 1977.

Johnson, Emery. "Statement on Indian Health Programs, March 2, 1981." In *Documents of United States Indian Policy,* 2d exp. ed., edited by Francis Paul Prucha, 298–300.

Kane, Robert, and Rosalie Kane. *Federal Health Care (With Reservations!)* New York: Springer Pub. Co., 1972.

Kane, Robert, and P. Douglas McConatha. "The Men in the Middle: A Dilemma of Minority Health Workers." *Medical Care* 13, no. 9 (September 1975): 736–43.

Kelly, William H. "Applied Anthropology in the Southwest." *American Anthropologist* 56 (1954): 708–16.

King, John. Interview by author. Ganado, Ariz., 2 October 1992.

Kirk, Ruth Falkenburg. "Indian Welfare: The Navaho." *Public Welfare* (April 1946): n.p.

Kluckhohn, Clyde. *Navaho Witchcraft.* Cambridge, Mass.: The Museum, 1944; Boston: Beacon Press, 1967.

Kluckhohn, Clyde, and Dorothea Leighton. *The Navaho,* rev. ed. Garden City, N.Y.: The Natural History Library/Anchor Books/Doubleday, 1962.

Konner, Melvin. *Medicine at the Crossroads: The Crisis in Health Care.* New York: Pantheon Books, 1993.

Kosik, Fran. Interview by author. Tuba City, Ariz., 4 February 1993.

Kunitz, Stephen. *Disease Change and the Role of Medicine: The Navajo Experience.* Berkeley: University of California Press, 1983.

———. *A Survey of Fertility Histories and Contraceptive Use among a Group of Navajo Women,* Lake Powell Research Project Bulletin, edited by Priscilla C. Grew. Los Angeles: University of California, Collaborative Research on Assessment of Man's Activities in the Lake Powell Region, Research Applied to National Needs, National Science Foundation, 1976.

Kunitz, Stephen, and Jerrold E. Levy. *Drinking Careers: A Twenty-Five-Year Study of Three Populations.* New Haven, Conn.: Yale University Press, 1994.

———. *Navajo Aging: The Transition from Family to Institutional Support.* Tucson: University of Arizona Press, 1991.

Lang, Jim. Interview by author. Window Rock, Ariz., 13 November 1992.

Larson, Janet Karsten. "And Then There Were None: Is Federal Policy Endangering the American Indian 'Species'?" *The Christian Century* (26 January 1977): 61–63.

Lee, Philip R. "Reinventing Public Health." In *Health Care Reform in the Nineties*, edited by Pauline Vaillancourt Rosenau, 74–82.

Left Handed, recorded by Walter Dyk. *Left Handed, Son of Old Man Hat: A Navajo Autobiography*. 1938; Lincoln: University of Nebraska Press, 1996.

Leighton, Alexander H., and Dorothea C. Leighton, recorders. *Lucky: The Navajo Singer*, edited and annotated by Joyce J. Griffen. Albuquerque: University of New Mexico Press, 1992.

————. *The Navaho Door: An Introduction to Navaho Life*. Cambridge, Mass.: Harvard University Press, 1944; New York: Russell and Russell, 1967.

————. "Therapeutic Values in Navajo Religion." *Arizona Highways* 43, no. 8 (August 1967), 2–13.

Leighton, Dorothea. "As I Knew Them: Navajo Women in 1940." *American Indian Quarterly* 6, nos. 1–2 (spring/summer 1982): 34–51.

Leighton, Dorothea, and Clyde Kluckhohn. *Children of the People*. Cambridge, Mass.: Harvard University Press, 1947.

Levy, Jerrold E., Raymond Neutra, and Dennis Parker. *Hand Trembling, Frenzy Witchcraft, and Moth Madness: A Study of Navajo Seizure Disorders*. Tucson: University of Arizona Press, 1987.

Lewis-Kratsik, Don. Interview by author. Fort Defiance, Ariz., 5 March 1993.

Loughlin, Bernice. "Aide Training Reaches the Navajo Reservation." *American Journal of Nursing* 63 (July 1963): 106–9.

McDermott, Walsh, Kurt Deuschle, John Adair, Hugh Fulmer, and Bernice Loughlin. "Introducing Modern Medicine in a Navajo Community." *Science* 131 (22 and 29 January 1960): 197–205, 280–87.

McKenzie, Taylor. Interview by author. Gallup, N.Mex., 5 February 1993.

McNeill, William H. *Plagues and Peoples*. Garden City, N.Y.: Anchor Press, 1976; New York: Anchor Books/Doubleday, 1989.

McNeley, James Kale. *Holy Wind in Navajo Philosophy*. Tucson: University of Arizona Press, 1981.

McPhail, Jasper L. "American Indian School of Medicine," *Arizona Medicine* 34 (April 1977): 270–72.

Means, Florence Crannell. *Sagebrush Surgeon*. New York: Friendship Press, 1955.

Mitchell, Frank. *Navajo Blessingway Singer: The Autobiography of Frank Mitchell, 1881–1967*, edited by Charlotte J. Frisbie and David McAllester. Tucson: University of Arizona Press, 1978.

Moore, William Haas. *Chiefs, Agents, and Soldiers: Conflict on the Navajo Frontier, 1868–1882*. Albuquerque: University of New Mexico Press, 1994.

Morgan, William. "Navaho Treatment of Sickness: Diagnosticians." *American Anthropologist* 33, no. 3 (July-September 1931): 390–402.

Moses, L. G., and Raymond Wilson, eds. *Indian Lives: Essays on Nineteenth- and Twentieth-Century Native American Leaders*. 2d pbk. printing. Albuquerque: University of New Mexico Press, 1993.

Mullan, Fitzhugh. *Plagues and Politics: The Story of the United States Public Health Service*. New York: Basic Books, 1989.

Mulligan, Wallace. "The Navajo Nation Health Foundation: The Sequel to Salsbury." *Arizona Medicine* 33 (January 1976): 52–54.

Munn, Barbara. Interview by author. Window Rock, Ariz., 4 March 1993.

Murbarger, Nell. "White Man's Medicine in Monument Valley," *Desert Magazine* 21 (July 1958): 5–10.

Nakai, Peggy. Interview by author. Window Rock, Ariz., 5 March 1993.

Naswood, Elton. Interview by author. Tempe, Ariz., 21 July 1997.

Navajo Community College Newsletter. "Four Graduate from Nursing Program." *Navajo Community College Newsletter* 1 (January 1973): 1.

Navajo Health Authority. *Annual Report, 1973*. Window Rock, Ariz., 1973.

———. *Annual Report, 1975*. Window Rock, Ariz., 1975.

———. *Pictures of the Navajo: Their Health and Environment in 1980*, edited by Barbara Bayless Lacy. Window Rock, Ariz., 1980.

———. *Resolution 4R-1, Navajo Health Authority, Statement of Goals, Functions and Philosophy*. Window Rock, 1973.

The Navajo Nation. "A (Local) Doctor in the House." *The Navajo Nation* (Window Rock, Ariz.), n.d., 31.

Navajo Nation Health Foundation. "Navajo Nation Health Foundation, 1990 Annual Progress Report." Ganado, Ariz.: Foundation, 1991.

Navajo Times (Window Rock, Ariz.), 3 May 1961–28 April 1999.

Navajo Tribal Council. *CMY-57-70, Resolution of the Navajo Tribal Council: Establishing a Navajo Area Indian Health Advisory Board, 12 May 1970*. Window Rock, Ariz., 1970.

———. *CJN-62–72, Resolution of the Navajo Tribal Council: Rescinding Navajo Tribal Council Resolution CMY-57-70, and Creating a Navajo Area Indian Health Board and Eight Navajo Indian Health Service Unit Boards in Lieu Thereof, 15 June 1972*. Window Rock, Ariz., 1972.

———. *Navajo Tribal Council Resolutions, 1922–1951*. Window Rock, Ariz., 1952.

———. *Navajo Tribal Council Minutes, Major Council Meetings of American Indian Tribes*. Frederick, Md.: University Publications of America, 1991.

———. *Navajo Tribal Council Resolutions, 1922–1951*. Window Rock, Ariz., 1952.

Navajo Uranium Miner Oral History and Photography Project. *Memories Come to Us in the Rain and the Wind: Oral Histories and Photographs of Navajo Uranium Miners & Their Families*. Boston, Mass.: Author, 1997.

Negri, Sam. "When Things Go Awry, Relax, Here Comes Muttonman." *Arizona Highways* 73 (July 1997): 32–35.

Nelson, Mary C. *Annie Wauneka: The Story of an American Indian*. Minneapolis, Minn.: Dillon Press, 1972.

Newcomb, Franc Johnson. *Hosteen Klah: Navaho Medicine Man and Sand Painter*. Norman: University of Oklahoma Press, 1964.

New York Times, 12 March 1949–3 April 1977.

Ortiz, Alfonso, ed. *Southwest*. Vol. 10, *Handbook of North American Indians*, edited by William C. Sturtevant. Washington, D.C.: Smithsonian Institution, 1983.

Parker, Dorothy Ragon. "Choosing an Indian Identity: A Biography of D'Arcy McNickle." Ph.D. diss., University of New Mexico, 1988.

Parman, Donald L. *The Navajos and the New Deal*. New Haven, Conn.: Yale University Press, 1976.

Parsons, Talcott, and Evon Z. Vogt. "A Biographical Introduction." In *Navaho Witchcraft*, edited by Clyde Kluckhohn, ix–xxii.

Payer, Lynn. *Medicine and Culture: Varieties of Treatment in the United States, England, West Germany, and France*. New York: Penguin Books, 1988.

Perrone, Bobette, H. Henrietta Stockel, and Victoria Krueger, eds. *Medicine Women, Curanderas, and Women Doctors*. Norman: University of Oklahoma Press, 1989.

Peter, Doug. Interview by author. Window Rock, Ariz., 5 March 1993.

Philp, Kenneth R. *John Collier's Crusade for Indian Reform, 1920–1954*. Tucson: University of Arizona Press, 1977.

The Phoenix Gazette, 29 September 1988–10 February 1994.

Prucha, Francis Paul. *Documents of United States Indian Policy*. 2d ed. Lincoln: University of Nebraska Press, 1996.

————. *The Great Father: The United States Government and the American Indians*. Abridged ed. Lincoln: University of Nebraska Press, 1986.

————. *The Indians in American Society: From the Revolutionary War to the Present*. Berkeley: University of California Press, 1985.

Raup, Ruth M., for U.S. Public Health Service, U.S. Division of Public Health Methods. *The Indian Health Program from 1800 to 1955*. Washington, D.C.: GPO, 1959.

Reichard, Gladys A. *Navaho Religion: A Study of Symbolism*. New York: Pantheon Books, 1950; Tucson: University of Arizona Press, 1983.

Roessel, Mary. Interview by author. Shiprock, N.M., 6 August 1997.

Roessel, Robert. Interview by author. Round Rock, Ariz., 29 July 1997.

————. "Navajo History, 1850–1923." In *Southwest*, edited by Alfonso Ortiz. Vol. 10, *Handbook of North American Indians*, 506–23.

————. *Navajo Education in Action: The Rough Rock Demonstration School*. Chinle, Ariz.: Navajo Curriculum Center, Rough Rock Demonstration School, 1977.

The Rough Rock News. "Navajo Mental Health." *The Rough Rock News* (18 March 1970): n.p.

Salsbury, Clarence G., with Paul Hughes. *The Salsbury Story: A Medical Missionary's Lifetime of Public Service*. Tucson: University of Arizona Press, 1969.

Salsbury, Cora. *Forty Years in the Desert: A History of Ganado Mission, 1901–1941*. Chicago: Press of Physicians' Record Co., n.d.

Sandner, Donald. *Navaho Symbols of Healing*. New York: Harcourt Brace Jovanovich, 1979.

Sasaki, Tom T. "Socioeconomic Survey of the Many Farms and Rough Rock Navajos." In *The Navajo Yearbook, 1951–1960*. Vol. 8, edited and compiled by Robert W. Young. Window Rock, Ariz.: Navajo Agency, 1961, 103–13.

Schackel, Sandra K. "'The Tales Those Nurses Told!': Public Health Nurses among the Pueblo and Navajo Indians." *New Mexico Historical Review* 65 (April 1990): 225–49.

Schwarz, Maureen Trudelle. "The Explanatory and Predictive Power of History: Coping with the 'Mystery Illness,' 1993." *Ethnohistory* 42 no. 3 (summer 1995): 375–401.

Skocpol, Theda. *Boomerang: Clinton's Health Security Effort and the Turn Against Government in U.S. Politics*. New York: W. W. Norton & Company, 1996.

Smith, Paul Chaat, and Robert Allen Warrior. *Like a Hurricane: The Indian Movement from Alcatraz to Wounded Knee*. New York: New Press, distributed by W. W. Norton & Company, 1996.

Spencer, Steven. "They're Saving Lives in Navaho Land." *Saturday Evening Post* 227 (April 1955): 30–31, 96.

Spicer, Edwin H., ed. *Perspectives in American Indian Culture Change*. Chicago: University of Chicago Press, 1956; Chicago: University of Chicago Press, 1961.

Staff of the Navajo Health Education Project, University of California School of Public Health. For U.S. Department of Health, Education, and Welfare. U.S. Public Health Service. Division of Indian Health. *Orientation to Health on the Navajo Indian Reservation: A Guide for Hospital and Public Health Workers*. Washington, D.C.: GPO, 1961.

Stapleton, Will, and Patricia Heredia. "A History: Churches Contribute to Navajo Nation Health Care." *Navajo Times* (8 April 1976): B10–13.

Starr, Paul. *The Social Transformation of American Medicine*. New York: Basic Books, 1982.

Steiger, Brad. *Indian Medicine Power*. Gloucester, Mass.: Para Research; Atglen, Pa.: Whitford Press, 1984.

Stewart, Omer C. *Peyote Religion: A History*. Norman: University of Oklahoma Press, 1987.

Stirling, Betty. *Mission to the Navajo*. Mountain View, Calif.: Pacific Press Publications Association, 1961.

Tapahonso, Luci. *Sáanii Dahataal, The Women Are Singing: Poems and Stories*. Tucson: University of Arizona Press, 1993.

Temkin-Greener, Helen. "Surgical Fertility Regulation Among Women on the Navajo Indian Reservation." *American Journal of Public Health* (August 1969): 405–6.

Todacheeny, Thomas. Interview by author. Gallup, N.M., 4 February 1993.

Tolan, Sandy. "Uranium Plagues the Navajos." *Sierra* 68 (November/December 1983): 55–60.

Tomchee, James. "President James Tomchee, Native American Church of Navajoland" (Interview). *The Maazo Magazine: Navajo Life Stories* 1 (spring 1986): 30–45.

Trennert, Robert. "Indian Sore Eyes: The Federal Campaign to Control Trachoma in the Southwest, 1910–1940." *Journal of the Southwest* 32 (summer 1990): 121–49.

———. "White Doctors Among the Navajos, 1868–1928." Paper presented at Western History Association Annual Meeting, Tulsa, Okla., October 1993.

———. *White Man's Medicine: Government Doctors and the Navajo, 1863–1955.* Albuquerque: University of New Mexico Press, 1998.

U.S. Department of Health, Education, and Welfare. U.S. Public Health Service. *Health Services for American Indians.* Washington, D.C.: GPO, 1957.

———. *History, Mission, and Organization of the Public Health Service.* Washington, D.C.: GPO, 1976.

———. *The Indian Health Program: The U.S. Public Health Service.* Washington, D.C.: GPO, 1963.

———. *The Indian Health Program: The U.S. Public Health Service.* Washington, D.C.: GPO, 1972.

U.S. Department of Health, Education, and Welfare. U.S. Public Health Service. "After Antibiotics: The Fire Dance." *Medical News* (10 June 1959): n.p.

U.S. Department of Health, Education, and Welfare. U.S. Public Health Service. Health Services and Mental Health Administration. Indian Health Service. *Indian Health Trends and Services, 1970 Edition.* PHS Pub. No. 2092. Washington, D.C.: Office of Program Planning and Evaluation, Program Analysis and Statistics Branch, January 1971.

U.S. Department of Health, Education, and Welfare. U.S. Public Health Service. Division of Indian Health, Navajo Area Office. *Health Highlights: Trends in DIH Facility Workloads, Navajo Area.* Albuquerque, N.M.: Albuquerque Area Program Analysis Branch, 1968.

U.S. Department of Health and Human Services. U.S. Public Health Service. Indian Health Service. *Indian Health Service: Comprehensive Health Care Program for American Indians and Alaska Natives.* Washington, D.C.: GPO, 1992.

———, prepared by the National Indian Health Board and American Indian Technical Services. *The Indian Health Service's Implementation of the Indian Self-Determination Process.* Washington, D.C.: GPO, 1984.

———. Office of Planning, Evaluation, and Legislation, Division of Program Statistics. *Indian Health Service: Trends in Indian Health, 1992.* Washington, D.C.: GPO, 1992.

———. *Regional Differences in Indian Health, 1992.* Washington, D.C.: GPO, 1992.

U.S. Department of Health and Human Services. U.S. Public Health Service. Navajo Area Indian Health Service, Chinle Hospital Steering Committee. *Dedication: Chinle Comprehensive Health Care Facility, August 28, 1982, Chinle, Navajo Nation.* Washington, D.C.: GPO, 1982.

U.S. Department of Health and Human Services. U.S. Public Health Service. Navajo Area Indian Health Service, Office of Program Planning and Development. *Navajo Area Indian Health Service, Area Profile, 1992.* Washington, D.C.: GPO, 1992.

U.S. Department of Justice, Civil Division. "Proposed Rules, Radiation Exposure Compensation Act." *Federal Register* 62 (23 May 1997): 28393–96. Microfiche.

U.S. House. "Debate on Transferring Maintenance and Operation of Hospital Facilities for Indians to Public Health Service, H.R. 303." *Congressional Record.* 83d Cong., 2d sess., 1954. Vol. 100.

U.S. House and Senate Joint Committee on Navajo-Hopi Indian Administration. *Legislation Concerning the Navajo Tribe: Hearings before the Joint Committee on Navajo-Hopi Administration on General Legislative Matters Concerning the Navajo Tribe of Indians*. 86th Cong., 2d sess. (29 January 1960). Washington, D.C.: GPO, 1960.

U.S. House Committee on Indian Affairs. *Statements on Conditions among the Navajo Tribe: Hearings before the Committee on Indian Affairs, House of Representatives*. 79th Cong., 2d sess., 9 March 1946, 15 May 1946. Washington, D.C.: GPO, 1946.

U.S. Senate Committee on Indian Affairs. *Issues of Indian Health and Health Care Reform: Hearing before the Committee on Indian Affairs on the National Health Care Reform and Its Implications for New Mexico Indian Health Programs at the Reservation and Urban Level*. 103d Cong., 2d sess., 8 April 1994, Shiprock, N.Mex., Washington, D.C.: GPO, 1994.

U.S. Senate Select Committee on Indian Affairs. *Hearings before the Select Committee on Indian Affairs on S. 2482, to Amend the Indian Health Care Improvement Act and to Authorize Appropriations for Indian Health Programs*. 102d Cong., 2d sess., 1 April 1992. Washington, D.C.: GPO, 1992.

U.S. Senate Subcommittee on Indian Affairs of the Committee on Interior and Insular Affairs. *Indian Self-Determination and Education Program: Hearings Before the Subcommittee on Indian Affairs on S. 1017 and Related Bills*. 93d Cong., 1st sess., 1 and 4 June 1973. Washington, D.C.: GPO, 1973.

Vaillancourt Rosenau, Pauline, ed. *Health Care Reform in the Nineties*. Thousand Oaks, Calif.: Sage Publications, 1994.

Vogel, Virgil J. *American Indian Medicine*. Norman: University of Oklahoma Press, 1970.

Vogt, Evon C. "Navaho." In *Perspectives in American Indian Culture Change*, edited by Edwin H. Spicer, 278–376.

Wekesser, Carol, ed. *Health Care in America: Opposing Viewpoints*. San Diego, Calif.: Greenhaven Press, 1994.

White House Domestic Policy Council. *The President's Health Security Plan: The Complete Draft and Final Report of the White House Domestic Policy Council*. New York: Random House, 1993.

White, Patricia. "Forced Sterilization Amongst American Indian Women." *Journal of Indigenous Studies* 1, no. 2 (1989): 91–96.

Winship, Henry W., III. "Pharmacy Goes West: Cultivating the Navajo Indians." *Journal of the American Pharmaceutical Association*, n.s., 4 (December 1964): 594–99.

Witherspoon, Gary. *Language and Art in the Navajo Universe*. Ann Arbor: University of Michigan Press, 1977.

Wunder, John R. *"Retained by The People": A History of American Indians and the Bill of Rights*. New York: Oxford University Press, 1994.

Wyman, Leland. "Navajo Ceremonial System." In *Southwest*, edited by Alfonso Ortiz. Vol. 10, *Handbook of North American Indians*, 536–57.

Yazzie, Sonya. "Lifestyle Changes among the Navajo: Cause for Diabetes?" Paper presented at the 9th Annual Navajo Studies Conference, Fort Lewis College, Durango, Colo., 1996.

Young, Robert W. Foreword to *The People's Health*, by Adair, Deuschle, and Barnett, xi–xv.

———, ed. and comp. *The Navajo Yearbook, 1958*. Vol. 7. Window Rock, Ariz.: U.S. Department of the Interior, Bureau of Indian Affairs, Navajo Agency, 1958.

———. *The Navajo Yearbook, 1951–1961*. Vol. 8. Window Rock, Ariz.: U.S. Department of the Interior, Bureau of Indian Affairs, Navajo Agency, 1961.

Young, Robert W. Telephone interviews by author, 5 April 1992, 8 February 1993.

▾ INDEX ▴